SISTERHOOD & SOLIDARITY
Feminism and Labor in
Modern Times

Sisterhood & Solidarity

Feminism and Labor in Modern Times

By
Diane Balser

South End Press **Boston, MA**

First edition, second printing
Typesetting, layout, and design by South End Press
Cover photo credit: Culver Pictures

Copyrights are required for book production in the United States. However, in our case, it is a disliked necessity. Thus, any properly footnoted quotation of up to 500 sequential words may be used without permission, so long as the total number of words quoted does not exceed 2,000. For longer quotations or for a greater number of total words, authors should write to South End Press for permission.

Library of Congress Cataloging-in-Publication Data

Balser, Diane.
   Sisterhood and solidarity.

   Bibliography: p. 233
   Includes index
   1. Women in trade-unions—United States—History. 2. Feminism—United States—History. I. Title.
   HD6079.2.U5B34   1987   331.4   87-4733
   ISBN 0-89608-278-4
   ISBN 0-89608-277-6 (pbk.)

South End Press, 116 St. Botolph St., Boston, MA 02115

Table of Contents

Acknowledgements

There are many people who helped me and supported me with this book. My parents and family (my sister and brother and their families) have always had confidence in me and my abilities.

The many women that I worked and grew with in the early stages of the women's movement are always with me. The emerging sisterhood of the late 1960s and early 1970s changed my life and prompted me to dedicate my life to the liberation of women and of all peoples.

During the 1970s and 1980s, there have been thousands of women who I have either met or read about, from nations throughout the world, who have been models for me. They have inspired me to continue my commitment to cooperatively building an international women's movement.

In addition to the women's movement, I have continually learned from the women and men of the labor movement.

Much appreciation needs to go to the faculty and students of the Sociology Department at Brandeis University who encouraged me to combine my activism and my intellectual needs. In particular, Gordie Fellman, chair of my thesis committee and good friend, Ann Lane, and Carmen Sirianni, members of my committee who encouraged me to write a feminist doctoral dissertation. This book came from my thesis.

Pam Roby, Professor of Sociology and Women's Studies at the University of California, Santa Cruz, has been a most dedicated friend and colleague throughout the writing of my thesis and this book.

I owe much to Barbara Brandt who edited the thesis, and then helped me transform it into a book. She spent countless hours with me going through different drafts.

Karen Slaney, Angela Krimsky, and Harriet Wilby assisted me with the editorial work.

The staff at South End Press, in particular, Cynthia Peters and Michael Albert, worked hard on and had confidence in this publication. Carol Baker, Jade Barker, and Ellen Herman also contributed their valuable skills toward the book's production.

I am grateful to the Arthur and Elizabeth Schlesinger Library on the History of Women in America, Radcliffe College, for its collection of the magazine, *Revolution* (1868-1871). Also, I am thankful to the leaders of the Coalition of Labor Union Women and Union WAGE for the many interviews they gave me and the materials and archives they allowed me to use.

A special thanks goes to the thousands of co-counselors in the Re-evaluation Counseling Communities who have supported me and have had faith in me. Most especially, I deeply appreciate Harvey Jackins who has been my mentor and ally during the past fifteen years.

Introduction

The late 1980s offer new challenges for those who are serious about political change in the United States and throughout the world. It is time for the women's liberation movement and other progressive movements to search for new directions.

This decade has brought all of the difficulties of the Reagan administration, as well as, paradoxically, new sources of hope. In the early part of the decade, organizations working for peace and those advocating the rights of women, labor, minorities, the disabled, the elderly, and gay people concentrated on defeating the policies and programs of the Reagan administration. Despite the major setbacks which accompanied Reagan's election in 1980, hope was inspired by the growth of progressive coalitions that developed in response to the rightward swing in American politics. And hope was further encouraged by the appearance of the Gender Gap—the emergence of women as a recognizable political force.

Women have a long history of empowering themselves through collective organizing, and between 1982 and 1984, it seemed that they finally had the strength to defeat a U.S. president and change the political agenda of the government. After the 1984 election, however, a malaise overtook the feminist movement. Joan Walsh, in a 1985 article, "Feminism's New Frontiers," summarized the feeling well when she said,

> After the trouncing of Geraldine Ferraro, the defeat of every non-incumbent female congressional candidate, the shrinking of the gender gap and the re-election of Ronald Reagan,

anybody who'd been starry-eyed over the transformative potential of the women's vote felt foolish, if not a little crazy.[1]

Within a year of the 1984 presidential election, a discussion emerged in the women's movement concerning what had gone wrong and what should happen next. During the summer of 1985, there was a major struggle for leadership in the National Organization for Women (NOW). Judy Goldsmith, who had worked closely with Mondale and Ferraro, lost the presidency to Eleanor Smeal, who promoted a return to greater militancy and independence from traditional electoral politics. In November 1985, Betty Friedan wrote an article in the *New York Times*, "How to Get the Women's Movement Going Again," in which she urged feminists to deal with and organize around the actual realities of women today, particularly the economic reality of poverty.[2] This challenge inspired even further dialogue and examination.

Today's political and economic situation demands broad and sweeping changes. This book is about that search for new strategies for major change. We live in a time of tremendous military escalation, when the threat of nuclear war is omnipresent and there continues to be great disparity between those who have wealth and those who do not. At the same time, the world has more than enough resources and available technology to build a rationally organized and just society. Social justice movements have historically challenged inequalities, demanded change, and promoted visions of a fundamentally different society. In the 1930s and 1940s the trade union movement initiated progressive labor reforms. Since World War II, national liberation movements (particularly in third world countries) have caused great upheaval, challenging the global domination of the superpowers and attempting to create new societies. Despite their recent discouragement, women have emerged as a group with the potential to play a leading role in the struggle for social change throughout the world.

The feminism that exploded in the 1960s and 1970s involved (and still does) a broad philosophy and program for political and social transformation. It contains a vision of a world free of female subordination and free of oppression. Despite the setbacks of the 1980s and the alienation of some feminists from political life, the goal of political power—not the power to oppress others, but the power to change societal institutions—remains the driving force of feminism.

How can we make real the feminist aspirations for freedom? How do we develop women and their allies into an organized force with a program and strategy that can win both the short-term goals of legal equality, reproductive rights, etc., and the long-term goal of a liberated society?

The focus of this book is the attainment of economic power and its relationship to political power. It is concerned with attempts to organize women both as workers and as an oppressed sex, and it is also about building alliances between feminist organizations and unions. In the late nineteenth and early twentieth centuries, feminists once emphasized political change through suffrage; and more recently, some feminists have advocated change through the support of certain political candidates. But feminists have not yet organized women in a way that allows women to gain economic control over their lives or gives them sufficient power to reconstruct society according to their own economic and social needs.

In the last few decades there have been tremendous changes in women's lives, their relationship to work, and their role in society. Yet the devaluation of women's work continues as a central element of women's oppression. Women have been the majority of working people particularly when parenting and housework are considered legitimate forms of work. However, since World War II, women have become the fastest growing segment of the wage-work force and the labor movement, and this fact makes possible new forms of collective organization and political strength. This book is based on the idea that the revolutionary changes in the relationship between gender and work occurring today can serve as a bridge between all groups of women (women of different races, classes, ethnic groups, etc.) and between women and working people. Organizing women around gender and work can create the possibility of stronger and larger women's organizations and, at the same time, lay the foundation for a resurgence of unionization in the United States. These are the seeds for a new power—the power to set things right in the world.

Political
Power
for Women

1

The 1980s mark the third decade of this generation's women's liberation movement—a movement international in scope and larger and stronger than any movement of women preceding it. From the early consciousness-raising groups in the United States, to more than 100,000 women in Italy marching for abortion rights, to women refusing to wear their veils in the early stages of the Iranian revolution, women of many nations, races, and classes have developed an understanding that they suffer a common oppression, and that, as women, they need to organize politically to fight that oppression.

Feminism flourished during the 1970s, particularly in the West. There was an upsurge in feminist journalism, research, literature, and music. Women organized networks around issues such as rape, domestic violence, health care, and childcare. The number of issues has proliferated, spanning the spectrum from equal rights to reproductive freedom, from the elimination of sexual violence to ending sexual discrimination in work, religion, education, and politics. Economic issues such as pay equity, the unionization of women workers, and increased social benefits have also become part of the larger women's liberation movement.

Many groups have addressed the double oppressions of being both female and a member of a minority group—Asian, black, working class, Hispanic, Jewish, disabled, etc. Sexism in a variety of forms and cultures has been examined. Women's activities in third world nations have increased dramatically, and the interconnection of sexism, racism, and nationalism is being explored from the unique viewpoints of the women involved.

More than just a series of activities or a spontaneous explosion in consciousness, feminism has grown into a strong political force for change and freedom. The Gender Gap has become a recognized phenomenon in many Western nations. Women are leading the international peace movement. Political organizations for women and female political leaders have increased in number. At the 1985 United Nations Conference in Nairobi, Kenya (which ended the "Decade for Women"), a consensus was reached for the first time on a general program of women's issues and it was adopted by many countries throughout the world.

Throughout the history of feminism there has been an understanding that gaining political power—in order to change society and control one's life—is essential to free women from oppression. Feminist leaders' have generally believed, from the earliest stages of the movement, that institutionalized powerlessness underlies female servitude. The central demand of the early feminist movement, in both England and the United States, was for the political right of suffrage. Suffrage was considered key to political power; since women are a majority of the population, if they could vote and if they voted as a bloc, it was assumed that there was nothing they could not change.

During the days of the suffrage movement, feminism was very much a minority movement among women. Winning the vote was an advance, but, in and of itself, it did not gain political power for women. In the contemporary women's movement, which is significantly larger than its predecessor, gaining political power, outside as well as inside the voting booth, has been a recurrent theme.

An example of this renewed interest in garnering political power was shown as early as 1968. A group of feminists called Radical Women helped plan the Jeanette Rankin Brigade action in which 5,000 women demonstrated against the Vietnam War. During the Brigade protest in Washington, D.C., Radical Women staged a demonstration called "The Burial of Traditional Womanhood." Part of their statement explaining this action went as follows:

> You have resisted your roles of supportive girl friends and tearful widows, receivers of regretful telegrams and worthless medals of honor. And now you must resist approaching Congress playing these same roles that are synonymous with powerlessness. We must not come as passive supplicants begging for favors, for power cooperates only with power... Until we have united into a force to be reckoned with, we will be patronized and ridiculed into total political ineffectiveness. So if you are really sincere about ending this war, join us tonight and in the future.[1]

Feminists in the 1960s and 1970s spent much time and energy grappling with the concept of power and attempting to redefine its meaning. The women's movement did not want to emulate traditional forms of power often associated with men, such as the power to oppress others; it wanted to strive towards a politics of change and liberation. "The Personal is Political" became a favorite slogan of early contemporary feminism. It meant that even women's personal and emotional issues were political in the larger sense of the word, and that politics needed to explore the effects of oppression in women's most intimate, personal lives. This redefinition of "political" provided the meaning and driving force in building the consciousness of this new mass movement.

The politics of feminist liberation has contained two major components: the growth of a mass consciousness of oppression and liberation, and the organizing of specific political struggles and actions. Both components have been responsible for the growing power of the women's movement.

The shared awareness or consciousness of female oppression has included the ideas that women as a group are oppressed; that they are institutionally victimized and forced into subservient relationships to men; that despite differences, women share a common gender identity and that the heart of women's fight is a quest for freedom from all subservient roles. Moving from subservience to freedom; transforming dependency and subordinate relationships into self-definition, purpose, and autonomy; changing institutions which foster oppression into institutions based on equality and respect—these are the goals of liberation, the ideas comprising the consciousness of female liberation.

While it is true that there is not one feminist ideology, there are common themes in contemporary feminism which form the basis of a shared consciousness. From what has been termed "mainstream" feminism to "radical" feminism and "socialist" feminism—from Betty Friedan to Simone de Beauvoir and Shulamith Firestone—basic change both in women's personal lives and in societal institutions that affect them have been and still are shared as common goals. At the end of *The Feminine Mystique*, written in 1963, Betty Friedan states,

> Who knows what women can be when they are finally free to become themselves? Who knows what women's intelligence will contribute when it can be nourished without denying love? Who knows of the possibilities of love when men and women share not only children, home and garden, not only the fulfillment of their biological roles, but the responsibilities and passions of the work that creates the

human future and full human knowledge of who they are? It
has barely begun, the search of women for themselves. But the
time is at hand when the voices of the feminine mystique can
no longer drown out the inner voice that is driving women on
to become complete.[2]

Other feminist spokeswomen believe that women's liberation
implies not only fundamental changes for women, but also freedom for
all people. Many feminist theoreticians have struggled with the relationship between feminism and other theories of social change. The
beginnings of contemporary feminist theory developed out of a dialogue
with Marxism such as that created by Simone de Beauvoir, Juliet
Mitchell, Shulamith Firestone, and others. In the eyes of these feminists,
Marxist theory did not include an adequate analysis of female oppression. In practice, too, Marxist movements often did not allow women,
either as individuals or as a group, to play a major role in worldwide
social change. Feminists have also begun to integrate the complexities of
racism, as well as other forms of oppression, into their understanding of
gender oppression. This has challenged feminists to understand the
many different ways women experience oppression and has broadened
our understanding of what women's liberation could mean. The idea
that women's liberation implies and necessitates the liberation of all
people, the dream of women leading *all* people towards a better, more
peaceful world, fills the pages of feminist writing and has become an
essential piece of feminist consciousness.

The action component of the women's movement has involved mass
struggles for women's rights and for changes in the institutions which
affect women's lives. These struggles have included the fight for equal
legal and reproductive rights, ending sexual violence, and many others.
In the United States the battle for the Equal Rights Amendment (ERA)
helped to establish the women's movement and build it as a mass
movement with majority support. In countries throughout the world,
organizing mass demonstrations, creating national political organizations, running political candidates on a women's rights program, and
grassroots organizing for institutional change, have all been a part of
women's struggle for political power.

Both elements—consciousness and action—are interconnected.
They have shaped each other and have contributed equally to the growth
of a political movement. The earlier battle for suffrage and the
contemporary battle for equal rights were inspired by and furthered
women's quest for a new life. Barbara J. Berg in her work *The
Remembered Gate: Origins of American Feminism, 1800-1860*, defines
feminism by stating,

For the purposes of this study, feminism is used to describe a broad movement embracing numerous phases of woman's emancipation. It is the freedom to decide her own destiny; freedom from sex-determined roles; freedom from society's oppressive restrictions; freedom to express her thoughts fully and to convert them freely to actions. Feminism demands the acceptance of woman's right to individual conscience and judgment. It postulates that woman's essential worth stems from her common humanity and does not depend on the other relationships of her life.

Woman's rights, however, implies a demand for particular privileges. At different times in the history of this country, the rights for which women struggled have included the right to vote, the right to equal educational and employment opportunities, the right to be treated by physicians of their own sex, the right to be served at male clubs and restaurants. Each specific request is rooted in the basic ideology of woman as an autonomous being. But this collection of isolated rights does not add up to feminism.[3]

Each separate struggle gives concrete expression to the larger dream and provides a tool for translating that dream into an actual program. In their inceptions, suffrage, the ERA, and a woman's right to choose abortion were specific vehicles which conveyed a rich and broad picture of women's freedom. Concurrently, the larger consciousness has inspired the fight for the many particular rights.

During the first wave of feminism, as in this generation, feminists articulated a total vision of feminism. Several early feminists revealed a deep understanding of female subjugation and a knowledge that basic societal change would be needed to achieve women's freedom. Susan B. Anthony and Elizabeth Cady Stanton were the two feminist leaders who most embodied this understanding. "We call for nothing less than emancipation from all political, industrial, social and religious subjugation,"[4] said Susan B. Anthony. Similarly, Elizabeth Cady Stanton stated: "We are in the midst of a social revolution, greater than any political or religious revolution that the world has ever seen, because it goes deep down to the very foundation of society."[5]

The larger vision was usually combined with a list of demands—individual rights that made up the basis of a feminist program. During the mid- to late 1800s those rights included property rights, marriage rights, inheritance rights, and others. Out of those demands, suffrage emerged as the critical issue. In the eyes of its early advocates, suffrage was the key to realizing the larger program of freedom and equality. For Stanton and Anthony, for example, suffrage was a vehicle both for liberating women as independent, self-determining individuals, and for institutional liberation. Although the suffrage movement was split from the start and, in the latter phase, a more conservative wing was often in the leadership, the vision symbolized by suffrage was nevertheless the motivation for the larger feminist movement. According to Ellen DuBois in her pioneer work, *Feminism and Suffrage: The Emergence of an Independent Women's Movement: 1848-1869*, the battle for suffrage initiated the first independent feminist movement.

> Approached as a social movement, rather than as a particular reform, suffrage has enormous contemporary relevance. It was the first independent movement of women for their own liberation. Its growth—the mobilization of women around the demand for the vote, their commitment to gaining increased power over their own lives—was itself a major change in the condition of those lives.[6]

Suffrage was also crucial because, given the views of liberal democracy, the vote was (and still is) seen by many as the key to political power and access. If women could vote, so it was believed, they could win their own issues and make other desired changes.

Furthermore, suffrage was key because it was a gain that, if won, would affect *all* women, cutting through divisions of race and class. This is one of the reasons black women, working-class women, and immigrant women worked on the issue despite the biases within the existing suffrage movement. Unfortunately, those active in the cause of suffrage were never able to work out conflicts over class, race, ethnicity, etc. While suffrage was won and eventually supported by many, the movement did not develop a feminism that spoke for all women; a united women's voice was not created. Creating that voice remains an ongoing challenge for feminism today.

The ERA and women's right to choose abortion were two central feminist demands during the 1970s. They provided the means to unite a mass base of women and conveyed a dream of equality and decision-making for women. However, there were two significant differences between these issues and suffrage. While suffrage had grown out of a series of demands and remained the key feminist political demand for over fifty years, the struggles for the ERA and abortion rights helped proliferate many other issues (such as pay equity, childcare, affirmative action, an end to sexual violence, reproductive health rights, and peace) which formed an overall feminist agenda. Secondly, while the ERA and the right to abortion helped create a mass movement (as did suffrage) and strengthen women as a political force, they did not directly stand for gaining access to overall political power. However, the defeat of the ERA in 1980 caused feminist political leaders to change their strategies, making the attainment of political power through the ballot, and through the election of pro-female candidates, the key issue for feminism in the 1980s. Thus, gaining political power has resurfaced as a major goal of contemporary feminism.

The year 1980 represented a major turning point for the women's movement. The election of Ronald Reagan, the rise of right-wing governments throughout the world (often with anti-women agendas), the defeat of the ERA in the United States, and the emergence of the Gender Gap were all crucial phenomena. The power that the women's movement had developed during the 1970s was acknowledged by the explicitly anti-feminist backlash of Reagan and the New Right. No presidential candidate had ever made women's issues (such as *anti*-ERA, *anti*-choice, and *return* to the "traditional family") so prominent as Ronald Reagan did.

When Reagan came into office, his programs had a disastrous effect on women. The military budget increased tremendously and domestic programs, which disproportionately affect women and children, were cut. The ERA was defeated and federal programs to fight job and educational discrimination were weakened.[7] Reagan, working hand-in-hand with the New Right, has continued to attack a woman's right to choose abortion. And it became obvious in the early 1980s that women were the fastest growing poverty group in the United States.

At the same time, however, women's political influence was growing. During the early years of Reagan's first administration a new political phenomenon was observed—the Gender Gap. Prior to the 1984 presidential election, the Gender Gap in the United States was described through the following set of observations: women are the majority of the voting population; since 1980 women have voted differently from men; since the 1980 elections, fewer women than men have approved of Reagan's performance on a whole host of issues such as women's rights, the economy, the environment, Reagan's military policies, etc.; in 1982, women's votes were found to be the deciding factor in several important elections.[8]

These facts were observed not only by feminists. According to pollster Louis Harris, "One of the major developments of the 1980s will be the full-blown emergence of women as a powerful new force in American politics."[9] Even Ronald Reagan was compelled, during his first term and re-election campaign, to give lip-service to women's issues (without, of course, changing his basic position).

The dream that existed during the battle for suffrage, if not before, that women, with the vote, could exert significant political influence, appeared to be coming true. Ellie Smeal observed that by 1980, 64 percent of all American women supported the efforts of the women's rights organizations.[10] This was a turning point for feminism. For the first time in history, women's issues were supported by a majority of women in the United States, whether or not they considered themselves to be feminists. Feminism had arrived as a majority movement; the challenge to feminist political leaders was clear.

As Bella Abzug stated in her book *Gender Gap*:

> Women are a majority of Americans, and for the first time in our history they are at odds with their government on almost every important issue of foreign and domestic policy.
>
> Today in our vaunted democracy, we have a government that does not represent us and that actually works against policies favored by a majority of Americans. We women must get used to thinking of ourselves as a mighty multitude, with important allies among men and underrepresented groups. Although women are a majority of that coalition-in-the-making, we are not even now being recognized as such. We can change that. We can learn to become political leaders and activists, or we can sit back and let a minority of men in government, backed by powerful money and military interests, run our country and try to run the whole world. It's up to us.[11]

The existence of the Gender Gap (and the need to defeat Ronald Reagan) caused women leaders to predict that women would and could elect the next president of the United States. According to Eleanor Smeal, in her work *Why Women Will Elect the Next President:*

> The message is clear: The 1984 elections—and all other presidential, statewide, and congressional races in the future—could be determined by the women's vote. As women's votes increasingly come to constitute the margin of difference, women's political power will continue to grow.[12]
>
> Women *will* elect the next president of the United States.[13]

The nomination of Geraldine Ferraro as Democratic vice-presidential candidate in 1984 reflected the political strength of the women's movement and was at least a partial fulfillment of feminist political aspirations. Having a woman run as a vice-presidential candidate on a major party ticket on a woman's rights platform was truly an historical event.

However, as the 1984 election turned out, Ronald Reagan was not defeated by women, or by anyone else. Predictions notwithstanding, there was no significant difference in voting patterns between women and men. This did not mean that the Gender Gap, or its potential, did not exist. It did mean, however, that women were not voting as a majority in their own interest (nor in the interests of other oppressed peoples).

There have been several theories put forward as to why women did not defeat Ronald Reagan in 1984. One was that Walter Mondale was not a very good alternative to Reagan and did not emphasize women's issues, or any other significant issues for that matter. Second, women did not have sufficient organizational strength; feminist leaders had relied too heavily on women's spontaneous outrage at Reagan. Third, while some feminist issues gained majority support, the ideas central to women's liberation had not yet reached all women. Feminism is still a minority movement. Finally, factors of race and class were not significantly considered by many feminist leaders. It was in fact poor people and black people who voted in largest percentages against Reagan. Certainly these elements did play a role in the outcome of the 1984 election.

Despite the setbacks of 1984, the international women's movement is growing. There is still a visionary feminist agenda which, if implemented, would mean a transformation of society. While many feminists, particularly radical feminists, believe that working within the traditional political system will only lead to co-optation, the need to *win* is greater than ever before. The dream of women leading the world towards a better society is still in the hearts and minds of many women and men. Feminism has the potential to be a vibrant theory and practice for wide political change and there is every indication that many major issues, particularly the peace issue, will depend on female initiative and leadership. The key question and challenge remains: how does the women's movement grow from one that has great force and momentum to one that actually takes political power and uses it to change society?

Women
and Work

Chapter 1 established that gaining political power is crucial for women's liberation, and that women are coming ever closer to implementing their potential power. Political power, in this context, means the ability to shape society according to one's own needs and one's own vision of the way things should be. There are four major sources of political power for women.

1) Women constitute a majority of the population. While this fact carries with it the clear potential for achieving a comprehensive program of women's rights, this potential has not yet been realized because women do not vote as a unified majority. In addition, political power has not yet been recognized as a common goal even by all feminists (many of whom still dislike the "political process").

2) The growth of a feminist consciousness which is international in scope. This consciousness assumes a unity among women, demanding a transformation of both societal institutions and women's personal lives. This consciousness, however, has not yet led to political power for two reasons. First, although it is spreading, it is still shared by only a minority of women. Second, it has not yet articulated a comprehensive set of ideas, programs, and goals around which the vast majority of women can be organized.

3) Women are members of every group in society, and in particular most other oppressed groups (they experience "double" or "multiple" oppressions). Every woman has multiple identities. In addition to her gender identity, each woman is also a member of an ethnic group,

nationality, age group, religious persuasion, economic class, occupational category (paid and/or unpaid), sexual preference, a state of physical ability or disability, etc. As such, women make up the majority of most oppressed groups—i.e., older people, the poor, the working class, third world nations, people of color in the West, the physically disabled, etc.

The fact that all women share a single gender identity and simultaneously are members of all other oppressed groups is a source of both conflict and power. While these differences between women can and do precipitate conflicts, each group of women also adds a unique perspective and richness to the total understanding of the female experience. Most important, women have access to every other oppression. Thus women cannot really end their own oppression without ending the oppression of all other peoples. Likewise every other oppressed group must tackle sexism in order to be liberated.

Women are only at the beginning stages of recognizing the existence and potential power of these "multiple" oppressions. From the late 1960s to the present, there has been, within the women's movement, a much greater awareness of the complexity of oppression. Conferences and organizations of women of color, Jewish women, older women, disabled women, lesbians, and others have increased. In addition, feminists have a greater international perspective than ever before. However, there is also a long way to go in developing programs that will unite all women, build strength among the particular multiple oppressions, and unite women with other groups. While feminists have increased their ability to work in political coalitions (for example with labor groups, civil rights organizations, etc.), they still have not taken the initiative in building the kinds of comprehensive multi-sided coalitions necessary for real political change.

4) The last source of women's political power stems from the fact that women possess massive and still largely untapped economic power, based primarily on their ever-increasing role in the wage-work force. This book focuses on women's economic power, both because it has been so frequently ignored, and because its potential, once recognized and organized around, could be so strong and immediate. Real economic power for women means organizing women in such a way that they can gain control over their economic lives, end inequality, and share fully in the society's material wealth and decision-making.

In recent years, more attention has been paid to women's economic status, although the focus has been primarily on observing and analyzing their economic plight, not their potential economic power. It is becoming more commonly recognized that the growing poor are women and children, that there is a disproportionate distribution of wealth and income between women and men, and that economic crises throughout the world affect women more than others. According to the United Nations, "women comprise half of the world's adult population, yet perform nearly two-thirds of all work hours, receive only one-tenth of the world's income, and own less than one-hundredth of the world's property." In the United States, two out of three adults in poverty are women; three-quarters of the nation's poor are women and children; 50 percent of female-headed households—and 75 percent of homes headed by black women—live below the poverty line; three-quarters of the elderly poor are women.[1]

Several feminists have recently suggested that the elimination of poverty become the basis for a feminist political agenda. For instance, in an article entitled "Feminism's New Frontiers," written shortly after Reagan's 1984 re-election, Joan Walsh stated, "The realization that gender alone makes women statistically vulnerable to desperate poverty is helping feminism find a new focus."[2] However, while this new focus on women's economic status is a major step in the right direction, it only calls attention to woman as victim at a time when there is a much greater need to recognize women's potential economic *power*.

Feminists have not given enough attention to women's economic status and women's economic power, a weakness that is part of a long and widespread trend among feminists, as well as most other political activists. It is a trend that is only now beginning to change. For example, in the early years of contemporary feminism there was often an ideological war between Marxism and feminism. Of the many issues under contention, the most important was the relationship between gender and class. Marxism (and most other theories of class relationships) has invariably given primacy to the wage-work force, in particular the male wage-work force. For many Marxists and other people committed to social change, the male working class was (and still is) the primary vehicle of basic societal change. Although Marx (and Engels) analyzed women's oppression, it either remained on the outskirts of the theoretical discussion or was subsumed under the rubric of class.

In contrast, early contemporary feminists identified the family and the sexual power relationships within it as the basis of their studies. Much of feminist theory attributed women's political and economic powerlessness and sexual victimization to their roles in the family. As Ellen DuBois stated, "The major contribution of contemporary feminism has been the location of the family as a central institution of women's oppression."[3]

Recently, a whole new wave of literature and new feminist theories about work and class has been developing. Women's work and women as workers (even if their primary work is in the home) have become central themes of this research. From many feminist articles and books on this topic, a new shared conception of women's work is emerging.

It is now assumed by most feminists that women have always worked, and that the kind of work women have performed has been part of their oppression. Even women's role in reproduction—pregnancy, childbirth, and childraising—has consistently been used to shape women's exploitation.

In this new look at women as workers, women's role as unpaid houseworker has received considerable attention. While the idea of women's enslavement in the home is not new, its growing importance in feminist theory, and the creation of a more developed analyses about it are new. For example, Ann Oakley, a British feminist, in *Women's Work: The Housewife, Past and Present* studies the creation of the modern housewife, the myths of domesticity which reinforce her role, and the kind of work she performs in industrial society.

> A vast number of books have been written about men and their work; by contrast, the work of women has received very little serious sociological or historical attention. Their unpaid work in the home has scarcely been studied at all. This book is an attempt partially to redress this balance. Its perspective is feminist; it challenges the set of conventional values which label work a masculine activity and assign women to the home.[4]

Oakley and others believe that the "universal entrapment of women in the home" was the byproduct of industrial capitalism. Before industrial capitalism, the family as it functioned within the context of the household, village, or manor, was the basic economic unit; women's productive labor (such as making clothing) was integral to that unit. Under industrial capitalism, the wage-worker was seen as the productive laborer; and women's work was hidden and devalued behind a series of myths such as "a woman's place is in the home." These myths both reinforced her role and denied its exploitative nature.

Initially the predominant feminist literature on women's work was on work within the home. Entrapment in the home was the basis of feminist novels, theory, movies, etc. Ironically, Marxists, feminists, and social scientists all neglected working-class women and other women in the wage-work force until very recently. In almost every publication about women as workers written during the last few years, reference is made to the *absence* of literature about working women in the majority of previous studies written either about women or about the working class.

For example, in her latest book, *The Rising of the Women*, Meredith Tax observes,

> Until the development of the women's liberation movement in the late 1960s, the most diligent searcher for women in the pages of United States labor history could find them only sporadically. They would suddenly appear, only to disappear again like the Cheshire Cat in *Alice in Wonderland*, leaving just a smile behind.[5]

And Philip Foner claims,

> Working women . . . do not loom large in the new scholarship dealing with the American women's movement just as they do not occupy an important place in most histories of the American labor movement. While women are not new to the American work force, their role in this capacity has been largely neglected.[6]

Recent studies, however, do look at women's work in the wage-work force, and the relationship between domestic labor and wage-work for women. To what can we attribute this growing awareness of women's role in the wage-work force? A primary factor seems to be the current reality, in which women are no longer predominantly houseworkers, but both houseworkers *and* wage-workers outside the home.

The facts about women's increasing participation in the wage-work force are striking. Women today are the fastest growing segment of the wage-work force, and the growth of industrialization has spurred this trend. In 1979, women were 42 percent of the wage-labor force, compared to 26 percent in 1940.[7] Today 51 percent of women sixteen years and older work for wages. Some have predicted that by 1990, over 50 percent of the wage-work force will be female. It is important to note that approximately one-eighth of women workers are racial minority members. (Forty-six percent of white women are wage-workers compared to 49 percent of minority women.)[8]

It is not an overstatement to claim that there has been a revolution in work in the last three decades and that the increase in female wage-workers in the U.S. labor force "is the single most important change in the labor force in this century."[9]

Along with the massive entry of women into the wage-work force, a parallel and equally revolutionary phenomenon has been the development of a *sex-segregated wage-work force*, with men, in general, occupying the higher status and better paid positions and the majority of women holding the lower status and lower paid positions.

The dramatically sex-segregated nature of the wage-work force is highly significant for the development of women's power for two reasons:

1) Until recently, sex segregation has historically obscured the recognition of women's participation in the wage-work force, by identifying their work as "unimportant," and women as "frivolous" rather than "serious workers."*

2) By grouping women into a distinct and clearly oppressed segment of the wage-work force, sex segregation offers unique opportunities around which to organize women at work.

Sex segregation in the workplace has gone hand-in-hand with the development of industrialization. For example, while women in the colonial era participated in a variety of occupations, manufacturing became predominantly male with the advent of industrialization. In 1890, a little less than 20 percent of the wage-work force was female.[10] The majority of these women were employed as domestic servants and operatives in textile or clothing factories—jobs that mirrored their roles in the family. Women worked in different industries from men and with segregated wage scales, or had different tasks within the same industry.

The idea was promoted that women, because of their "inferiority," could not do the same jobs as men. At best, they were temporary workers who should have been in the home, not "real workers" in the wage-work force. These myths about women were used to restrict them to certain kinds of labor and to justify the lower wages they were paid.

The sex composition of jobs was modified during different stages of industrialization in order to meet the needs of production and maximize profits. In an outstanding study of the changing composition of the clerical work force, Margery Davies found that in 1870, a time when there

---

*The existence and significance of sex-segregation at work is being recognized by an increasing number of feminist thinkers and activists. For example, in "Capitalism, Patriarchy and Job Segregation by Sex," Heidi Hartmann argues:

> It is my contention that the roots of women's present social status lie in the sex-ordered division of labor.[11]

> Job segregation by sex, I will argue, is the primary mechanism in capitalist society that maintains the superiority of men over women, because it enforces lower wages for women in the labor market. Low wages keep women dependent on men because they encourage women to marry. Married women must perform domestic chores for their husbands. Men benefit, then, from higher wages and the domestic division of labor. This domestic division of labor, in turn, acts to weaken women's position in the labor market.[12]

were relatively few clerks,[13] men comprised 97.5 percent of the clerical labor force. Clerical work was then considered fairly prestigious, skilled work. With modern industrial capitalism came an increase in business, the introduction of machines, and the need for many more clerical workers. By 1920, more than 90 percent of stenographers and typists were women; the entire clerical force had been feminized.[14] By this time a myth had developed that clerical work was well suited to the "female nature," while in reality women simply provided cheaper labor. The greater use of machinery and the increased need for less skilled labor usually meant that men moved towards the more skilled jobs and women towards the less.

Ironically, with the proliferation of women in the wage-work force, occupational segregation has not only remained, but increased. (The recent large increase in the number of women in the wage-work force has primarily been the result of a large expansion in the numbers of service and clerical workers.) According to a 1978 report by the Carnegie Corporation, "The rate of occupational segregation by sex is exactly as great today as it was at the turn of the century, if not greater."[15] In particular, the gap between women's and men's earnings has increased in the last twenty years. Today 80 percent of the female wage-work force is in the lowest paid and the least skilled jobs:

1) jobs in peripheral industries, including both peripheral manufacturing and retail trades (for example, light industrial as opposed to heavy industrial jobs),

2) clerical occupations,

3) health and education sectors (a carryover from women's role in the family), and

4) domestic service (another carryover from the family).[16]

These two phenomena—women's entrance into the wage-work force and the sex-segregation or "genderfication" of work roles—have brought about revolutionary changes in the lives of both men and women. It has been noted that,

> The postwar decades and especially the 1960's and the 1970's have seen dramatic changes in women's relationship to work. The vast increases in female labor-force participation which occurred in this period produced equally vast social and cultural shifts, transforming family relations as well as women's sense of "place" in the larger society. And the growth of a mass feminist movement led to enormous changes in

consciousness about gender—not only among movement participants, but in the population as a whole.[17]

Women's participation in the world of wage-work has given them a greater sense of self, higher expectations, and greater independence from men. When women were mainly houseworkers and had little or no money for themselves, they were completely dependent upon men. While poverty and low incomes are still major problems for many working women, their greater autonomy and participation in the world outside the home are giving women a greater potential for leadership and greater initiative in world affairs.

Historically, the majority of working people have been women; this is especially true when one considers work done primarily in the home. Today, under industrial capitalism women increasingly make up the majority of the group that directly produces our society's economic wealth. Throughout history, women as workers have always had the potential for economic power; today, women as the fastest growing segment of the wage-work force are close to realizing that potential.

Moreover, the overlap between gender and class, greater than ever before, carries with it the seeds of liberation and power. Since almost all jobs in our society are defined by gender, women function within this society both as an oppressed gender and as an oppressed group of workers. This double identity, or double oppression, carries with it the potential for women to unite with other groups of workers around crucial issues of common interest. It also provides a way to unite all groups of women despite the differences created by multiple oppressions. Women of all races, classes, ethnic groups, ages, sexual preferences, etc. share a common oppression as workers. Despite differences in income and the kinds of work performed by black women in comparison to white women, women from middle-class backgrounds in comparison to women from working-class backgrounds, there are deep commonalities along the dimensions of gender and work. This is particularly true as women's labor becomes less defined by husbands and fathers. Eighty percent of all women who work outside of the home are in non-professional, low paying, low status jobs. This phenomenon is partly responsible for the feminization of poverty.

It is the thesis of this book that integrating and organizing around these two categories—women as an oppressed gender and as an oppressed group of workers—can help women realize their major source of political power. It can also be vital to the larger picture of social change. Not only do feminists need to understand and organize around the economic dimensions of all women's lives, they also need to integrate a feminist and a class perspective. As I will show, beginning in the next chapter and continuing throughout the rest of this book, the relationship between the feminist movement and the union movement is a key factor in this effort.

The Relationship Between Feminism and Unions

3

Bringing together the feminist and union movements could be a major key to broad societal change. We have already discussed women's potential power to bring about changes not only for themselves, but also for other oppressed people. And because women make up a majority of the working class, and are close to becoming 50 percent of the wage-workers, we need to make ourselves aware of the potential power that would come from organizing women as workers.

Even today, with union membership declining and unions in a confused and weak state, unions are still the only organizations specifically designed to represent workers. In the 1930s, unions were behind all of the major progressive changes for workers in the United States, and, despite weaknesses on issues of race and sex, led the progressive agenda for change. While unions are certainly not the organizations they were in the 1930s, there exist no other organizations in our society today with their potential power. Some observers, such as Andrew Levison, author of *The Working-Class Majority*, argue that labor is still a major force for progressive domestic legislation today.[1]

Historically women, as well as people of color, have had a rough time in relationship to unions. Yet today women are the largest growing membership in unions, just as they are the largest growing segment of the wage-work force.

> The postwar decades were a period of feminization for the labor movement, even as organized labor as a whole declined in strength. In 1956 women were 18.6 percent of all union members; by 1978, they comprised 24.2 percent of the total.

When employee associations are also included in the figure,
the proportion of women is even higher, rising from 23
percent in 1973 to 30 percent in 1980. Indeed in the 1970s,
almost all of the growth in labor organization membership
was comprised of women workers.[2]

Perhaps because of this fact, there is a growing interest by feminists
not only in issues of women and work, as described in the previous
chapter, but in labor unions as well. This has taken place along with the
dramatic changes in the gender composition of the work force, the
emergence of a new working women's movement, the increase of women
in unions, and the development of many more union activities for
women.

However, most feminist literature dealing with feminism's relationship to the union movement has focused on the past. A major
contribution of this focus has been an analysis of the historical sexism of
the trade union movement. The work of such feminist thinkers as Linda
Gordon, Barbara Wertheimer, and Alice Kessler-Harris, among others,
reveals the exclusionary and/or discriminatory policies of many unions
over the years. These writers show (as do other commentators) that the
very first unions in the United States were set up by skilled craftsmen and
were for men only. Not only did men exclude women from their unions,
they tried to prevent women from entering the trades. For close to a
century, the major struggles fought by wage-working women were to
establish their right to organize and to gain acceptance as workers. In the
early days of unions, women, excluded from the male unions, organized
into separate unions which, incidentally, led many militant struggles.

Towards the end of the nineteenth and the beginning of the
twentieth century, when the number of women wage-workers increased
as a result of industrialization and immigration, women became
permanent members of the wage-work force. The struggle that they now
faced was to become part of the exclusively male trade union movement.

The dominant trade union organization at this time was the
American Federation of Labor (AFL), which was ambivalent towards
wage-working women at best, overtly hostile at worst. Most if not all of
the AFL leadership was convinced that "a woman's place is in the
home." The *American Federationist*, the AFL newspaper, published
many articles during these years condemning the presence of women in
the wage-work force and demanding women's exclusion from industry.
An international union head warned: "Keep women out of the trades,
and if not, out of the union."[3] At the 1898 and 1914 AFL conventions,
several resolutions were almost passed against women in the wage-work
force. Feminists and others have argued convincingly that the union

demand for equal pay for equal work was a method that male unionists used to eliminate employers' economic incentive to hire women and thus keep women out of wage labor. Although many unions at the time did not explicitly exclude women, they used other methods to prevent women from joining unions: high initiation fees, restrictive apprenticeship programs, etc. For instance, the Molders Union charged a fifty-dollar fine to any member who instructed women in the trade. Also, initiation fees ranged from twenty-five dollars to five hundred dollars, excluding almost all women from participating.[4]

The union movement's sexism had a noticeable impact on women as well as on the development of trade unions.

> In the period from 1897 to 1920, the A.F. of L. underwent dramatic expansion. It consolidated and confirmed its leadership over a number of independent unions, including the dying Knights of Labor. Membership increased from about 265,000 members in 1897 to more than four million by 1920, and included four-fifths of all organized workers. In the same period, the proportion of women working in the industrial labor force climbed rapidly. Rapid and heavy expansion offered a golden opportunity for organizers. That they didn't take advantage of it by including women among their membership is one of the most important facts in the history of labor organizing in America.[5]

Exposure of the union movement's sexist practices has led some feminists to see male unions as enemies of women. For example, in a 1971 article, "The Men are as Bad as Their Masters.... Socialism, Feminism, and Sexual Antagonism in the London Tailoring Trade in the Early 1830s," Barbara Taylor quotes from an editorial in a short-lived newspaper, *The Pioneer.*

> However loudly the men may bellow for their own liberties, they will never bestow what they obtain upon woman until she demands it from her masters, as they have done for theirs; and whenever that struggle arrives, the men will be as tenacious of giving up their domination as is any other power of relinquishing its authority.

Several feminists have argued that unions and employers worked together to keep women subservient to both male workers and their bosses. In "Capitalism, Patriarchy and Job Segregation," Heidi Hartmann argues that,

Men's ability to organize in labor unions—stemming perhaps from a greater knowledge of the techniques of hierarchical organizations—appears to be key in their ability to maintain job segregation and domestic division of labor.[7]

She cites the exclusionary policies of unions, their fight for equal pay for equal work, and later, for protective legislation which either excluded women from wage-work and/or limited them to less skilled, poorer paid work.

In "Where are the Organized Women Workers?" Alice Kessler-Harris explains the role that organized labor, and particularly the AFL, played in dividing "the working class firmly along gender lines and to confirm women's position as a permanently threatening underclass of workers who finally resorted to the protection of middle-class reformers and legislators to ameliorate intolerable working conditions." She describes the many ways the AFL tried to exclude women from unions and the wage-work force. When they were not successful, she claims, the unions tried to control women from within. "When the AFL did organize women, its major incentive was often the need to protect the earning power of men. Women were admitted to unions after men recognized them as competitors better controlled from within than allowed to compete from without."[8]

Not only does the bulk of feminist writing portray unions as sexist, but there is also an assumption that there is an inherent conflict between feminism and class analysis, between feminism and labor organization. For instance, Robin Miller Jacoby, in "The Women's Trade Union League and American Feminism," argues that:

Feminism and class consciousness are obviously complex notions in themselves, and very little serious theoretical attention has been paid to the relationship between them. Feminism simultaneously complements and conflicts with the ideology of the primacy of class identity. It is complementary in that it implies equal rights and opportunities for women within sexually mixed, class-based settings such as labor unions; it is conflicting in that it also implies that gender identification creates solidarities transcending class divisions.[9]

While there have been conflicts between women and male trade unionists and there has been a history of sexism within the union movement, neither the conflict nor the sexism is inevitable. Despite the sexism of male unions, unionization has been vital for women. Moreover, there has been an evolution of cooperation between unions and women. The present period of time represents the possibility of a synthesis with crucial possibilities.

There have been at least three processes in the movement towards cooperation between feminism and unionism:

1. Growth of unionization among working women.

2. Steps taken towards bringing a feminist perspective to unionization and towards integrating gender and work issues (double oppression of women).

3. Steps taken towards the resolution of the direct conflicts between feminists and unions.

The Unionization of Women Workers

Throughout the history of wage-working women, there has always been a significant impulse towards unionization. Although male unions and bosses put obstacles in their way, working women have managed to create a significant union history of their own. However, many feminists have questioned whether unionization has furthered the interests of women as women. Have unions conflicted with women's need to free themselves from male domination? When women have unionized, it has very much furthered their interests both as workers and as women. Unions have given women at least some power and offer the potential for much greater economic empowerment. For women, earning wages has been one step towards economic independence from men, even when those wages went back into a male-headed family. Women who work for wages are better off economically than women who do not, and women who are unionized are better off than women who are not. Secondly, almost all unionization efforts have required women's initiative and leadership. Thirdly, at times, women organizing themselves into unions have recognized that unionization was an act of self-assertion and power. In many union activities, women have revealed a feminist consciousness, as shown by the following:

UNION IS POWER

Our present object is to have union and exertion, and we remain in possession of our unquestionable rights. We circulate this paper wishing to obtain the names of all who imbibe the spirit of our Patriotic Ancestors, who preferred privation to bondage, and parted with all that renders life desirable—and even life itself—to produce independence for their children. The oppressing hand of avarice would enslave us, and to gain their object, they gravely tell us of the pressure of the times, this we are already sensible of, and deplore it. If any are in want of assistance, Ladies will be compassionate and assist them; but we prefer to have the disposing of our charities in our hands; and as we are free, would remain in possession of what kind Providence has bestowed upon us and remain daughters of freemen still.[10]

These principles accompanied a petition that strikers in February 1834 distributed to other women operatives in a Lowell, Massachusetts mill. The Working Woman's Union, organized in 1878 by leading women unionists Lucy Parsons and Elizabeth Rodgers, presented another example of the feminist consciousness of female union activity. According to Meredith Tax,

In 1879 the Chicago Eight-Hour League held a three-day festival, culminating in a Fourth of July parade. The Working Woman's Union had a pink float, bearing banners with slogans that showed both its labor and feminist aspects: "In a union of strength we seek the strength of union" and "When woman is admitted in the council of nations, war will come to an end, for woman more than man, knows the value of life."[11]

Several periods of women's unionization history are memorable because of the initiative and independence that women demonstrated in the unionization process. The early days of the trade union movement and the women's movement were such a time. Female working-class organizing first began in the early to mid-nineteenth century with a number of strikes organized and led by women from the New England textile mills. This began labor organization for women and helped start the first women's unions. (Women usually built separate unions because they were excluded from men's unions.) Although many early women's unions were short-lived, they produced outstanding leaders and were often involved in many militant struggles. Women from the Lowell Female Labor Reform Association initiated the struggle for a ten-hour day.

Although there were continuous efforts to organize women workers, not until the early twentieth century did women unionize again on a mass scale. At that time, many unorganized workers were organized into permanent, stable unions, and women were included in some male unions. Between 1903 and 1917, the first major unions made up of mainly women were formed.[12] Although only a small percentage of women belonged to unions and the AFL made it difficult for women to join, tens of thousands of women went out on strike to defend their rights as workers.

It is not surprising that militant activity originated in the garment trades since a high percentage of workers were women operating in extremely exploitative conditions. Perhaps the most significant women's strike in United States history was "the Uprising of 20,000." In 1909, at the Triangle Shirtwaist factory in New York City, 150 workers were locked out after they joined the Ladies' Garment Workers Union. When the women went out on a picket line, thugs, hired by the owner, attacked and beat them. However, it was the strikers who were arrested. They appealed to the Women's Trade Union League (WTUL) and many women from the League (including wealthy allies) joined the picket lines. On November 22, 1910, a mass meeting of garment workers was held at Cooper Union. A young woman, Clara Lemlich, in a militant speech, called for a general strike.

At least 20,000 unorganized workers responded. The next day women came out of every shirtwaist factory in Manhattan and Brooklyn. It was described as "like a mighty army rising in the night and demanding to be heard." When the strikes began, every shop in New York was non-unionized, but after it was over, thirteen weeks later, 312 shops had full union contracts. There had been approximately 100,000 garment workers on strike at the same time. It was the first "general strike" of its kind and the first large strike of women workers. It brought into existence the complicated machinery of the modern strike.[13]

What happened in the garment trades was of tremendous significance in the history of labor, the history of women workers, and the history of women in general. This strike in New York City was the largest women's strike in American labor movement history. These workers had previously been considered unorganizable, yet they proved themselves capable of united economic action and leadership, and won important gains. The period of militant strikes by both women and men in the garment trades lasted for four years. During that time, more working women joined unions than ever before and garment workers' unions became mass organizations.

The famous Lawrence Strike of 1912, in which the Industrial Workers of the World (the Wobblies) led 20,000 textile workers, most of them immigrants, was also one in which women played a key role. Elizabeth Gurly Flynn, along with Big Bill Haywood, provided excellent leadership. Women carried banners proclaiming, "We want Bread and Roses, too!"—a slogan which became famous because it captured women's dream of a better life in all ways.

Between 1920 and 1960, in contrast to earlier years, there was no significant independent working women's movement or feminist movement. There were, however, major changes for women and labor. In the

1930s, with the tripling of organized labor, militant labor struggles, and the New Deal, came government endorsement of unionism. In 1935, the Congress of Industrial Organizations (CIO) split off from craft union-ism. The CIO's organizing of industrial unions marked a significant change for women. No longer excluded as they had been by the AFL, large numbers of women were recruited into unions. However, sexism remained a problem. Men still ran the unions, and separate seniority clauses and pay scales for women remained unchallenged by the unions.

Women's ability to deal with their double oppression underlies the ability of feminists and unionists to unite. Often working-class women have infused feminist demands and a feminist consciousness into their organizing. Moreover, feminists have often seen work related issues and the cause of working-class women as an important part of a feminist program.

Feminism Among Union Women

Periods in which there was a high feminist content to female union struggles have usually been times when there was an active feminist movement even if it was separate from the working women's movement.

The earliest period of women's unionization was such a time. There were several reasons that female wage-workers developed a feminist awareness. It was considered unfeminine for women to organize and go out on strike (originally called "turning out"). In 1824, the *Boston Transcript* described the first strike by women as "an instance of woman's clamorous and unfeminine declaration of personal rights which it is obvious a wise providence never destined her to exercise."[14] William Austin, agent of the Lawrence Company, described the march of operatives out of the Lowell mills in 1834 as an "amazonian display." He wrote in a letter that "this afternoon we have paid off several of these Amazones [sic] & presume that they will leave town on Monday."[15]

In the early days of U.S. industrialization, women were the first factory workers. In 1810, women and children were 87.7 percent of the U.S. factory labor force. Since men were engaged in farming and skilled trades in which they got higher wages, either young, unmarried women and/or entire families worked in the textile mills. Although this period of female dominance in factory work lasted for a short time, it gave women an early start in unionization. Further, there was an active feminist movement with some participation of women workers. Women workers were influenced by the ideas of Mary Wollstonecraft, Frances Wright, and other leading feminists. Last, the basic union structures for women were separate organizations which provided greater unity and leadership among women.

As a result of these circumstances, many women workers were aware that their struggle was simultaneously one of sex and class. In an 1876 strike, when the Factory Girls' Association was formed in the Lowell mills, women sang their own version of a popular song:

> Oh! Isn't it a pity that such a pretty girl as I
> Should be sent to the factory to pine away and die?
> Oh, I cannot be a slave,
> I will not be a slave,
> For I'm so fond of liberty
> That I cannot be a slave.[16]

During the strike they claimed: "As our fathers resisted unto blood the lordly avarice of the British ministry, so we, daughters, never will wear the yoke which has been prepared for us.[17]

In 1834 the Lowell mill announced a wage cut and hundreds of women walked off the job. One woman "mounted a stump and made a flaming Mary Wollstonecraft speech on the rights of women and the inequities of the 'monied aristocracy.'"[18] In a speech in September, 1846, Mehitable Eastman, a leader of Manchester's Female Labor Reform Association, combined a vehement protest against the industrial system and female oppression within it.

> Much has been written and spoken in this country in a woman's behalf, yet a large class are destined to servitude as degrading, as unceasing toil can make it. How long can this state of things exist? . . .
> . . . [N]ever with the awful facts of female degradation, under our present system of industry, staring us in the face; never, while we are conscious of powers under developed, affections hemmed in, energies paralyzed, privileges denied, usefulness limited, influence impaired, honors forfeited, and destiny thwarted. No. Never shall we hold ourselves exempt from responsibility, never shall we cease our efforts in the warfare against evil.[19]

There were several publications which represented the voice of militant mill women and dealt with women's issues. There were articles on equal pay for equal work and even a proposal for "affirmative action." There were articles on equal rights for women and ones which deplored male-dominated laws and institutions. In "Rights of a Married Woman," the principle that men and women should function as complete equals in marriage was expressed.

While this period stands out, there have been other periods where working women brought together issues of sex and class. For example, the Women's Trade Union League pioneered feminist methods of organizing women by training them in leadership and organizing skills. Also, the League combined a program of work-related demands and gender issues. From historical documents, it appears that there were women who knew that, to be successful in their fight for equality, they must integrate an understanding of their double oppression. The existence of a feminist movement was vital to this understanding and so was an independent working women's movement.

Integrating Gender and Work Issues

For the most part, the middle-class women's movement for women's legal rights and the working women's movement for women's economic rights operated independently of each other. However, they deeply affected each other's development. There were working women and black women who were outspoken suffragists. Lavinia Waight in 1831, secretary of the United Tailoress' Society, demanded the vote for women and women's right to sit in legislatures. Among the few wage-working women attending the first women's rights Convention in Seneca Falls in 1841, Charlotte Woodward, a glove sewer, said,

> We women work secretly in the seclusion of our bed chambers because all society was built on the theory that men, not women, earned money and that men alone supported the family.... But I do not believe that there was any community in which the souls of some women were not beating their wings in rebellion. For my own obscure self I can say that every fibre of my being rebelled, although silently, all the hours that I sat and sewed gloves for a miserable pittance which, as it was earned, could never be mine. I wanted to work, but I wanted to choose my task and I wanted to collect my wages. That was my form of rebellion against the life into which I was born.[20]

Working women and their leaders continued to be active in the struggle for suffrage. At Cooper Union, Rose Schneiderman replied to a New York state senator who thought women might lose their femininity if they voted, saying,

> We have women working in the foundries, stripped to the waist if you please because of the heat. Yet the Senator says nothing about these women losing their charm. They have got to retain their charm and delicacy, and work in the foundries. Of course you know the reasons they are employed in foundries is that they are cheaper and work longer hours

than men. Women in the laundries for instance, stand for thirteen or fourteen hours in the terrible steam and heat with their hands in hot starch. Surely these women won't lose any more of their beauty and charm by putting a ballot in a ballot box once a year than they are likely to lose standing in foundries or laundries all year round. There is no harder contest than the contest for bread, let me tell you that.[21]

Suffrage was won with, and perhaps because of, the active support of working-class and immigrant women. Despite racism, black women mobilized for the vote and working-class women were crucial in winning trade union support for women's right to vote. Interestingly, the suffrage movement was most limited and ineffective in the later part of the nineteenth century when its base was mainly limited to white, middle or upper class, Anglo-Saxon Protestant women. During the last fifteen years of the suffrage movement, that movement extended itself to support wage-working women's issues. By 1905, the Ohio Woman's Suffrage Association, for example, affirmed "the right of all wage-earning women to organize for the purpose of protecting their industrial interests."

A similar development has taken place with the ERA. In the last decade the trade union movement and trade union women leaders have been among the ERA's most active allies.

Resolving the Tensions Between Feminism and Unions

The overall relationship between feminists and trade unionists has often been seen as a conflict between middle-class feminism and male-dominated unions. The usual analysis is that feminists' class bias prevents them from allying with working people, while male unionists gain too much from their sexism to support women's liberation. However, in reality, their relationship and its history has been much more complicated. Although many feminists have expressed anti-union attitudes, there have been some feminists who have helped or supported unions. For instance, Lucy Stone of the early American Women Suffrage Association originally opposed unions, yet in the early 1850s Lucretia Mott, another active suffragist, helped the Philadelphia Sewers organize an industrial union. There were leading feminists, such as Frances Wright, who were ardent supporters of labor.

Similarly, unions have served both a positive and negative role in relationship to women. From feminists' point of view, the lack of alliance has been the fault of unions. While the history of neglect and discrimination by unions is well established, their history of support is less well known. Terence Powderly, Grand Master of the Knights of

Labor, was a full supporter of suffrage and temperance. President Frances Willard of the National Women's Christian Temperance Union joined the Knights. The 1886 Temperance Convention proclaimed solidarity with the Knights of Labor, initiated a labor department, and advocated an eight-hour day. Susan B. Anthony was brought back in contact with the labor movement when Powderly initiated her into the Knights.[22] (She had been asked to leave the National Labor Union for promoting scabbing during a strike.) Powderly welcomed other suffrage delegates into Knight assemblies.

Almost from its inception the AFL pledged itself to universal suffrage. The *American Federationist* often printed articles in favor of women's suffrage and AFL conventions usually passed favorable resolutions. In 1914, when the leader of a national organization opposed to women's suffrage was refused permission to speak before the AFL Executive Council, Samuel Gompers stated: "You might as well have a discussion with some person who is opposed to trade unionism as to have an argument against equal suffrage."[23] The Women's Trade Union League worked hard to gain the AFL's support for suffrage. In the opinion of Mary Dreier, one-time president of the Women's Trade Union League, labor played a key role in the 1917 suffrage victory in New York. Unions were an important ally in the final victory of suffrage.[24]

Union support for other gender issues was sparse until after World War II, with some notable exceptions. The IWW was the only labor organization to discuss the issue of birth control.[25] This was a significant pioneer effort. Unless women were able to decide when and if to have children, their ability to participate as wage-workers was severely limited. Many years later, the Coalition of Labor Union Women (CLUW) would take a position on women's right to choose abortion.

For a long period of time, the major gender demand that unions made within the work force was equal pay for equal work. Feminists have correctly criticized labor's use of this demand contending that unions advocated equal pay in order to limit or exclude women's participation in the work force. It was assumed that if an employer had to pay women equal wages to men, men would always be preferred. While this may have been true, the demand was one that women's groups also advocated; it was one of the key demands of the Women's Trade Union League (WTUL). While many unions did use it to curb competition from women in the wage-work force, the demand for equal pay set the stage for a future challenge. Lower wages for women have been the basis of a sex-segregated work force. They have been the fundamental way that divisions between men and women in the work force have been perpetuated. The movement for pay equity in its present formulation—

equal pay for work of "comparable worth"—has its roots in this earlier demand.

Unions have not been a monolithic force. There have been differences among unions as there have been differences among male trade unionists. Meredith Tax believes that the differences between unions determined the extent of women's success organizing at work.

> The way women are organized depends on the character of the labor movement at the time. When trade union men have been eager to help them organize, not only have women built unions, but they have participated fully in the labor movement, using their organizations as a base from which to build and influence the united front of women....
>
> Even when the labor movement's leadership has been more conservative and indifferent to the need to organize women, it has still been possible for women to organize themselves into unions. In this situation working women often turned to the feminist movement for help.
>
> When the labor movement has been actively hostile to the organization of women, it has been extremely difficult for women's unions to survive, even with help from feminists. Unions that were heavily infiltrated by racketeers, such as the construction unions and the United Garment Workers, seem to have been particularly antagonistic to women, since their leadership was threatened by a popular upsurge that could not immediately be controlled and channeled for purposes of private graft.[26]

There has been a history of male unionists who have supported women workers. Early male trade unionists such as Seth Luther and William Sylvis were clear advocates for women workers and opponents of sexism in the wage-work force. Most feminists have argued that union resolutions (in the AFL in particular) on behalf of working women reflected union hypocrisy and were designed to hide the sexism of unions. While in many cases this is true, these resolutions also reflected the contradictory attitudes that have permeated the entire labor movement. Many trade union leaders, like Samuel Gompers, believed both that women should stay at home and that women, at least those in some industries, should be unionized. The practice and rhetoric of both progressive and established unions have always been very contradictory.

Unions' history of conflict and tension over women's issues reflected, in large part, a more general pattern of conflict within labor. There have been unionists who believed that unions should represent *all* workers, organized and unorganized, of all races, and both sexes. Others, of various ideologies, defended a trade unionism that represented only a segment of the labor force; the latter were usually dominant in the labor movement. The former, those who wanted to organize the unorganized, were usually much more sympathetic to women—the IWW, the insurgent garment industry unions, and the industrial unions of the Congress of Industrial Organizations (CIO) in the 1930s are all examples. These unions were not free of sexism. Their top leaders were men; women workers' special needs often were not taken into account and women's occupations were often left unorganized. However, all of these unions organized substantial numbers of women, a major break-through for the union movement. More women were in the leadership of these unions than in any others.

These progressive unions did not organize women out of charity. Since women workers have usually made up a sizeable percentage of the unorganized, they represent a potentially large force for the unions. Also, once organized, women have tended to be a militant and progressive force within the union movement, fighting for more democratic and open unions. There are many ways that unions have significantly advanced with women's participation.

The labor movement has changed over the years in its relationship to women workers; the history has not been a static one. There have been several stages and each stage has represented an improvement in the relationship between women and labor. Unionism's early years were characterized by male unions. Though there were some important exceptions, these unions excluded women from membership and often attempted to exclude or limit women's participation in the wage-work force. (Many analyses that assert that unions have been women's enemies are rooted in studies of unions from the earliest period.) In the early twentieth century women began to join previously all-male unions. Although there were still attempts to exclude women from the wage-work force, they were generally unsuccessful. Industrialization was bringing women into factories and women were organizing on their own. This time they were included into unions as permanent members. During the wave of industrial unionization in the 1930s, workers organized on an industrial rather than craft basis. This wave of organizing included the largest number of women ever to be organized and was a major step forward in working women's history.

Present Situation

The present situation for women and unions is a new and complex one. Women, as stated before, make up a greater proportion of union membership than ever before (30 percent in 1980). In the 1970s, women workers were responsible for almost all of the growth of new union membership.[27] This corresponds to the general growth of female dominated jobs in the public and social service sectors. Public sector unions, like the American Federation of State, County, and Municipal Employees (AFSCME) have grown dramatically.

The 1970s saw intense activity by union women, such as developing women's caucuses and women's committees within unions, and organizing union women in and with women's liberation organizations. Women in unions and unions themselves started raising important issues—such as pay equity, affirmative action, childcare, and sexual harassment—in collective bargaining and legislation.

Working women's organizations have proliferated. Organizations that are outside the union movement, such as "9 to 5," have attempted to organize previously unorganized women. The inception of the Coalition of Labor Union Women (CLUW) within the traditional labor movement (as the largest union women's organization in U.S. history) has strengthened the power of women within the labor movement. Furthermore, there has been a definite increase in female labor leadership, and the labor movement has become one of the women's movement's chief allies on important feminist issues such as the ERA. (In 1973, the AFL-CIO reversed its previous position and endorsed the ERA.)

Women, however, are still severely underrepresented in total union membership. "In 1980, only 15.9 percent of the nation's employed women were labor organization members compared to 28.4 percent of men."[28] The overwhelming majority of women workers are unorganized and are still in the lowest paid, most devalued jobs. Unions have developed in a few occupations, but that growth has not been the result of any commitment to organizing female workers because they are women.

> The feminization of the labor movement was not the result of any special commitment to organizing women workers as *women*. Rather, it was the unintended consequence of a series of efforts to offset the general decline in membership by organizing particular occupational groups—at one stage, teachers; later hospital workers; and most recently, public-sector clerical and service workers. As a result, the composition of the organized female work force today is very different from the traditional base of the organized labor movement. By 1980, nearly half of the nation's six million organized women workers were in three major employment categories; educational services, medical services and public administration. Only a quarter were in manufacturing, labor's traditional stronghold.

The expansion of unionism among women workers has been quite selective, so that while some occupational categories are now highly organized, others—most importantly, private-sector clerical, service, and sales occupations, remain largely outside the labor movement. In the public sector, management opposition to unionization is generally less formidable than in comparable private-sector workplaces, and frequently public employees are already organized in associations (without collective bargaining rights), so that unionization victories are often considerably easier to achieve than in private industry. Consequently, many unions have rushed to organize public workers in order to boost membership levels—and dues—at a time when both are sorely needed. But there have been very few efforts to extend unionism to the millions of "pink collar" workers in such private industries as banking or insurance. Unionism among private-sector clericals remains very limited, and most of it involves clericals employed by manufacturing firms with organized blue-collar work forces.[29]

Given the growth rate of women in unions, women are still vastly underrepresented in union decision-making and leadership. While there has been some increase in female union leadership, particularly on the local level, male leadership still predominates.

The contradictory situation for women workers is related to the general difficulties unions are now facing. The growth of female union membership has taken place at a time when overall union membership has declined and the traditional stronghold of union membership—male dominated industrial workers—has weakened. According to a February 1985 report by the AFL-CIO Committee on the Evolution of Work,

...[D]espite their accomplishments, unions find themselves behind the pace of change. During the 1960s and 1970s the American work force grew in an unprecedented way—adding 1.3 million new workers per year in the 1960s and 2.1 million new workers per year in the 1970s—whereas the labor movement's membership remained static as gains made in organizing were offset due to job losses in basic industries. In the 1980s, union membership has shown a decline in absolute numbers as well as in percentage terms. The proportion of workers who are eligible to join a union and who in fact belong to a union has fallen from close to 45 percent to under 28 percent since 1954; using the measure of percentage of the entire work force, the decline has been from 35 percent to under 19 percent.[30]

First, the growth of the work force has occurred, and will continue to occur, principally in those sectors of the economy that have not traditionally been highly organized. Manufacturing and construction, for example, currently account for 50 percent of the AFL-CIO's membership, but those sectors have declined relative to others and currently employ only 22 percent of the civilian work force. In contrast, the service sector of the economy has had, and will continue to have, the largest growth. During the 1970s about 90 percent of all new jobs were added in service organizations. By 1990, service industries will employ almost three-quarters of the labor force. Yet, less than 10 percent of the service sector is organized, and only 20 percent of the AFL-CIO membership is in unions representing workers primarily in the service industries.[31]

The report fails to mention that these changes in the work force are accompanied not only by occupational shifts, but also by shifts in gender composition. The fastest growing segments of the wage-work force are female-dominated; the declining sectors are male dominated.

The union movement's weakened state, however, is not only due to the change in the wage work force. Other factors, such as heavy red-baiting and destruction of progressive trade unionism in the 1940s and 1950s, the concentration of industries, the growth of multinational corporations throughout the world, the increased use and exploitation of third world labor and markets, increased global competition, and the anti-union policies of the current U.S. administration, are all critical factors.

The union movement needs rebuilding. The previously mentioned report by the AFL-CIO committee, "The Changing Situation of Workers and Their Unions," is the first major public acknowledgement by the AFL-CIO leadership that important changes are needed. Some of the recommendations made in that report include:

Experimentation with new approaches to representing workers and addressing new issues of concern to workers. (The report explicitly mentions pay inequity as one such issue.)

Establishment by the AFL-CIO of a pilot project of an experimental organizing committee to find out the best ways to organize the unorganized.

Renewed committment to organizing (greater involvement on the part of union leadership).

Experimentation by unions with new organizing techniques.

Finding new ways for unions to involve both union members and non-union members.[32]

The report also fails to talk about women explicitly. However, women are in the best position to play a leading role in making these changes happen. Women are not only the most rapidly increasing group of workers but, in addition, many new union issues combine aspects of gender and work. The feminist movement has much to contribute to new ways of organizing, such as an understanding of the relationships between individual, personal, and group change.

At precisely the time that the labor movement needs rebuilding and is becoming "feminized," the feminist movement is at a crossroads. Since the defeat of 1984, feminists are grappling with the need to reinvigorate feminism and actualize its potential power. A major theme of this book is that for feminism to actually build economic/political power for broad change, it must unionize women workers. Similarly, labor will have to develop a totally new relationship to women if it is to become a real force. The integration of feminism and unions, the organization of women both as a gender and as workers, are the needed next steps.

Working Women's Organizations

In this exploration of the means necessary for women to actualize their economic and political power, we turn our focus to working women's organizations. Historically, working women's organizations have been almost the only vehicles for organizing women both as women and as workers.

Today, groups organizing women in the workplace include independent working women's organizations (such as "9 to 5"), women's caucuses within mixed-sex unions, and special conferences and organizations just for trade union women. By examining some working women's organizations, both past and present, we can gain a better understanding of the components needed to realize women's economic power.

The United States has a rich history of working women's organizations. Many of these groups came about as a result of alliances between working-class and middle-class women, often achieving a variety of beneficial results for working women. For example, working women's organizations in the late nineteenth and early twentieth centuries were crucial in passing legislation to protect working women and in unionizing unorganized women workers.

One such organization was the Working Women's Association (WWA) of 1868, an alliance of the leading feminists of the day— Elizabeth Cady Stanton and Susan B. Anthony—with women union leaders. In a very short time, it achieved several significant accomplishments. With the support of the middle-class WWA, women typesetters formed their own union and were among the first women to be admitted into a previously all-male union. Also, the WWA established an alliance with the National Labor Union, a leading male labor

organization of the time. For a short time, feminists advanced unionization as a major feminist issue; as a result of their efforts, trade union
men committed themselves to challenging sexual discrimination in the
workplace.

Another successful working women's group was the Illinois
Woman's Alliance (IWA) of the late 1880s, which brought together every
significant women's organization and the city federation of trade unions
in Chicago. Formed by socialists, feminists, and trade unionists, the
IWA encouraged trade unionism and social legislation on behalf of
women workers and workers in general. The IWA conducted a massive
survey of sweatshops; it formulated model laws for compulsory education and the regulation of work conditions in places employing women
and children; it ran campaigns pressuring for more schools in poor
neighborhoods, and defended the legal rights of street-walking
prostitutes.[1]

Another working women's organization was the American Women's
Trade Union League (WTUL), formed in 1903 in Boston by representatives of labor women, trade unionists, and the settlement house
movement. The League was an alliance of wealthy women ("allies") and
working women who combined a philosophy of social reform with trade
union concern. The League's platform called for the organization of all
workers, equal pay for equal work, an eight-hour day, a living wage, and
full citizenship for women (i.e., the vote). The League played a
significant role in aiding major women's strikes from 1903 to 1917. It
provided the backbone of support for the great Shirtwaist-maker's Strike
of 1909, helped thousands of women to organize and unionize, provided
leadership training for many working women, and supported some of
the outstanding women labor leaders of the time.[2]

The New York WTUL is the subject of a recent in-depth study by
Nancy Schrom Dye, "Feminism or Unionism? The New York Women's
Trade Union League and the Labor Movement." Dye's purpose in
studying the WTUL was to examine the problems faced in "synthesizing
a commitment to the women's movement with a commitment to
organized labor."[3] Her article explores and analyzes the many problems
which the WTUL faced attempting to carry out this goal, and envisions a
unionism which could include all women and integrate a feminist
perspective into its other concerns.

The issues Dye discusses can be applied to all working women's
groups, past and present. These include, on the one hand, the proper
relationship between women and the union movement, between feminist concerns and the process of unionization of women; and on the
other, the attempt to integrate women's oppression as women with their
oppression as workers in order to deal with that double oppression.

As Dye explains, the first years of the WTUL were devoted to unionizing unorganized women workers. The group made significant contributions to that goal and was vital in building permanent and stable unions for women. However, during its early years the League faced a number of problems in its relationship to the American Federation of Labor (AFL). Many specific AFL practices were contradictory to building a labor movement based on gender equality and organizing unorganized workers.

> By trying to follow A.F. of L. practices, the New York League was caught in a double bind. League members were well aware of the A.F. of L's discriminatory practices and negative attitudes toward women, yet given the structure of the early twentieth-century labor movement, they had little choice but to push women to join A.F. of L. unions. In their efforts to integrate women into the male-dominated labor movements and in their desire to appear as respectable trade unionists to the A.F. of L., League members were often forced to subordinate their commitment to feminism for a conservative trade union philosophy that was usually incompatible with their constituents' needs as workers and as women.[4]

The League had specific feminist goals regarding the unionization of working women. It wanted to organize working women into unions, integrate women as equals into the established labor movement, and train women to be active union participants and leaders. AFL policies, including overt discrimination, inhibited these goals in many ways. For example, the AFL organized workers into craft unions on a shop-by-shop basis. Such unions were designed for skilled workers; most women workers were unskilled or semi-skilled. In addition, the AFL required that all unions organized by the League affiliate with AFL unions. This posed many problems for women workers because of high dues, and the curtailment of local autonomy (women often organized into small, independent unions).

AFL and the League came into conflict in many instances, and the Lawrence Strike of 1912 was a major example. This strike, one of the largest and most militant in United States history, involved a working population that was at least 50 percent women and children. (Because of the strength of female participation, Bill Haywood, a leader of the strike, claimed that "women won the strike.") The AFL opposed the Lawrence Strike and required that the League oppose it, too. (The AFL only supported its own local union, the United Textile Workers, which organized craft workers and would have nothing to do with the immigrant, unskilled working people of Lawrence.) League leadership was torn, but felt that it had to comply.

Dye poses the question of whether the League had any other options. On the one hand, women were more successful when they organized small, independent unions in which they were able to lead. However, Dye argues that the League did not have any real alternative to the AFL.

> The Women's Trade Union League might have worked for the formation of industrial unions rather than adhering to the increasingly irrelevant craft union model....It would have been impossible, however, for the WTUL to have launched a campaign for industrial unionism in a labor movement that had no significant industrial tradition....The fact is in the early twentieth century United States, the American Federation of Labor represented the only model for successful trade unionism, despite its obvious and severe disadvantages for female workers.
>
> ...Thus the Women's Trade Union League of New York had little success in creating unions that were effective, stable labor organizations and that met the WTUL's feminist objectives of giving women opportunities for self-assertion and responsibility. Alternatives such as separate women's unions or women's federal unions, while perhaps attractive from a feminist standpoint, made little sense from a trade unionist point of view. Yet the course the League pursued of attempting to integrate women into the labor movement by following the principles and practices of the A.F. of L. was rarely satisfactory. Moreover, given the attitudes of male trade unionists, the structure of the early twentieth century labor movement, and the weak economic position of most working women, neither A.F. of L.-style craft unions nor independent women's organizations could meet female workers' needs. The Women's Trade Union League's goal of creating a feminist labor movement remained unrealized.[5]

The question of organizational affiliation has not been an easy one for working women, and Dye's study of the WTUL gives some reasons why. In an effort to understand some of the difficulties encountered by the WTUL, Dye looks at the League's unsuccessful attempt to reconcile dual oppression by trying to reconcile women workers' commitment to both the labor movement and the women's movement.

> The women who made up the organization were never able to reconcile their dedication to women as an oppressed minority within the work force and their commitment to the labor movement as a *whole*. Belief in sisterhood, they discovered, was not always compatible with a belief in the importance of

class solidarity. In other words, members were unable to develop a solution to the problem of women's dual exploitation: were women workers oppressed because they were workers or because they were female? In effect, many controversies which troubled the organization were in large part a reflection of this struggle as well as ideological ramifications for many members.[6]

The dilemma of not being able to resolve its dual commitment strongly affected the League's development. Some of its members were committed to looking at the problems of women workers from their special interest as women, while others looked at such problems from the vantage point of their identities as workers. One major debate in the League was whether to emphasize unionization for women workers or focus on winning protective legislation for women. This debate reflected the underlying tension between viewing women workers as women or as workers.

These conflicts have been raised again and again in the history of every working women's organization, past and present. How should feminists and women workers relate to existing institutions? Should women organize their own independent unions or join the large established unions? And how can working women integrate an understanding of their oppression as women and as workers? Is this at all possible? In the rest of this book these questions will be explored by looking at three organizations for wage-working women which have explicitly attempted to integrate both feminism and trade unionism, gender issues and women's work issues. The organizations to be examined are: the Working Women's Association (WWA), founded in 1868; Union WAGE, formed in 1971; and Coalition of Labor Union Women (CLUW), formed in 1974.

The WWA of 1868 is examined as an important historical example. While it was short-lived, it is one of the best and earliest examples of a working women's feminism. Through the association, two parallel alliances were formed: one with the National Labor Union (NLU), and the second within WWA itself, between middle-class feminists and working-class women typesetters.

The WWA came about when Susan B. Anthony and Elizabeth Cady Stanton, editors of the *Revolution*, the first radical feminist journal in the United States, became involved with a group of female typesetters who had been excluded from the existing all-male National Typographical Union (NTU). The alliance between these feminist leaders and working-class typesetters made possible the formation of a women's typesetting union and put pressure on the NTU to accept that union, thereby becoming one of the first unions to admit women. At the same time, Anthony and Stanton were growing closer politically to the leaders of the NLU. The two feminist leaders developed a highly sophisticated analysis of the relationship between wage labor and sexism both inside and outside the wage-work force. The *Revolution* also carried many articles supporting the activities of the NLU. The NLU, in return, took the most advanced position on women workers of any group of labor unions up to that time.

Both Union WAGE (recently defunct) and CLUW are contemporary organizations. While almost all other feminist-oriented case studies of unions have looked at the past, I have chosen to emphasize these two because their development reveals the unique opportunities for integrating feminism and unionism at the present time. CLUW and Union WAGE, in contrast to other contemporary working women's organizations, have attempted to bring together labor and feminist issues.

Like the WWA, Union WAGE was a pioneer organization. Formed in the early 1970s, it was the first organization of that generation to understand the importance of integrating women's liberation and trade unionism. Founded by a small group of women who had been active trade unionists, and leftists,* WAGE addressed the neglect of working women by the existing feminist movement. WAGE's major goal was to bring women's liberation to the workplace and the organization's emphasis was on women as wage-workers. While WAGE leaders understood the need to organize around women's issues in the workplace, their focus was on "women as workers," and they continually emphasized the need for the women's liberation movement to incorporate an understanding of wage labor and unionism for women. The organization remained relatively small, but in its early years in particular it had a significant impact on the West Coast as the major advocate for trade union women.

This book will trace the three major struggles that went on within the WAGE organization, each of which reveals another dimension of the process of integrating women's liberation and trade unionism. One struggle revolved around the historical conflict between protective legislation and the ERA. Another conflict was between the trade union women who had originally formed WAGE, and a group of women who entered the organization afterward. Coming out of the radical feminist and socialist feminist movements, this second group questioned WAGE's original focus on unions and wage-work. The struggle between these two factions is one of the best examples of the "woman as woman" versus "woman as worker" positions.

*Left and left-wing will be used to refer to groups that identify as left in the political spectrum and/or explicitly work for radical social change.

The third major debate within WAGE concerned the strategy for building unions that would be best able to meet the needs of women workers. While WAGE leaders were pro-union in principle, they were quite critical of the existing trade union movement because of its history of sexism and racism. In light of this, WAGE debated whether the best way for women workers to organize was to form their own independent union, or to work for change within the established trade union structure. The WAGE newspaper contained one of the most illuminating debates on this question, one that had been troubling working women for years.

In contrast to Union WAGE, which worked outside the existing union movement, CLUW was the first modern organization of union women to operte within the established trade union structure. While CLUW is not a union itself, it represents union women and has become the largest national organization of union women ever to emerge in the United States.

During the first two years of CLUW's existence—1974-75—its leadership, composed of prominent female trade unionists, was engaged in a fight with left-wing groups for control of the organization. Critical of the established labor movement, the leftists believed that CLUW should be independent of the AFL-CIO, Teamsters, and all other existing unions, and should be open to non-union women as well. The union-based leadership of CLUW, while critical of some aspects of the established trade union movement—especially the sexism—nevertheless believed that women needed to work within existing structures.

After a two-year struggle, the left-wing faction was defeated and CLUW became, as intended, an organization open only to union women in conjunction with the existing union movement. Since the mid-1970s, CLUW has operated as a strong pressure group for women's rights within the labor movement.

CLUW's major success to date has been to bring gender issues to the labor movement. Yet much of the labor movement is still run by men, and most women workers remain unorganized. A study of CLUW makes it clear that certain important questions are yet to be answered. How will complete equality for women be won within the union movement? Can CLUW maintain a cooperative relationship with the AFL-CIO and still assert independence in key areas? What is needed to organize all unorganized women workers? Through my analysis of these case studies, I will attempt to discover answers to these questions.

Analytical Structure

Four major criteria will be used to measure the effectiveness of each organization. The organization's:

1. theory and practice around the double oppression of women;

2. approach to the unionization of women, particularly from a feminist perspective;

3. approach to stimulating change within the existing labor and feminist movements, facilitating direct contact between unions and feminism;

4. broader political programs for change.

Working women's organization need to develop both a coherent theory and practice relating to women's double oppression if they are to empower women. It is helpful if the theory is explicit, but it does not have to be so.

In terms of practice, there are four categories of issues that have been addressed by working women's organizations—moving from issues which affect all workers to issues which affect women exclusively, including those outside the wage-work force:

1. work issues that women share with men, such as wages, job security, etc.;

2. work issues that are distinctly female, such as organizing unorganized women workers;

3. gender issues in the work force, such as maternity leave, pay equity, affirmative action, etc.;

4. gender issues outside the work force, such as the ERA, which affect all women but also have implications for the work force.

A given organization will most likely lean to one side or the other of this continuum of issues. To be effective, though, it needs to see the equal and related importance of both gender and work issues. To gain power, working women's organizations need to deal adequately with all four categories of issues.

Empowering women depends on unionizing *all* women as workers. The strength of any working women's organization therefore depends on the ability to unionize. In addition, the process of unionization for women is enhanced by, if not dependent on, its ability to address gender issues and to build democratically run unions on a grassroots level.

To facilitate change within the existing labor and feminist movements, working women's organizations must serve as a bridge between feminism and unions, building alliances between the two; and they have to change both movements at the points where the conflicts occur. That is, they have to change both the anti-union attitudes and practices of the existing feminist movement, and the sexist attitudes and practices of existing union movement.

Changes need to occur in the labor movement regarding its almost all-male leadership, its failure to organize unorganized workers, and its forms that make it difficult for women to participate. The feminist movement needs to recognize the importance of unionization, organize unorganized working women, and ally with working-class people over issues of concern to both women and men.

Forums for such broad political change include collective bargaining, legislative reforms, and electoral activity. At the height of its strength, the trade union movement was the driving force behind major political changes in the United States and was responsible for forging the most progressive domestic legislation. With adequate organization, this could happen again.

In comparison to feminist organizations that do not work on labor issues, working women's organizations have tended to articulate much more comprehensive social and economic programs for fundamental social change. In trade unions, working women are often at the forefront of progressive change.

Today, feminists are in a position both to forge a coalition of all oppressed groups and to articulate a comprehensive economic and social program. Feminists will be able to accomplish these ambitious goals when women are organized on the basis of their economic power.

Working Women's Association of 1868

5

From the beginning of the women's rights movement in the 1840s, its advocates put forward a sweeping vision which understood that basic change was necessary to achieve women's freedom. This transforming vision was articulated particularly by Susan B. Anthony and Elizabeth Cady Stanton.

This larger vision was usually combined with a list of specific demands for women's rights. This two-pronged approach—the vision and the concrete program—was exemplified at the 1848 Seneca Falls Convention, which has often been viewed as the official starting point of modern U.S. feminism. At this convention, *A Declaration of the Rights of Sentiments*, modeled after the Declaration of Independence, was drawn up. It called for a broad scope of rights for women, including: equality in marriage, property rights, the right to earn equal wages, to have child custody, to make contracts, to testify in court, to inherit property, and the right to vote. The document also included a long list of injuries which clearly attributed women's subordination to the domination of men over women.[1] Women's freedom, as expressed at Seneca Falls and in the writings of several feminist leaders, was seen simultaneously as the fight for specific rights as well as for a fundamentally changed society.*

*Zillah Eisenstein, in *The Radical Future of Liberal Feminism*, analyzes the connection and tension between radical feminism and the fight for legal rights, which was often accompanied by a liberal-Republican philosophy.

Suffrage: Key
Demand of Feminism

Following the Civil War, suffrage became the specific link between reformist and radical visions of feminism. There were several reasons why, out of many demands, the vote emerged as the pivotal issue of the women's rights movement.

The vote had become the key issue for blacks after the abolition of slavery. Given the basis of liberal democracy, citizenship meant very little without it. Disenfranchisement was a symptom of black people's political powerlessness; gaining the vote was the route, or so it seemed, to legal equality. Suffrage proved important in ensuring the gains of Reconstruction.

Early feminists worked to eliminate individual property ownership of women by men. The second step was to fight women's exclusion from institutions outside the family. After women made certain gains, especially around property rights, the vote became crucial. It appeared to be necessary for entrance into the public world, without which other demands for legal equality could not be won. When the Fourteenth Amendment of 1866 granted the vote to black men but not to women of any race, women were forced to make suffrage a central demand.

In her pioneer work, *Feminism and Suffrage: The Emergence of an Independent Women's Movement in America: 1848-1869*, Ellen DuBois argues that the vote was a radical demand; from the beginning, it significantly challenged male authority and was meant to establish women's public life outside the family. Thus it was the most controversial demand in the early program for women's rights. DuBois observes that while women were winning property rights, they were consistently denied the vote.[2]

In my opinion, there was another crucial factor that made the vote, at least symbolically, the most radical feminist demand of that time. Although a demand put forward by white, middle-class women, the vote was a goal that could potentially unite *all* women and one which would directly affect working-class, black, and immigrant women. Other reforms, especially those related to property rights and higher education, primarily affected only middle- and upper-class white women. While many critics of the suffrage movement claimed that suffrage was mainly in the interests of middle-class women, the vote was at various times supported by working-class, black, and immigrant women. For its time, it at least raised the possibility of a women's movement that could begin to cut through the boundaries of class and race. In its original conception, suffrage stood for the emancipation of *all* women as *women*.

Also, suffrage came to represent much more than it actually was. It stood for female power. Suffrage appeared to link a specific right (the vote) with a picture of freedom from all forms of institutional sexism, and it held the promise that women as a united force could bring about major political changes both for themselves and for other oppressed groups.

It should be noted that there was a split in the suffrage movement almost from the start, and that in the faction led by Susan B. Anthony and Elizabeth Cady Stanton, suffrage was part of a much larger program of freedom and equality. For Stanton and Anthony, suffrage was a vehicle both for the individual liberation of women as independent, self-determining individuals, and also for institutional liberation from economic, political, and social oppression.

After the Civil War, as the U.S. Constitution was being amended to allow newly freed male slaves to vote, the suffrage movement split over the issue of black male suffrage. The proposed Fourteenth Amendment was written so as to grant all *male* citizens the right to vote. (This was the first time that the word "male" had been used in the Constitution.) The proposed Fifteenth Amendment explicitly stated that the vote could not be denied "on account of race, colour, or previous condition of servitude." While some members of the women's suffrage movement fought to add the word "sex" to those conditions, other members of the women's rights movement, who primarily identified themselves as abolitionists, were willing to work for black male suffrage and postpone the issue of women's suffrage until the Fifteenth Amendment was passed. This group, led by Lucy Stone, Henry Blackwell, and others, formed the American Woman Suffrage Association in 1869. The other side, led by militant feminists Stanton and Anthony, believed that women's needs should not be postponed, and opposed the Fifteenth Amendment while proclaiming its belief in universal suffrage.[3]

The two groups were not able to reconcile their differences. While the abolitionists articulated the needs of black men often at the expense of women (both white and black), suffragists who argued on women's behalf often used overtly racist arguments. This racism went hand-in-hand with a growing anti-male sentiment. Stanton and Anthony even argued that black men might be more tyrannical than white men and that white women would be better voters than black men.[4] Eventually, the Fourteenth and Fifteenth Amendments were passed, granting the vote to all male citizens, but saying nothing about the rights of women.

Not surprisingly, the Stone-Blackwell group was much more conservative than the Stanton-Anthony group on nearly all other questions as well. After the passage of the Fifteenth Amendment, Stone and Blackwell concentrated solely on gaining the vote for women, refusing to combine suffrage with any other feminist issues because they feared alienating middle- and upper-class women. Their newspaper, the *Woman's Journal,* was geared mainly to professional women and women of leisure, while the *Revolution,* Stanton and Anthony's paper, presented a radical feminist program with female suffrage as its central component.[5]

It is ironic that the feminists who stood firm on the question of female emancipation were not able to integrate an understanding of racism and its interconnection with sexism. The dilemma has remained a crucial issue throughout the history of feminism. Women are members of all races, classes, and ethnic groups. *In order for women to be freed as women, they must fight against all oppressions, including those that affect men.* In other words, for feminists to support the interests of black women, they must fight the effects of racism on black men too.

The specific case of the Fifteenth Amendment is just one example of a dilemma that the women's movement still faces today, as it struggles for the liberation not only of women, but also of other oppressed groups.

New Allies and a New Constituency

The conflict between the abolitionists and other suffragists compelled Elizabeth Cady Stanton and Susan B. Anthony to search for a new base and new allies. This search led to one of the most important episodes in early feminist history; the feminists allied themselves with the all-male National Labor Union, forming the first major feminist/union alliance. This in turn led them to join with wage-working women to build a working women's feminist organization. These new political alliances were accompanied by the development of a fresh theoretical perspective about feminism.

In January 1868, Stanton and Anthony started the newspaper *Revolution,* which was the most exciting feminist journal of its time.* Within its pages, theory, vision, and analysis of female oppression and emancipation were developed. The *Revolution*'s motto, "Principle, Not Policy—Justice, Not Favors—Men Their Rights and Nothing More— Women Their Rights and Nothing Less," symbolized a new independence after their break with the abolitionists.[6]

> The *Revolution* was not the first American periodical dedicated to the improvement of women's status...However,

*George Francis Train, an outspoken racist, was the original financial backer for the *Revolution.* Old allies from the abolitionist camp were deeply upset and criticized accepting aid from Train, but the feminists replied that since Train's was the only support they had, they were willing to take it.

the *Revolution* was certainly the least trammeled and most daring feminist paper that had yet—and perhaps has ever— appeared. In its pages, the editors—Stanton, Anthony and Parker—convey a complex sense of women's oppression and a rich vision of their emancipation. "Take the Revolution," Stanton advised, "in which not only the ballot, but bread and babies will be discussed." The *Revolution* reported on female farmers, inventors, sailors, and thieves, or any woman who disproved that "nature contended [sic] them all for the one mission of housekeepers." The editors wrote and reprinted articles on prostitution, infanticide, and the nonmonoga- mous practices of Oneida communitarians and Utah Mormons. They published the writings of Frances Wright and Mary Wollstonecraft and discovered feminist heritage that was many centuries old. Friends advised them to change the paper's name to something more in keeping with the genteel tradition of women's journalism, but only the *Revolution* would suit them. It indicated their goal of building woman suffrage into a movement that promised women total revolution in every aspect of their lives.[7]

All aspects of female oppression were discussed in the *Revolution*, including analyses of marriage, religion, and the economy. Suffrage was often discussed as the vehicle for advancing the entire cause of female liberation.

The radical vision of the *Revolution*'s editors led them to one of their most significant advances: an economic analysis of the oppression of both women and working people. Previous feminist thought had included some understanding of the economic aspects of women's lives. For example, the Seneca Falls Declaration included a section about excluding women from access to jobs and money, but emphasized the exclusion of women from the professions. In 1866, the Woman's Rights Convention accepted a report by Caroline H. Dall about the broader need for female employment, job training, better working conditions, and equal pay for equal work.[8] This set the stage for Stanton and Anthony to go beyond what had already existed in the feminist movement. The *Revolution* included a pioneer article on women's unpaid domestic labor and its importance in the larger work force.[9] In addition, Stanton and Anthony analyzed the exploitation of wage labor under capitalism an its relationship to sexism. The addition of a radical economic analysis to a feminist theory that had previously emphasized only the legal aspects of female oppression was a major step forward. And it had clearly developed from the growing alliance between feminists and the leaders of the National Labor Union.

The National Labor Union

In 1866, two years before the founding of the *Revolution,* the National Labor Union (NLU) was created. One of the first national labor federations in the United States, it was composed of trade unionists and labor reformers.

Historically, trade unions had functioned to protect skilled white male workers from management and from other workers. Skilled white men, a minority of the working population, were often hostile to unskilled or semi-skilled workers, women, and blacks. Since these workers were a potentially competitive force (and were often consciously used that way), skilled workers organized to protect their interests. A major goal of the National Labor Union was to change that tendency. To broaden the labor movement's constituency, the NLU made a point of allying itself with women and blacks, bringing organized labor into the world of independent political change. Although there would be continued conflicts within the NLU between the largely conservative representatives of the skilled trades and the more progressive reformers, the overall NLU was part of the early group of working class liberationists who understood that there could be no victory for workers without challenging the divisions among workers.

The NLU had two common grounds with the feminists of the *Revolution.* First was their common interest in the cause of working women. The National Labor Union was the first national labor federation that pledged support to working women. Second, both groups had become disillusioned with the two major political parties. They both envisioned an independent political program that would unite their interests, contribute to wide social change, and perhaps lead to a third party.[10]

William Sylvis, a major NLU leader, was its most outstanding advocate for working women. Although, like almost all other trade unionists at the time, he believed that women did not belong in the wage labor force, Sylvis became convinced that the labor movement needed to be united. According to him, this meant including women and blacks. Under Sylvis's leadership, the 1866 National Labor Convention pledged "individual and undivided support to the sewing women, factory cooperatives, and daughters of toil."[11] One year later, the NLU recommended that working men endorse equal pay for equal work and help women form labor organizations. Although the pledge to working women and statements of support may have had little direct influence on most unionists (other than the Cigar Makers International Union, which was the first national union to admit women into membership), the pledge to working women opened the door for union alliance with radical feminists. It strengthened the position of progressive male trade unionists and expressed the potential of a labor movement that could represent *all* workers.

Beginnings of the Alliance Between Feminists and the National Labor Union

While the leaders of the National Labor Union and the feminists of the *Revolution* did not actually meet until the July 1868 Democratic Party Convention, there was important indirect interaction and several parallel developments occurred between the two groups.

The first issue of the *Revolution*, on January 8, 1868, announced a commitment to "suffrage, irrespective of color or sex; to equal pay for equal work; the eight-hour day; the abolition of party despotism; currency reform; unrestricted immigration; and the regeneration of American society," along with the slogan "Down with Politicians, Up with People."[12] From the start, many of the National Labor Union's ideas were accepted by the *Revolution*, and the NLU received a lot of publicity in this feminist magazine. As early as April 1868, the *Revolution* had declared, "The Principles of the National Labor Union are *our* principles. We see on the surface of this great movement the dawn of brighter days."[13] It even printed a biography of William Sylvis.[14] Most important, the *Revolution* endorsed all of the NLU's planks: the eight-hour day, land reform opposition to monopolies, producer and consumer cooperatives, currency reform, and trade unionism.[15]

From the beginning, the *Revolution* not only endorsed and supported the NLU, it also supported a political program more far-reaching than that of any other feminist organization. Just as the NLU understood the need for a political program more encompassing than its immediate trade union demands, the feminists were also seeing feminism in the context of greater social change. Susan B. Anthony and Elizabeth Cady Stanton saw themselves initiating the rudiments of a people's movement against oppression, in which feminists, working people, and blacks would ally against exploitation. (Despite their break with the abolitionists, Stanton and Anthony continued to speak against racial injustice.)

The development of the feminists' political platform was accompanied by their advancement of theoretical analyses concerning capitalism and the relationship between wage labor and sexism. In 1868, Elizabeth Cady Stanton delivered a speech, "On Labor," in which she stated,

> I find that the same principle degrades labor as upheld slavery.
> The great motive for making man a slave was to get his labor

or its results for nothing. When we consider that the slave was provided with food and clothes and that the ordinary wages of the laborer provide his bare necessities, we see that in a money point of view they hold the same position. And the owner of one form of labor occupies no higher moral status than the other because the same motive governs in both cases.[16]

Much of the speech condemned the life of wage-workers under capitalism.

Let us look deep down into the present relations of the human family and see if the conditions of different classes cannot be more fairly established. Under all forms of government, about seven-tenths of the human family are doomed to incessant toil, living in different degrees of poverty from the man who hopes for nothing but daily bread for himself and family, to the one who aims at education and accumulation.[17]

Stanton and her associates had developed a clear understanding of the relationship between capital and labor. One of the *Revolution's* editorials, "Capital and Labor," stated,

Behold one class, mid ease and luxury, dying out with ennui and excess, yet imagining itself made to mold the masses to its will, while the great unwashed, sullen with hardship and injustice, accept their condition, with occasional outbursts, as hopeless...You who boast that in this and all men are free, look for a moment at the laborer's lot. He rises early to a scant breakfast, with his wife and his children in poverty and rags, and with his dinner in hand goes forth to daily toil.[18]

The major link between the National Labor Union and the *Revolution*'s editors was their mutual interest in working women. This shared area of concern was one of the reasons why the feminists also developed a very sophisticated analysis of wage-working women's double oppression along with their understanding of the exploitation of wage labor under capitalism. The matter was put this way in one of the earliest issues of the *Revolution*:

Look in the world of work. In trade and commerce disfranchised class and outlaws, Ishmaelites. Credit and Captial are to them impossible—hence women are crowded out of all profitable and honorable employments with no choice in life but a marriage of necessity, prostitution, or starvation. The capitalist is, today, using the cheap labor of women to grind to powder the man by her side, thus violating the laws of nature by creating antagonism between men and women where, in the nature of things no real antagonism exists. A disfranchised class degrades and cheapens every branch of labor it enters...hence it is to the interest of the laboring man to dignify the woman by his side to give her the ballot that when she strikes for higher wages, capitalists and politicians knowing the discontent of woman, too, can find expression at the ballot box, will take heed to a strike that has a vote behind it. In those factories where women work beside women, they work more hours than where men work alone...A disfranchised class cheapens whatever labor it touches. The employments of women are uniformly considered degrading for men— hence the tailor, the man milliner, the hairdresser and the work are sneered at.[19]

Feminists realized that sexism was an integral part of class experience. While all workers, male and female, were exploited as workers, women workers were used as cheap labor, segregated in a few overcrowded professions, and discriminated against or excluded from other jobs. *The feminists did not blame the male workers or see them as enemies. They saw that the natural relationship between men and women was one of unity and it was the capitalist, using women as cheap labor, who created the conflict.* Feminists urged working men to support women's causes (including suffrage, equal wages, and employment opportunities), claiming that it was not in men's interest to have capitalists use women as cheap labor. The solution for working men was not sexism, but equality with women. During the short period of time that feminists worked with organized labor and working women, such issues as unionization, equal pay, job training, and equal employment opportunities were seen as crucial feminist issues. This program laid the basis for a working women's feminism.

In a parallel development, there was growing support and sympathy for working women within the National Labor Union. On July 2, 1868, leading NLU officials passed the following resolution:

Resolved, that the low wage, long hours and damaging service, to which multitudes of working girls and women are doomed, destroy health, imperil virtue, and are a standing reproach to civilization; that we would urge them to learn trades, engage in business, join our labor unions, or use any other honorable means to persuade or force men to render unto every woman according to his works.[20]

Feminists and labor leaders were in agreement about sexual inequality within the wage-work force, but not necessarily outside it. The feminists understood that the double oppression of working women was caused by the situation of women both at home and in the wage-work force; they were concerned with the situation of all women, not just wage-workers. Labor leaders shared an analysis, and eventually a common program, with the women's movement which challenged the mistreatment of wage-working women, but they continued to believe that a woman's place was in the home. While some members of the National Labor Union were in favor of suffrage, many were not; as an organization, they never endorsed suffrage.

The Formation of the Alliance

In July 1868, the *Revolution*'s editors and the NLU labor leaders met at the Democratic Party presidential convention. While neither group was able to get the Democratic Party to support their platforms, they were able to cement a relationship with each other, based on their mutual commitments to labor reform, the cause of working women, and the possibility of building a third political party.

Meanwhile, the *Revolution* invited all unions and organizations that worked for the "amelioration of the condition of those who labor for a living," to attend an upcoming NLU convention. The editors of the *Revolution* particularly urged women to attend, noting that the NLU convention call was "addressed to workingmen only; the voice and action of some former meetings and the liberal tone of the newspaper devoted to the interests of the Union lead us confidently to believe that working *women* also will be admitted to the body if they make the proper application."[21]

At the National Labor Union's convention of September 1868, Susan B. Anthony made sure that women would be represented by attending with three other suffragists, Mary Putnam, Mary McDonald, and Elizabeth Cady Stanton. All four requested delegate status. With the exception of Stanton, they all had credentials from labor organizations that were formed before the convention. Stanton was the only woman whose credentials were challenged because she came from a suffragist organization. Delegates, mainly from the building trades, argued that Stanton should not be admitted because she did not come from a labor organization. They made it clear, however, that what they really opposed was her stand on suffrage. Sylvis argued on behalf of Stanton, stating that she is "one of the boldest writers of her age ... [who] has done more than anybody I know to elevate her class and my class, too and God knows they need elevation."[22] However, he also made it clear that seating Stanton did not mean an endorsement of women's suffrage. Stanton was seated on the first vote, but delegates from the building trades threatened to walk out if she remained. A compromise was negotiated by passing a resolution that stated, "By admission of Mrs. Stanton as a delegate to this body, the National Labor Congress does not regard itself as endorsing her particular ideas or committing itself to the question of Female Suffrage."[23]

Suffrage reappeared as an area of conflict later in the convention. The Committee on Female Labor rejected a recommendation that its resolution should call for "securing the ballot." Still, major steps were made towards fighting sexism within the work force. J.C. Whaley, the retiring President of the NLU, stated that "the question of female labor is one of paramount importance to the industrial classes and merits the attention of trade organizations, local and national."[24] Addressing sexual competition in the work force, he argued that working men should respond to the use of women as competition not by excluding them, but by working with them to raise their wages.

The report made by the Committee on Female Labor was historic. It urged the extension of the eight-hour day to women workers and trade unions for working women. It also encouraged women "to learn trades, engage in business, join our labor unions, or form protective unions of their own, and use every other honorable means to persuade or force employers to do justice to women by paying them equal wages for equal work."[25]

When the report (minus any reference to women's suffrage) was adopted by the convention, the National Labor Union became the first labor federation in the world's history to vote for equal pay for equal work. Indeed, to Karl Marx, this stand made the NLU one of the most significant organizations in the world labor movement. Thus he wrote to a friend in America,

> Great progress was evidenced in the last Congress of the National Labor Union in that among other things it treated working women with complete equality while in this respect the English, and the still gallant French, are burdened with a spirit of narrow-mindedness. Anybody knows, if he knows anything about history, that great social changes are impossible without the feminine ferment. Social progress can be measured exactly by the social progress of the fair sex.[26]

The convention also adopted as a goal the creation of an independent, labor-based political party. Stanton believed that the major accomplishments of the convention were the formation of a national party and the recognition of women. "They have inaugurated the grandest movement of the century, proved themselves wise in reading the signs of the times, and cunning in securing the only element of faith and enthusiasm that will make the NEW NATIONAL PARTY OF AMERICA...triumphant in 1872."[27] Continued enthusiasm was expressed in the pages of the *Revolution*.

> The Admission of four women as delegates marks a new era in Workingmens [sic] Conventions. And the appointment of Mrs. Catherine Melaney, President of the Collar Laundry Union of Troy, composed of five hundred women, as assistant Secretary, whose duty it will be to organize Labor Unions all over the country, shows the recognition of woman to be the future policy of the National Labor Congress...The producer—the workingmen, the women, the negroes—are destined to form a triple power that shall speedily wrest the centre of government from the non-producers—the land monopolists, the bondholders, the politicians.[28]

Combined with a sense of achievement for women, suffragists celebrated the potential power of an alliance between themselves, labor, and blacks. In the above quote, it is clear that in their eyes, the "enemy" was government and big business.

Everyone involved agreed that important steps were taken at the convention for the progress of both women and working people. From the feminists' point of view, the primary loss was suffrage. It was rejected partly because it was viewed as a middle-class reform but also because, despite their advanced views on women workers, Sylvis and the other progressive male trade unionists believed that women's natural place was the home. Suffrage, at least on a symbolic level, questioned traditional male and female roles and symbolized a radical equality between men and women.

The major gender issue accepted by both labor and women leaders was equal pay for equal work. However, given the fact that most women did very different work than men, that demand could not be won without changing the segregated nature of the work force. Furthermore, genuine equality in the work force meant that both sexism at home and gender roles in the wage-work force would have to end. No one but the feminists of the *Revolution* and perhaps a few others were ready to take the steps needed to accomplish that kind of equality. Even the advances made for women workers at the National Labor Union's convention were accepted by most of the men present because they feared competition from women workers, rather than because they were ideologically committed to women's freedom.

What suffragists learned at the convention was that men could be won over as allies, at least in the fight for women's rights within the wage-work force. And the feminists had played a crucial role in moving labor forward.

The Formation of the Working Women's Association #1 _____

The Working Women's Association #1 was formed immediately prior to the 1868 National Labor Union convention for the express purpose of providing Anthony and the others with delegate credentials. Although the Association turned out to be short-lived (September 1868 to December 1869), it did much more than merely qualify feminists to attend a labor convention. It could be considered the first working woman's feminist organization in the United States.

Establishing a statement of beliefs was among the first activities of the Association. Its platform began: "The working women today, like those of the past, belong to a large class of manufacturing and distributing producers, and as such are entitled to recognition and adequate remuneration in the great army of the world's work." It went on to say that, because of a lack of "just estimate" of women's work, no definite wage had ever been fixed in the departments of women's special industries, and this had given rise to various abuses, particularly "the oppression of working women by corrupt and avaricious employers," which caused "poverty, misery and death. . . Hence the necessity of association in order that we may attain enlightened views, devise plans for cooperation, and establish our position on an equitable basis."[29]

The members of the Association understood that women workers experienced a special oppression. Gaining recognition for their labor, recognizing their right to organize themselves as workers into unions, and fighting for adequate pay were all fundamental to their struggle.

A major theme continually expressed in the Association was the fight against class and gender inequality. At a meeting of the Association's Local One, held in September 1868, Emily Peers, a typesetter, and one of the Association's Vice Presidents said,

> As a working woman—one who has accepted its conditions, desiring to carry out the idea of this association, "The amelioration and elevation of working women"—I feel a freedom to briefly outline my thoughts, believing they are shared by many of my sisters in toil, as well as sex.
>
> In this city where not only the poor of our land, but the ignorant, the degraded of all nationalities are herded together, forced by the instinct of self-preservation to the sharpest of

competition one with another, it is especially necessary that efforts, organized and persistent, should be put forth by every well-wisher of humanity to better their condition.

And upon the very threshold of this movement, looking to the improvement, social, moral and physical of women, having only her welfare in mind, it becomes us to carefully, dispassionately consider what are her needs... Inequality between the sexes, as well as in the sex itself, we know have always existed. There has been inequality of wealth, of social status, of all that divides and makes caste in life...

I want to see labor dignified; I want to see my sex elevated; I want to see all of my inequality removed and in the growing intelligence of the age, in the moral forces of the public mind, I build my faith that all will be accomplished.[30]

This commitment to integrating the issues of sex and class into the cause of working women made the Working Women's Association a pioneer organization. Emily Peers clearly saw the mutually dependent relationship between class and gender injustice.

From the start, the Association was an alliance between working women and the middle-class feminists Stanton and Anthony. Its initial purpose in the beginning was to establish unity between both classes of women in order to fight the discriminatory and exploitive practices of industry and management, as well as the sexist practices of trade unions. However, the middle-class suffragists had an additional agenda. They strongly believed that suffrage was a crucial solution to the problems of working women, that economic inequality could be remedied with the ballot. The editors of the *Revolution* stated,

Yes, labor and the ballot go hand in hand. As soon as workingmen come to understand how the disfranchisement of women cheapens all labor...they will demand the ballot for her...[31]

We would call the attention of working men...that the cheap labor of woman cheapens their labor also...Give woman the ballot, you dignify and exalt her, make her labor valuable...[32]

Working women did not agree. They consistently felt that the priority for working women was to improve their economic conditions, and they did not see suffrage as the solution to their problems. As Emily Peers claimed, the vote was not "the great panacea for the correction of all existing evils." They also thought that supporting suffrage would make them look too radical.

At the very first meeting of the Association the issue of suffrage was prominent.

Miss Anthony stated the object of the meeting to be an organization of working women into an association for the purpose of doing everything possible to elevate women, and raise the value of their labor...

The meeting was then organized by the election of Mrs. Anna Tobitt as President, Miss Augusta Lewis, Miss Susan Johns and Miss Mary Peers as vice-presidents. Miss Elizabeth C. Browne as Secretary and Miss Julia Browne as Treasurer... Miss Lewis works upon the newly-invented typesetting machine. Miss Johns and Miss Peers are both able compositors and profitably employed. The Misses Browne are clerks in the *Revolution* office...

Mrs. Stanton thought it should be called the Working Women's Suffrage Association.

Miss Augusta Lewis said that woman's wrongs should be redressed before her rights were proclaimed, and that the word "suffrage" would couple the association in the minds of many with short hair and bloomers and other vagaries. She thought that the working women should be brought together for business purposes, after which they could be indoctrinated with suffrage or any other reform.

Mrs. Macdonald coincided with Miss Lewis.

Mrs. Stanton said that redressing woman's wrongs before her rights were asserted was placing the cart before the horse...

Notwithstanding Mrs. Stanton's argument, it was decided that the word "suffrage" should not be inserted and the Working Women's Association was adopted as the title.

Miss Anthony said that if those present did not feel that the ballot was the fulcrum by which they could gain their ends, she was sorry; but did not desire them to pass resolutions beyond what their present mental status sanctioned.[33]

Although the vote remained a tense issue between middle-class suffragists and working-class women, the two groups were able to work together in the same organization for some time. In the beginning, suffragists were willing to put aside their demand for the vote and work in areas where there was common agreement. The unionization of wage-working women, and opposition to sexual discrimination by both trade unionists and employers became the most important concerns of the Working Women's Association. As Peers said to Stanton and Anthony, "You and I may hold an entirely different opinion, but waiving what is problematical, there is a broad common ground upon which we can stand, agreeing fully and entirely. We can reach out, one to another —the highest to the lowest—the hand of fellowship. We can make theory and practice go hand in hand...working closely up to our convictions."[34]

The Formation of the Women's Typographical Union

The Working Women's Association #1 was open to all women in the wage-work force. However, women typesetters who had come to the suffragists earlier for support (in their relationship with the all-male, New York-based Local No. 6 of the National Typographical Union) made up a significant part of the Association's membership.

Historically, the National Typographical Union had tried to exclude women from the printing industry by refusing to organize them. At the same time, management had attempted to use women as scabs during strikes in order to break the power of the union. In December 1867, Local 6 had called a strike against the *New York World*. In order to fight the union, the *World* trained and hired many women to set type on the job. Augusta Lewis and Emily Peers, who shortly thereafter partici-pated in the formation of the Working Women's Association, had worked at the *World* during the strike. When the *World* and Local 6 reached a settlement, all the women were fired. When the women pro-tested, the employers claimed that they had been incompetent.

The *Revolution* had covered the strike in a manner critical of the male union. It published an article urging women to keep their jobs and learn new skills, and claimed that the male printers' union had colluded with the employers to fire women and to intentionally keep them out of the trade. The women of the *Revolution* ultimately saw their lack of suffrage as the cause of sexist discrimination by the unions.[35]

The initial impulse on the part of women typesetters to form an alliance with middle-class feminists and organize the Working Women's Association resulted from sexual discrimination by male trade unionists. When a member of Local 6 suggested that the president of the National Typographical Union come to a meeting of the Association, his offer was rejected by the women. "I think the women can organize without the help of the men," Peers said. She characterized the male unions as associations committed to "the exclusion of women from the hardly earned avenues of labor she has entered,"[36] and concluded that women needed to unionize on their own.

At first, the women of the Association concentrated on trade union organizing and the development of producer cooperatives.*[37] As early as

*It was not unusual in the post-Civil War era of the labor movement to try to form cooperatives.

late September 1868, notices began to appear in the *Revolution* calling meetings of women workers to organize into trade unions. A typical notice was the following:

> The Working Women's Association #1 invite the women compositors of this city and Brooklyn to attend their next meeting to be held at the offices of the *Revolution*, Monday evening, September 28 at 7 and a half o'clock, to form a Woman's Typographical Union. Officers and members of the men's unions promise to render every possible aid in securing to themselves equal pay for equal work.[38]

Despite earlier sentiments, members of the Working Women's Association did invite representatives from Local 6 of the male union to meet with them, prior to formation of the women's own local. The *Revolution* reported on the discussion which took place.

> Mr. Alexander Troup, a delegate to the National Labor Congress from Typographical Union No. 6, denied that the association of which he was a member was in hostility to the female compositors...If the female compositors will work together with members of the Union, they will get an equal remuneration for their labor.
>
> Miss Peers—Will the Union allow ladies to join their ranks as members?
>
> Mr. Troup—I never knew of any woman applying for admission. I can speak for Mr. McMechanies, the present foreman of the *World* and President of the National Typographical Union as being in favor of women working at ease with equal rights and privileges as the men. But he is not in favor, nor am I, of women coming in to undermine the prices paid to men.
>
> Miss Anthony—How much is the initiation in this union of yours?
>
> Mr. Troup—One dollar.
>
> Miss Anthony—Oh, that is not much: I guess our girls can stand that (laughter).
>
> Miss Peers to Mr. Troup—Will you take my initiation fee now? If you please?
>
> Mr. Troup—Yes of course I shall; and will propose you as a member...[39]

The dialogue allowed the women to pose an important challenge to the male union. It also indicated the possibility of support for the women from the male unionists.

On October 12, 1868, the Women's Typographical Union (WTU), intended to be both a union and a producers' cooperative, was founded. The union was not designed to replace the Working Women's Association, which would continue to initiate and support a variety of working women's activities. The formation of the union was a tremendous step forward; despite severe sex discrimination, women had now unionized in one of the most skilled trades. Susan B. Anthony applauded this event as a feminist victory. At the union's first formal meeting she said,

> Girls, you must take this matter seriously now, for you have established a union, and for the first time in woman's history in the United States, you are placed, and by your efforts, on a level with men as far as possible, to obtain wages for your labor. I need not say that you had taken a great momentous step forward on the path to success. Keep at it now, girls, and you will achieve full and plenteous success.[40]

Robert Clark, Secretary of Typographical Union Local 6, also addressed the gathering:

> I will state here that it is necessary for the new Women's Typographical Union to have on their roll eleven names of compositors in good standing before applying for a charter from the National Union, under whose jurisdiction the new association will come. When admitted, we will sustain and stand by them in every sense, providing that they establish a scale of prices and stick by them. We have no desire to work against the women or exclude them.

Clark went further than mere acceptance of the Women's Typographical Union. On behalf of Local 6, he offered them assistance:

> We have agreed to hire a hall for your meetings, furnish you with books, stationery, etc. and assume all other expenses which it may be necessary for you to incur in getting your Association into working order, and to continue to do so until your Union shall be in a condition to support itself.[41]

The new women's union showed its strong solidarity with the labor movement on several occasions. For example, soon after its formation, members of the Women's Typographical Union were sought out by some employers for the purpose of providing cheap labor. The women refused, and Susan B. Anthony praised their action.

Shortly thereafter, in January 1869, Local 6 called a strike in the book and job printing sections of the printing industry in order to raise typesetting rates. The WTU completely cooperated. Not wanting to repeat its experience of the year before when women hired during a strike were fired immediately after, the WTU worked very hard not to have women used as strikebreakers. With help from the women, the strike was settled quickly, and in return for that help the WTU was admitted into the National Typographical Union at the summer 1869 NLU National convention. This was a major victory both for women and for workers. By admitting the Women's Typographical Union as its first female local, the National Typographical Union became the second trade union to accept women.

Further Activities of the Working Women's Association

As a result of their initial success with women typesetters, the Working Women's Association tried to organize women workers in other occupations. In September 1868, Susan B. Anthony and several National Labor Union leaders attempted to organize another local, Working Women's Association #2, this time with female garment workers. At an organizational meeting attended by more than 100 women, most of them sewing machine operators, women got up and reported their wages, hours and working conditions. This recitation of grievances could be considered a precursor of latter day consciousness-raising groups. For instance,

> A girl looking very ill and weak in voice—I am a carpet sewer. I work for one of the largest carpet houses in the Bowery. The Brussels carpets are very stiff sometimes, and I blister my hands very badly (showing her blistered fingers). I worked nearly three days, and sewed fifty yards of carpet, and when I asked him to pay me for sewing the border, which is additional work, he laughed and said it was "chucked in."[42]

The presence of National Labor Union leaders at the meeting was one of several instances in which the NLU actively supported the unionization of women. NLU representative Lewis Hines addressed the meeting:

> There is probably within a stone's throw a great many young women tonight who are stitching their eyes out, for a less compensation than what we have heard of tonight. A great many here there are who make $8 to 10 a week... The importance of laboring unions must be plain to you all. It is the only means of lifting you from this misery. Get together and form associations and establish scales of prices... These meetings will also be a means of making sanitary inquiries and injuries after your bodily health.[43]

Susan B. Anthony gave a talk expressing her support for unions but also continued to emphasize the need for suffrage. She felt this dual program—unions and suffrage—would combat the double oppression of working women.

Anthony actively continued trying to unionize women workers. At another meeting—this one held at the office of the *Revolution*—Anthony again urged garment workers to organize a union. Soon afterward, a Sewing Machine Operator's Union was formed. Unfortunately, this union failed for several reasons. Low wages and lack of steady work in the sewing trades made it very difficult for women garment workers to form unions. Moreover, most suffragists did not work in those occupations, and could be only resources and not organizers. Unlike women typesetters, garment workers were in an occupation which men had not already organized. Finally, despite the fact that individual leaders of the National Labor Union were supportive, the skilled male trade unions were not ready to become involved with unskilled or semi-skilled female workers.

Because of the many difficulties in organizing the unorganized women in female occupations, the Working Women's Association began to shift away from trade unionism, and moved towards investigatory work and publicizing the conditions of working women. The height of that work was the Hester Vaughn case, which began around late 1868.

Hester Vaughn was a domestic servant who had been seduced by her employer and became pregnant. She was convicted of infanticide after she gave birth unattended and her dead infant was found by her side. The Working Women's Association actively organized in her defense, including holding a mass meeting of women workers in New York City, giving speeches, petitioning, and sending a delegation to visit Vaughn in jail.[44]

The case presented an opportunity to raise many issues connected not only to working women but to all women. It was one of the first, if not the first, case of public opposition to sexual harassment. Clearly Vaughn's sexual vulnerability was intimately related to her economic exploitation. The whole incident was another example, in the eyes of the feminists, of women's powerlessness in a society that completely excluded women from the entire judicial proceedings. Eventually Vaughn was pardoned and deported to England.[45] The work of the Working Women's Association was never really acknowledged, but it had been crucial to Vaughn's pardon.

The Collapse of the Working Women's Association _____

While the Vaughn case was important because it exposed the deep injustice symptomatic of working-class women's general oppression as women, it also marked a change in the Working Women's Association from a working women's organization to a middle-class one.

The difficulties encountered by the suffragists in assisting wage-working women to unionize led them to turn their focus to an examination of working women's oppression as *women*. In previous organizing attempts, gender issues were of low interest to wage-working women, while middle-class women were more open to examining that dimension. In addition, investigatory and publicizing work was more in line with an older tradition of social aid. As a result of the new focus, the Working Women's Association attracted more middle-class and some wealthy and professional women, even while increasingly excluding the industrial wage-workers who had been its original constituency. Instead of being an organization in which working-class women were fighting on their own behalf, it became more of a "helper" organization. Stanton came to believe that perhaps the best hope for working women might be to get "women of wealth, education and leisure" working in their behalf.[46]

By the spring of 1869, the Working Women's Association was dominated by middle-class women. There were three major reasons for this shift in constituency and focus. One was the difficulty that women had in unionizing. Second was the lack of support for gender issues from other groups. Aside from the feminists, there seemed to be no other groups concerned with gender issues outside the wage-workplace. Furthermore, while there was a programmatic agreement among feminists, working women, and trade union men on some gender issues *in* the wage-workplace, there was no actual organizing done around them by either of the latter two groups. Third, the feminists' middle-class bias eventually precipitated a split between themselves and both the women typesetters and the National Labor Union. This break-up led to the ultimate collapse of the Working Women's Association.

During the beginning of the 1869 strike in which the Women's Typographical Union cooperated with Local 6 of the National Typographical Union, Susan B. Anthony had petitioned the book and job printing employers' association to contribute money for a women's typesetting training school. The publishers of the *Revolution* established a two-week training program. Although done in the name of philanthropy, it was the same technique of training and hiring women in order to defeat the men's union. While Anthony mainly saw it as an opportunity to get training and jobs for women, she showed a real lack of understanding of the basic principles of trade unionism. In practice, she had promoted scabbing during a strike and colluded with the interests of management.[47]

A variety of criticisms were levelled against Anthony, but it was John Walsh of Local 6 of the National Typographical Union who challenged Anthony's credentials to the National Labor Union at its August 1869 convention, on the grounds that the Working Women's Association was not a "bona fide labor organization" and that she had "striven to procure places for girls from which men had been discharged."[48]

When Anthony's credentials were being reported at the convention, John Walsh claimed,

> I am directed by Typographical Union No. 6 comprising of 2000 members to protest in their names the admission of Miss Susan B. Anthony. We claim she is not a friend of labor. I understand that the lady is here to represent a Working Women's Association of New York....I oppose her admission on the ground that she is a determined enemy of labor...In the first place, the lady is proprietor of a paper published in New York, called the *Revolution* and while the columns of that paper proclaim the principle of equal wages for men and women, its forms are gotten out by as notorious "rats" as we have in our trade, and who are opposed to our organization at every point. The ladies working upon that paper do not receive the same wages men receive, and this, too, notwithstanding the officers of our Union under the direction of that body called upon the proprietor of that paper and requested her to observe the same scale of prices which was observed in a union office. In the second place, during the struggle with their employers in which the Typographical Union No. 1 was engaged last spring—a meeting of our employers was held at Asto house and the lady...waited on those employers and solicited aid to furnish a room wherein females could learn to set type, thereby enabling our employers to defeat our just demands by throwing upon the market unskilled labor.[49]

Susan B. Anthony claimed that she did not know whether she was a "rat" or not, since her printer paid higher wages to women than they received in almost all other offices. However, Walsh continued:

> Why was the President of the Women's Typographical Union No. 1, a union which we support, turned out of the *Revolution* office a week ago?"

Miss Anthony—I did not know she was.

Mr. Walsh—I know that she was for being a union woman.

Miss Anthony—Oh, no.

Mr. Walsh—Well, she tells that.

Miss Anthony—Well, I cannot help it if she was. I am not responsible for anything in that office, except that I pay a job man for putting out my paper. My printer never told me that he had discharged the woman. Then again in regard to the employing printers. Last spring some one came into my office and said: "Miss Anthony, now is your time. You have been talking to your Workingwomen's Association about establishing a training school for learning girls to set type. Now is your time, while these employing printers are in distress to make them fork over some cash to establish a school." Well, of course, I am not in the Workingwomen's Association especially to advance men's wages: I am there...especially to help women out of the kitchen and sewing-room.[50]

There was a great deal of controversy over whether Anthony should be expelled from the NLU convention. Although she was criticized for her actions especially during the strike, many at the convention were eager for a compromise, and some believed that if William Sylvis (who had recently died) were still alive, a compromise would have been reached. Local 6 and Walsh pushed hardest against Anthony. They confirmed their charges against her with a letter written by Augusta Lewis, president of the Women's Typographical Union and former vice-president of the Working Women's Association, in which Lewis describes the changing character of the Working Women's Association.

The Working Women's Association was organized immediately before the last session of the Labor Congress. I was first vice-president. Mrs. Stanton was to have it a Working Women's Suffrage Association. It was left to a vote and defeated. The society at one time comprised over one hundred working-women; but as there was nothing practical done to ameliorate their condition, they gradually withdrew. I do not know who introduced the "Literary" in the society; but the debates and introduction of "suffrage" was introduced... After the adoption of the Constitution and by-laws several members of Sorosis [a New York women's group which started clubs for literary and intellectual self-improvement] on the committee to nominate officers which they did, ignored working women... Although the Society comprises many wealthy ladies, they raised 30 dollars for the laundresses of Troy. As a society either the want of knowledge or the want of sense, renders them as Working-womens' Association, very inefficient. I wish I could assist you in your protest more than I have, and it is not too late for the purpose.[51]

As Lewis said, the explicit class biases of the middle-class women who were increasingly dominating the Working Women's Association had driven out many of the working-class women. For instance, dues were raised and the meeting place was changed to a wealthier neighborhood in order to meet the needs of the new constituency. Furthermore, most of the new women were unfortunately anti-union, and by the time Anthony went to the August 1869 convention, the Working Women's Association was seen by both working women and working men as an anti-union organization.[52]

Anthony defended herself by pointing to the sexism of the trade union men. During her final pleas, she stated,

> There is an antagonism between men and women workers, and there must continue to be until men and women occupy an equal platform, civilly and politically (hisses and applause). I am not in a passion, gentlemen. I am here for women as I have been everywhere for women for the last twenty years, whether on the floor of a teacher's convention and woman's rights convention, or a labor organization. You have admitted black men to your councils but would you have admitted them...at any time prior to the issuance of that proclamation that enfranchised them? They hold in their hands that magic piece of paper, the ballot...Did I represent a class that held the ballot, my right never would have been questioned here.[53]

She defended her involvement with the printing employers' association on the grounds that the printers' union itself had been unwilling to train women. She said, "I want to ask the Cooperative Printers' Union of New York how many girls they have taken to learn the typesetting business? How many women have you ordered each department or establishment to take as apprentices and to train in the art of typesetting?"[54]

The debate between Susan B. Anthony and John Walsh of Local 6 continued, the class bias of the one exacerbating the sexism and racism of the other, and vice versa. In responding to Anthony's question, Walsh asserted, "If a girl is a member of our union, we will give her work...but we do not go outside our organization. You might as well ask why we don't sent for colored men or the Chinese to learn the trade. There are too many in it now."[55] He continued, "The lady [Miss Anthony] goes for taking women away from the kitchen and the worktub. Who in heavens are going to be there if these are not? I believe in man doing the working and taking a wife and supporting her and their children."[56]

In a parallel manner, Anthony revealed a strong class bias in her feminism. Not only did she continually express a lack of understanding of trade union principles, such as not scabbing during a strike, but her position became increasingly intertwined with anti-working class and anti-male sentiment. This was similar to the position she had taken towards black men in the debate about black male suffrage and was in sharp contrast to her earlier position in which trade union men were considered women's allies.

Susan B. Anthony was expelled from the National Labor Union at the 1869 National Labor Congress. It is important to note that the vote was very close as there were many who hoped that a compromise could be worked out. However, the split with the women typesetters and male trade unionists marked the end of the Working Women's Association. (The formal dissolution of the Association took place in December 1869.) It also marked the end of the alliance between middle-class feminists, working women, and male trade unionists until the early twentieth century. After Anthony's expulsion, the *Revolution* stated that "the worst enemies of Women's Suffrage will ever be the laboring classes of men. Their late action toward Miss Anthony is but the expression of the hostility they feel to the idea she represents."[57]

After the split, the Women's Typographical Union ran into problems. Although they were admitted into the National Typographical Union (at the same Congress that expelled Susan B. Anthony), the men's union continued to exclude them from jobs and from union apprenticeship programs. As a result of the latter they were not able to raise their wages to the level of men's. Augusta Lewis said,

> A year ago last January Typographical Union No. 6 passed a resolution admitting union girls in offices under control of No. 6. Since that time we have never obtained a situation that we could not have obtained had we never heard of a union. We refuse to take the men's situations when they are on strike, and when there is no strike if we ask for work in union offices we are told by union foremen "that there are no conveniences for us." We are ostracized in many offices because we are members of the union; and although the principle is right, the disadvantages are so many that we cannot much longer hold together...It is the general opinion of female compositors that they are more justly treated by what is termed "rat" foremen, printers and employers than they are by union men.[58]

The Women's Typographical Union was unable to recruit new members because they could not obtain the right to work in union shops or receive equal pay. Finally, in 1878, the provision under which the union had been chartered was revoked. The women were back to where they had been before they unionized.

The National Labor Union itself ended in 1873, due largely to its difficulty in keeping together so many diverse constituencies. In later years, other groups attempted to form national labor federations, but most of these subsequent attempts were initially, aimed exclusively at skilled white male workers.

The Next Stage of the Feminist Movement

Although it quickly failed as an organization supporting the economic concerns of working-class women, the Working Women's Association had nevertheless played an important role in the future of the feminist movement. Feminist historian Ellen DuBois notes,

> Ironically, the failure of the Working Women's Association alerted suffragists to an entirely different constituency, a middle-class one. They saw how strongly middle-class working women and other renegades from genteel ladydom were drawn to the ideology of female autonomy and equality that underlay both the Working Women's Association and the infant suffrage movement. Such women, organized on behalf of their own emancipation and not the uplift of their less fortunate sisters, were the people around whom an independent feminist movement would be built.[59]

With the collapse of their alliance with working-class women, middle-class feminists were able to develop an independent base and put suffrage into the forefront of their concerns. However, they stopped connecting women's oppression to race and class in any meaningful way. They lost the very crucial insight that unionization for women could be a major force in women's empowerment. Moreover, with only a middle-class and upper-class base, they became more conservative and isolated. During the late 1800s, suffrage sometimes became connected with "educated suffrage," an appeal based on preventing immigrants and other "lower class" groups from having too much political power.

Not only did feminists become more conservative on economic and class/race questions, they became more conservative on the idea of female emancipation itself.

In the earlier period suffragists had based their demand for political equality with men on the same ground as that on which their men had based their demand for political equality with their English rulers two generations before. If all men were created equal and had the inalienable right to consent to the laws by which they were governed, women were created equal to men and had the same inalienable right to political liberty. In asserting that natural right applied also to women, the suffragists stressed the ways in which men and women were identical. Their common humanity was the core of the suffragist argument. By the end of the century, however, many men of the older American stock were questioning the validity of the principle of "consent of the governed" as it applied to the new immigrants, the populations of the islands acquired by the United States in 1898, and the workers in the cities. The suffragists, belonging to the same native-born, white Anglo-Saxon Protestant, middle-class as the men who were re-thinking the meaning of natural right, also began to put less emphasis on the common humanity of men and women. At the time when the men of the group were taking new cognizance of the ways in which men differed from each other, new arguments for suffrage evolved, emphasizing the ways in which women differed from men. If the justice of the claim to political equality could not longer suffice, then the women's task was to show that expediency required it.[60]

The expediency argument, which became prevalent among suffragists, meant that women should gain the vote because *society* would benefit, rather than that it would free women from subservient roles. The early feminist program of multiple reforms and vision of equality got lost toward the end of the nineteenth century. It would be a mistake to say that the changes in the suffrage movement were simply the result of cutting ties with women of other classes. However, without their connections to working-class women, labor, blacks, abolitionists, and new immigrant groups, feminists stopped playing such an important role in initiating social change. The feminist movement no longer had a broad political program and a picture of freedom for all women.

Analysis

The Working Women's Association accomplished much in a short period of time. At the same time, several conflicts emerged that the

Association was unable to resolve, and which increased by the end of the group's existence. Following is an analysis of the Association in terms of both its successes and its difficulties.

The Working Women's Association's Theory and Practice Around Double Oppression
Opposing double oppression in theory

The Working Women's Association itself did not have a developed theory about the double oppression of women, although its activities raised critical issues about the sexual inequality of women in the workplace. However, the feminists of the *Revolution*, who had developed what for their time was a highly advanced understanding of women's oppression both as women and as workers, brought that analysis to the Association. Although Anthony and Stanton's analysis was not accepted in its entirety, ideas about double oppression served to unite these leading feminists with the working women and thus lead to the beginnings of a working women's feminism.

In their journal, the *Revolution*, Stanton and Anthony analyzed almost all forms of female oppression—in marriage, education, work, the economy, society's political institutions, and almost every other aspect of life. It was in the pages of the *Revolution* that capitalism was first identified as the source of both female oppression and the exploitation of all wage-workers. Feminists came to a profound understanding of the importance of women's domestic labor: even though the majority of women's work was unpaid labor at home, women were, as a result of that labor, a major segment of the working class. Furthermore, the wage labor of men was dependent on the unpaid labor of women. "How many of us must go supperless to bed if housewives claimed the eight hour demand as their own?" asked Parker Pillsbury in the *Revolution*.[61]

According to feminists, wage-workers of both sexes were exploited, but women wage-workers faced double exploitation. They were allowed access to only a few jobs and were paid less than men; they suffered from poor working conditions and went unacknowledged for the labor that they performed. By recognizing the existence of "women's work," Stanton and Anthony had a conception of the sex-segregated work force even if they did not use the term. Feminists also understood that the oppression of women in the wage-work force leaves them economically dependent and helpless in their domestic life: "Hence, women are crowded out of all profitable and honorable employments with no choice in life but a marriage of necessity, prostitution, or starvation."

The working women in the Working Women's Association and the men of the NLU did not, however, all share this understanding. There was agreement about the facts of sexual inequality in the wage-workplace, but little interest by either male or female workers in gender issues outside that sphere.

The Working Women's Association was based on its members' common opposition to women's lack of training, equal pay, union organization, respect and recognition for their labor, and decent working conditions. The WWA believed that economic discrimination resulted from both gender and their class oppression. For example, Emily Peers, one of the Working Women's Association's vice-presidents, said:

> I want to see labor dignified; I want to see my sex elevated;
> I want to see all of my inequality removed and in the growing
> intelligence of the age, in the moral forces of the public mind,
> I build my faith that all will be accomplished.[62]

The Working Women's Association's short period of success can be attributed to the fact that three groups—feminists, leading women working-class leaders, and trade union men—were in agreement about and willing to act on this particular aspect of female double oppression.

The Working Women's Association suffered, however, from the absence of a shared understanding regarding women's oppression both as workers and simultaneously as women outside of the wage-work force. Without a theoretical understanding of the nature and practice of the other major forms of double oppression, the activities of the Working Women's Association were inherently limited.

Opposing double oppression in practice

The case of the Working Women's Association demonstrates how an active program which opposes women's double oppression can be success-ful, but also that when this two-pronged approach is dropped, the group will lose its effectiveness.

From working women's point of view, the Association's two major successes were organizing the Women Typesetters' Union and gaining Hester Vaughn's release from jail. In each case, the Working Women's Association (with support from feminists) took action against some aspect of women's double oppression. In the case of the typesetters, the Association opposed women's unequal access to jobs, training, and decent working conditions, and equal pay. In the case of Hester Vaughn, the Association organized to defend a woman who had been harassed and victimized by her male employer. In both cases, the fight against women's double oppression rallied the support and interest of a wide constituency (including, in the case of the women typesetters, the male unionists), which led to victory.

By contrast, the working-class members of the Working Women's Association were not interested in fighting women's oppression outside the workplace. Though familiar with feminist sentiments, they showed no interest in taking action around pure gender issues. In particular, the working-class women did not see the feminists' major cause—women's suffrage—as particularly relevant to them.

In some ways, it is easy to see why the working women did not support suffrage. Although Stanton and Anthony continually argued that disenfranchisement was the reason for the unjust treatment of working women, they were, to a large extent, confusing a symptom with a cause. While suffragists claimed that working men had more power than working women because they had the vote, women's lack of economic and political power was the *reason* that women lacked the vote, rather than the result.

In addition, the middle-class women's emphasis on suffrage was partly an outgrowth of their liberal philosophy and belief in individual legal rights. There were good reasons why working women saw economic power as a more central concern; their emphasis on unionization, gaining entrance into male-dominated unions, and challenging economic and sexual discrimination in the wage-work force confronted their economic powerlessness more immediately than did suffrage. It should also be pointed out that working-class women may have believed that supporting women's suffrage would alienate potential labor allies who perceived female suffrage as highly radical and unacceptable.

Although working-class women may have had good reasons to avoid involvement with the suffrage issue and the larger feminist analysis of women's oppression, sticking to a narrow definition of women's oppression in the workplace limited the success of the Working Women's Association.

It is my opinion that at that time, the *joint* demands of unionization and suffrage were the best expression of the feminist desire to unite gender and class issues, by developing a program around the relationship of women's economic and political power. In fact, less than half a century later, working women, particularly in the Women's Trade Union League, fought for both women's unionization and suffrage. Unfortunately, Stanton and Anthony were less committed to unionizing women than they were to suffrage. When their program of unionization did not immediately work for women other than the typesetters, the middle-class women were ready to drop their attempts to organize unorganized women workers. Also, they were very quick to drop their support of the union men during the strike of Local 6 in January 1869. They did not understand that in order to support working-class women, they also needed to support working-class men, particularly during a labor strike.

The Working Women's Association's Approach to Unionizing Women

The major success of the Working Women's Association (WWA) was the creation of a women's union and the entrance of that union into the all-male typesetters' union. The independent initiative and strength created by an alliance of middle-class and working-class women were responsible for these two victories. Moreover, building the all-female union was perceived by the feminists as a *feminist* victory because women had organized in their own interests and had won a specific gain which moved them closer (at least so it seemed) to economic equality with men.

The WWA used feminist techniques and formats in the course of their organizing attempts. The creation of the WWA itself came about as the result of a hard-won consensus between the two groups of women. When the WWA tried to organize women garment workers, for example, they used the process of speaking out and reciting grievances—which preceded by 100 years a practice common in the world feminist movement today: consciousness-raising.

The alliance between working-class and middle-class women broke down because the middle-class feminists did not maintain the principles of labor solidarity. And when the male unionists turned on them, the feminists completely gave up their belief in the benefits of unionization for women. At the same time, when the male typesetters stopped functioning as allies, the women typesetters were unable to maintain an independent female base outside the male-dominated union movement, causing the collapse of their union.

This example suggests the importance of alliances between middle-class and working-class women in maintaining the strength of women's unions. The support of feminists had been crucial for the women typesetters in their unionization and inclusion in the National Typographical Union. Without this support, they were not able to maintain their rights as workers and fight sexism in the trade union movement. The key ingredients in their earlier success had been: 1) an autonomous organization; 2) an alliance with middle-class women; and 3) a combination of issues related to both sex and class. Without establishing women's unity both as an oppressed sex and as workers, the practice of a working women's feminism collapsed.

The Working Women's Association's Approach to Stimulating Change Within the Feminist and Labor Movements and Facilitating Alliances Between the Two Movements

Building alliances

One of the greatest successes of the WWA was that it stimulated an alliance between leading feminists of the time and a male-dominated national labor organization. During this time, union men in the NLU gave crucial support, including material support, to the unionization of women workers. The alliance with women strengthened the leadership of William Sylvis and the more progressive male leadership who believed that trade unions should represent and organize all workers. (They never, of course, included unpaid women workers.)

Stimulating change

Through their contact with the male trade union leaders and working women, the feminists, for a brief time, became increasingly pro-union. The existence of the Association provided hope that wage-working women could form the basis of an independent feminism, and that trade union men could be their allies. Feminists also developed a program in which labor and the needs of working women were a central part of their feminism. As a result of their relationship with the NLU, they saw that sexism could be challenged while areas of cooperation were being sought. Furthermore, they recognized that women, labor, and blacks were all victims of a common enemy and that all three working together could be effective agents of broad social change. Because of their contact with the NLU, the editors of the *Revolution* even adopted a comprehensive political program and saw the possibility of joining with labor in building a third political party. Finally, it was during the time of these alliances that a rich, unique feminist theory was developed.

Although the steps taken towards change within each movement were extremely significant, they were only a beginning, and their effects were not lasting. After this episode, the male leadership of trade unions did not include more women, the unions continued to organize skilled, predominantly white, male workers, the majority of workers remained unorganized, and women were still excluded from all-male unions. Furthermore, the progressive trade unionists were not able to permanently win other trade unionists to the causes they stood for, nor were the *Revolution* feminists able to involve many other feminists in their program with labor. During a time of crisis, the WWA was ultimately unable to mediate the conflict which arose between feminists and trade union men when John Walsh of the Typesetters pushed for the expulsion of Susan B. Anthony.

Development of a Broad Political Program

The total program put forward by the WWA included workplace issues specific to women as well as work issues of concern to both female and male workers. However, while the Association combined at least some gender and class concerns, the most significant advances for feminism were first raised in the *Revolution* as a result of its editors' involvement with the Association. In addition to its commitment to a wide variety of feminist issues, the *Revolution* also supported many NLU reforms, including the eight-hour day, land reform, producer and consumer cooperatives, control of monopolies, and the creation of an independent political party.

The editors of the *Revolution* and the NLU leadership were the most advanced elements of their respective constituencies. While neither had the power to fulfill their goals, their combined programs represented one of the broadest and most transforming political agendas of its time. The *Revolution*, especially, combined advanced feminist thinking with very progressive economic programs. The power of the *Revolution* and NLU alliance demonstrated the political potential which could emerge when unity is eveloped between feminism and working-class liberation.

The alliance initiated by the WWA, between feminist and union leaders, helped create an environment in which both groups were encouraged to think differently about issues such as sex discrimination, the relationship between class and gender, and the potential power of a full-scale alliance between women and labor.

This alliance helped generate new, revolutionary ideas about the economic and political empowerment of both workers and women, and stimulated the development of a mutual vision of a new and just society. Still lacking at that time was a wider base of support that could accept the ideas put forward by a few far-thinking leaders.

Union
WAGE

6

"A new force on the horizon is the tremendous upsurge of the working women's movement which will play a decisive role in democratizing the labor movement."

—Jean Maddox
The Fight for Rank and File Democracy

Introduction

Since the 1970s, important new changes have been taking place in women's lives, and the women's liberation movement has played an important role in these changes by articulating women's rebellion against traditional roles of subordination. This rebellion has occurred against a background of dramatic growth in women's participation in the world of wage-work.

This development has meant both an increase in the unionization of women and growing support for gender-oriented activities among union women. The intersection of women's concerns both as women and as workers is greater than ever before. At the same time, the potential for cooperation between unions and women's liberation organizations has been enhanced, with wage-working women serving as a bridge between the two.

During the last decade two organizations explicitly attempted to bring together women's liberation and trade unionism. The first was

WAGE,* a pioneer organization on the West Coast, formed in 1971 and disbanded in 1982. (The second organization was the Coalition of Labor Union Women—CLUW. See Chapter 7.) WAGE was the first organization since the Women's Trade Union League in the early 1900s to be made up of women unionists who advanced both in theory and in practice the importance of organizing wage-working women into unions as an essential part of both women's liberation and working-class liberation. Although WAGE remained relatively small, never becoming a national organization, it was pivotal in re-integrating class and gender, workers and women. It proposed that women's liberation should meet the needs of working women, and that working women could become a leading force in building a new trade union movement in the United States.

The Origins
of Union WAGE

The very beginnings of Union WAGE go back to 1971, at a conference sponsored by the National Organization for Women (NOW), held at the University of California at Berkeley.[1] When criticized for not including any working women in the program, the conference organizers developed a panel at the last minute featuring Jean Maddox and Ann Draper, both trade unionists and longtime social activists. The meeting of Maddox and Draper in the bathroom at that conference became a famous story among Union WAGE members. According to Jean Maddox:

> Ann and I hardly knew each other.... But we met each other in the women's bathroom and were complaining bitterly that there was no organization for working women and that, by God, we ought to have one. And Ann, who was always a great one to get people to do things, said, "Well, Jean, I'll tell you what to do. You announce that we're going to have a lunch hour meeting to talk about setting up a working women's organization." So I did, and 36 women came. Everybody agreed that we had to have an organization of working women.
>
> We hoped to stimulate women, to build their courage to stand up and fight for their place in the labor movement: to organize into unions, to demand that issues important to

*This group has used both spellings—"W.A.G.E." and "WAGE" in their literature. To be consistent, I use "WAGE" in talking about the group. In excerpts from its literature, however, I will use whichever form is used in the piece being quoted. Similarly, I will use "Union"; in excerpts the organization sometimes prints "UNION."

women be part of negotiations, and to assume leadership in their unions.[2]

Within two weeks the group formed and had a name—Union Women's Alliance to Gain Equality, or Union WAGE. Its first demonstration was on March 1971, at the state's Industrial Welfare Commission (IWC) in San Francisco. With help from other women and farm workers, Union WAGE, though a newly formed organization, had a picket line of over 100 supporters.[3]

The initial enthusiasm for Union WAGE was in part a response to the existing women's movement's complete neglect of class issues and the problems of working women. Women in the Bay Area who wanted to link women's liberation to labor had few if any places to go. The initial Union WAGE group, approximately sixteen women, shared a common political perspective on the questions of class, gender, and working women. They were able to reach political agreement almost immediately and that consensus allowed them to quickly form a coherent organization. Their comparatively unified political voice, especially in relationship to existing ideas about women's liberation, was grounded in their very similar histories. Many of the women had been (and some still were) members of Old Left political parties such as the Independent Socialists, Socialist Workers' Party, and the Communist Party. Despite the many differences and hostilities between these groups, those women shared a history of political involvement and action. In contrast to many new feminists of the 1960s and 1970s, these older women had shared a much more common perspective on such issues as class consciousness and the importance (or potential importance) of trade unions in regard to general social change.

Also, many of the women had highly developed skills in union organizing and leadership. Pam Allen, a feminist activist who became the editor of WAGE's newspaper and later broke with the women of the older consensus, was deeply impressed with the leadership skills of these women when she first joined WAGE. Coming out of the feminist movement, whose orientation was antagonistic towards "leaders," she claimed that there was "no way to understand the early years of Union WAGE without understanding the phenomenal skills the early women had."[4] Jean Maddox and Ann Draper were excellent leaders. They felt a responsibility, particularly to younger women, to provide the training and skills necessary for building rank and file caucuses, public speaking, and other such activities. Their union experiences trained them to lead meetings and to use parliamentary procedures. At the 1973 AFL-CIO California state conference, Draper led a training session on how to use procedure and how to win a proposal from the floor. It was as a result of

WAGE's efforts that a resolution was passed to hold a California-wide conference of women workers.[5]

The life stories of Draper and Maddox, both of whom died of cancer in the mid-1970s, epitomize the first generation of Union WAGE members.

Ann Draper, born in New York City, was an active socialist by the time she was fifteen years old, and much of her life was devoted to union organizing and activities in the Independent Socialist League. During World War II, she was a welder active in her local of the CIO Shipyard Union. At the end of the war, she became a local organizer for the Hatters and Millinery Union and continued organizing in other jobs in New York City and California.

In the late 1950s, Draper worked for the Amalgamated Clothing Workers as a director of the western states, a position she held until she died. She was an activist throughout her life, participating in the sitdown which began the Berkeley Free Speech Movement, organizing active support for farm workers, and opposing U.S. involvement in Vietnam. The last period of her life was spent in founding Union WAGE.[6]

When she died, the Union WAGE Executive Board published the following obituary:

Ann Draper 1917-1973

On March 25th of this year the labor movement and UNION WAGE lost one of the most dedicated and courageous heroines when Ann Draper succumbed to cancer in Oakland at the age of 56.

As a founder of UNION WAGE she sought to combine the energies of the women's liberation movement and the efforts of the labor movement to organize women workers.

Ann will be remembered for her diligent fight for the preservation of women's protective laws, a fight which continues today. She was one of the first to recognize the disastrous consequences of an Equal Rights Amendment which contained no safeguards for retaining state protective laws.

We in UNION WAGE miss her leadership, her friendship and her constant encouragement to take a greater part in the struggle for dignity, equality and justice for working people. Ann helped many of us to become involved in labor politics and the women's movement. Her ideas and the memory of her example will continue to inspire.[7]

According to those women closest to Draper, her greatest contribution was the encouragement she gave to women. Manja Argue, another of WAGE's founding members, recalls how Draper insisted that she (Manja) speak publicly even when she was tremendously frightened to do so.[8] Draper consistently urged other women to write and to speak, and was largely responsible for training the new generation of Union WAGE activists in leadership and organizing skills. This was especially important at a time when very few women took on that kind of responsibility.

While Ann Draper's strength lay in encouraging women to act, Jean Maddox led by example and inspiration. Pam Allen, who worked closely with Maddox, considered her to be one of the great women labor leaders.[9] According to Pam:

> Jean and I had planned to do a series of interviews on her
> life after the West Coast working women's conference,
> November 1975. It was consistent with Jean's approach to her
> work that she did not want the interviews to take time away
> from organizing the conference. Unfortunately, her health
> deteriorated seriously by late autumn.[10]

When Maddox died of cancer in 1976 at the age of sixty-one, the series of interviews had not been finished. However, Allen was able to put together a fairly complete account of Maddox's life, based on various articles and taped interviews found among her possessions.

The following is an abbreviated version of Allen's biography of Jean Maddox.

Maddox was born to very poor and hard-working parents in Idaho in 1915. Her father was part Native American—a heritage of which Maddox was always very proud. At seventeen, after her father's death, she went to work as a waitress. She spent the majority of her life as a union organizer, in particular organizing women workers, and was consistently concerned with issues of sexism in the workplace. (Maddox had also been a member of the Communist Party for more than ten years between the 1940s and 1950s.)

Her life was filled with exemplary actions aimed at organizing women workers to fight against their oppression as women and as workers.[11] For instance, Maddox worked (on a production line) in a soap factory as an organizer for a Local of the International Longshoremen's and Warehousemen's Union. At that time the men pushed the buttons to make the machines run and had the good pay, while poorly paid women did the work of lifting the soap off the production belts.

> I was elected shop steward in that department and one day
> it occurred to me that until I could prove to the women how
> much weight they were lifting each day, there would be no

hope to get them to organize to improve conditions and slow
down the production belts. The women were afraid of losing
their jobs; everyone was responsible for raising a family. I was
able to prove to them that they were lifting 2,000 pounds an
hour—one ton of soap every hour!

The stewards had been meeting with management
attempting to negotiate our grievances. But we were not
getting anywhere. So the women decided on a slow-down.
(This was before Taft-Hartley and other anti-labor legislation.) The slow-down began on a night shift. We would
pack only every other group of boxes. The men participated
with us wholeheartedly and kept using the machines to push
boxes away. When the night was over, soap and broken boxes
were piled all over the warehouse. The company had to close
the plant down for a day and a half to clean up the mess.

We went into a bargaining session with the employer and
won 17 new people in that department, a permanent rate of
speed to pack the soap and a lot of other goodies. It was a
major victory. The women were never the same after that.
They were militant as hell.[12]

Maddox also organized successfully against sexual harassment and,
in one instance, was able to get a foreman fired who had been forcing
women to sleep with him in order to keep their jobs.[13]

Maddox's major work was with Local 29 of the Office and
Professional Employees International Union (OPEIU). She joined
OPEIU in 1952 when she started doing office work. She soon became a
steward and part of the "struggle to build a strong, active rank and file
union."[14] In 1969, Maddox became President of Local 29, which, at that
time, was one of the largest office workers' locals in the country. During
Maddox's term, it became known as "the striking union."

In 1970, there was a major strike of clerical workers at Lucky
foodstores. "Our union was women," said Maddox, "and the employers
wouldn't talk with us. It was horrible. So right there at the negotiating
table we began to accuse them of discrimination against women, which
blew their minds. To my knowledge, it was the first time that a union
had ever raised this issue."[15] The clerical workers at Lucky's went on
strike and other unions in the store honored the picket lines.

Our striking women at Lucky were beautiful. . . . They
stood solid. They were determined that they were not going to
be treated as subhuman any longer. . . . The Lucky strike not
only brought the labor movement into the fight for equal
rights for women, it also brought the women's liberation
movement into the labor struggle.[16] I called every women's

liberation group in the area...I invited them to join the picket lines to give us a show of support. It wasn't very long before they had settled in and the women's liberation women began to understand the problems of the union women and union women began to understand the need to have a women's liberation movement. It was really great.[17]

Maddox continued to fight for women's rights in her union. At the 1968 and 1971 International Conventions of OPEIU she raised the demand for more women in leadership. After the 1971 International Convention, Maddox issued the following statement.

...Women must become more active in their own locals... Women must demand, not only equal pay and opportunity, but also a reasonable representation in their unions which will be responsible to the needs of working women.

Women must stop allowing themselves to be intimidated into believing that "they" aren't qualified, that "they" haven't had the experience or training to hold positions of leadership. Women must know within themselves, that given an opportunity to learn and participate in the affairs of their unions, they *can* become experienced and effective leaders in all levels of their union's structure.[18]

With Maddox's leadership, her local continued to be active on women's issues; it took stands on several important issues, including opposition to the Vietnam War; it was also concerned with the issue of rank and file participation in union decision-making. On many of these issues the local was in conflict with the International, and in June 1973, the International placed the local in trusteeship.

Trusteeship means that the leadership of a union is taken away from the local and put into the hands of the International. The practice of trusteeship was originally designed to deal with union corruption, but in fact it has often been used to stop rank and file organizing, and was obviously used to prevent grassroots independence in the case of Local 29. A long battle against that trusteeship began, with Jean Maddox taking an active part.[19]

While involved in that struggle, Maddox helped found Union WAGE and was elected its first president—a position which she held three times in all. Within WAGE she taught classes on union organizing and caucus building, and emphasized women learning leadership skills. More than Ann Draper, she was aware of the strengths of the modern feminist movement, although she also saw its limitations. Although critical of the women's liberation movement's failure to address itself to the problems of working-class and third world women, Maddox credited

the movement with raising her consciousness and raising the consciousness of women throughout the country on their need for equality.[20]

More than anything else, through her leadership in Union WAGE,
Maddox presented a vision of the role that the women's movement, based
in the working class, could play in trade unionism. "A new force on the
horizon is the tremendous upsurge of the working women's movement
which will play a decisive role in democratizing the labor movement,"[21]
said Maddox.

Union WAGE provided Draper, Maddox, and the other founders an
opportunity to put into practice what they had learned over the years
about unions and women. It was the advent of the women's liberation
movement which enabled them to take this new step for working women.

The Early Politics and
Political Program of Union WAGE

One of WAGE's first activities was to prepare a statement of purpose and
goals. The first issue of the WAGE newspaper, *Union WAGE*, published
in January 1972, stated:

> Women's liberation must be for the working women,
> beginning on the job. Our particular interest in this crucial
> area of female inequality has made our kind of organization a
> vital instrument in the battle for justice. Union WAGE hopes
> to break new trails in the fight for women's liberation in this
> society. Our tasks have just begun and we have a long way to
> go, but we will win!

Our Purpose and Goals:

> UNION WOMEN'S ALLIANCE TO GAIN EQUALITY
> (UNION W.A.G.E.) is an organization of women trade
> unionists organized to fight discrimination on the job, in
> unions, and in society. We are dedicated to achieving equal
> rights, equal pay and equal opportunities for women
> workers. Over 30 million working women endure double
> discrimination and exploitation: as women and as workers.
> Most carry the burden of two jobs; at work and then at home.
> Such is the pattern for most of California's 3 million women
> workers.

> Women workers constitute 40% of the work force but their
> pay averages 59 cents to the dollar paid to men workers for
> full-time work. Only one woman out of five is organized into a
> union; and women workers are clustered in the low-paying

jobs of society; clerical, service and manufacturing, and the women's work of nursing, teaching, housekeeping, etc. Trade unions are dominated by male leadership and largely ignore the needs of women workers.

1. Equal pay for equal work and equal opportunities, with jobs for all.
2. Stronger efforts for affirmative action programs for better-paying jobs.
3. Encouraging unionizing efforts to organize working women.
4. Urging women unionists to take leadership roles and greater responsibilities.
5. Raising special demands on behalf of women workers, e.g. paid maternity leaves with no loss of seniority and adequate maternity medical coverage.
6. Child care facilities; employer and government supported; parent-staff controlled.
7. Improvement and extension of state protective legislation to all workers.
8. Equal Rights legislation through Congress establishing equal rights under the law to maintain and safeguard state protective laws by extending them to men.
9. Minimum wage of $3 an hour guaranteed to all workers.
10. Work week of 35 hours or less at 40 hours' pay with double pay for overtime.*[22]

From the beginning, the primary focus of Union WAGE was on women as wage-workers. (This was not meant to exclude other roles that women played, such as mother, consumer, and houseworker.) The decision to focus on women as wage-workers came out of the ideological consensus of the group's original members. To them, the underlying basis of all oppression was class oppression. Since the wage economy was the class basis of capitalism, they reasoned, it was women wage-workers who were the key group among women. Therefore, the major basis of WAGE's program was to fight the double oppression of wage-working women by organizing women into unions and fighting for their needs as workers, *and* as women.

Despite their many criticisms of the existing labor movement, WAGE's leaders strongly believed it was crucial for women to organize into unions. Jean Maddox said:

*During the history of WAGE, various changes, to be described subsequently, were made in this statement.

> . . . We must constantly remember the main enemy is always
> the employer. Women must organize and join unions. Wages
> and working conditions are better for women in even the
> weakest union than they are in unorganized workplaces.
> Remember there is a class *struggle* going on.[23]

Ann Draper added that the goal for women is to "root our struggle in the
soil of the class struggle."[24]

The long-term goal of WAGE was the integration of trade unionism
and feminism. However, included in their political analyses were deep
criticisms of both the contemporary women's liberation movement and
current trade union practices. Throughout WAGE's history, especially
in the group's early years, the WAGE paper carried extensive critiques of
the "middle-class women's movement." In the late months of 1972,
Germaine Greer, author of *The Female Eunuch*, wrote reaffirming
WAGE's criticism of feminism.

> The concern of the liberal feminist to see that her sisters
> are allowed keys to executive washrooms must seem bitterly
> irrelevant to those three-quarters of America's female popula-
> tion who have an income of less than four thousand dollars a
> year. Professional women are startlingly articulate and even
> powerfully represented, but the women who outnumber men
> in the service industries and all the female classes of servants in
> private households who earn little more than 1,000 a year are
> still awaiting their champion.[25]

In an article titled "The Invisible Woman," *Union WAGE* looked at
Ms. magazine (November-December 1972) with biting criticism:

> This disregard for low-salary working and poor women,
> whether it be from ignorance or callousness—or both—results
> in a warped social viewpoint and some truly repulsive
> statements. Since women who work from necessity are in-
> visible to the editors and writers, the organizations whose job
> it is to protect these workers, the trade unions, are usually
> invisible too. When unions are mentioned, a rarity, they are
> dumped into the same viewpoint as business; big oppressors
> of women, institutions which keep women out of high paying
> jobs and in a subordinate political and economic status.[26]

The women of WAGE were also critical of what they considered an
anti-male bias of the middle-class women's movement. They saw this
attitude as part of modern feminists' anti-working-class stance and their
negativity towards unionism. To the WAGE women, class and society
were the enemy, not men. Sexism was a way of dividing working people,

and while men perpetrated sexist attitudes and structures, they were the *tools*, not the source, of sexism.

At the same time, WAGE leaders were equally critical of existing trade union organizations. They condemned most of the trade union movement leadership for its male domination, its frequent corruption and collusion with employers, its unresponsiveness to the vast majority of working people, its inability to organize unorganized workers, and its long history of sexism and racism.

The hope and vision of the early WAGE leaders were that women wage-workers would be the force to change both the women's movement and the trade union movement.

The Battle Between
Protective Legislation and the ERA _____

Protective legislation (laws pertaining only to women which are designed to protect women in the workplace) was one of the first and most important issues taken up by Union WAGE. It was addressed as a major issue largely because NOW was leading a highly successful campaign for passage of the ERA in California. The debate over the value of protective legislation, and its potential elimination by equal rights legislation, has actually been going on since the early 1900s and is one of the best examples of the ideological and structural differences that can emerge between liberal feminists and feminists with class-based politics.

Union WAGE got involved in the debate over equal rights because its members believed that passage of the ERA might eliminate protective legislation for women. Rules regulating hours and prohibiting over-time, for example, were products of an ideology that women are physically, intellectually, and emotionally weaker and therefore deserving of special protection in the wage-work force. After declaring a statute making a ten-hour workday maximum for bakers, the U.S. Supreme Court (in *Muller v. Oregon*, 1908) upheld a law which limited women laundry workers to a ten-hour day.[27] This ruling, which established the rationale for protective legislation, stated:

> The limitations which this statute places upon [a woman's] contractual powers, upon her right to agree with her employer as to the time she shall labour, are imposed not only for her benefit, but also largely for the benefit of all...The two sexes differ in structure of the body, in the amount of physical strength, in the capacity of long-con-

tinued labour, the influences of vigorous health, future well-
being of the race, the self-reliance which enables one to assert
full rights, and in the capacity to maintain the struggle for
subsistence. This difference justifies a difference in legislation.[28]

After the passage of women's suffrage in 1921, the National
Women's Party committed itself to adding an equal rights amendment to
the federal constitution. This attempt activated strong opposition to the
ERA by working-class women and their advocates. Since it was generally
assumed that equal rights legislation would lead to the elimination of
protective legislation, an extensive debate ensued. Most of the women
who supported protective legislation (and opposed the ERA) were
working-class women, while most of the women who opposed protective
legislation (and supported the ERA) were middle-class feminists.
Surprisingly, many supporters of protective legislation agreed with the
conservative ideas that women were indeed "weaker." For example,
many working women activists, in particular women in the WTUL and
the Women's Bureau, argued that women workers needed protection in
the workplace due to women's maternal nature and physical weakness.

The split over protective legislation was not, however, limited to
middle-class feminists and working-class women. During the early
twentieth century, most male trade unionists were also opposed to
protective legislation, and, in fact, to *any* worker-related legislation.
They felt that government interference would weaken unions' bargaining strength. It is interesting to note why, in this context, the WTUL
eventually came to support protective legislation. During its early years,
the WTUL's major strategy for working women was unionization.
However, after certain initial successes, it became increasingly difficult
to organize unorganized women workers due to sexism in the union
movement, women's double oppression, the often times temporary
nature of many "female" jobs, etc. As a result, the fight for protective
legislation gradually replaced the unionization of women workers as the
WTUL's central concern. (Interestingly enough, male trade unionists
eventually came around to supporting protective legislation—possibly
because they saw it as a less threatening alternative to organizing women
workers.)

The debate over protective legislation brought out some very
interesting questions, caused certain groups to align with each other
when they had previously been opposed, and exposed some fundamental
differences between working-class women and middle-class women—
differences that feminists are still struggling with today.

The supporters of protective legislation correctly saw protective legislation as the only available solution to improving working women's conditions, given women's mistreatment in the work force, poor working conditions, lower pay, and the fact that most working women were already unpaid houseworkers. However, many proponents of protective legislation did not deal with the issue of women's equality in general or the specific sexual inequality that women faced in the wage-work force. Many of them supported protective legislation not from a feminist perspective, but because they agreed with the sexist ideology that women are "weaker," and their solution to female exploitation was at best a band-aid approach to some of the very difficult conditions women faced at work.

Opponents saw protective legislation as a way of maintaining women's inferior political and social status. In the home, husbands or fathers were supposed to protect women; in the wage-work force women usually had no one to protect them. It therefore made sense—given sexist ideas about female nature—to call in the government to protect women and children.

> Women and children, for instance, were not accorded a legal status in the labor market (right of contract, etc.) equal to that of men, no doubt because employment in the industrial sector ran counter to the traditional view of their appropriate role in society. They were provided instead with an alternative set of rights in which the government, in effect, replaced the husband or father as the source of protection. Rather than give them the status of autonomous and independent individuals, the law offered them a new source of protection. Thus the motives underlying the introduction of protective labor legislation were highly conservative.[29]

Opponents of protective legislation who were also advocates of the ERA (primarily the NWP, under Alice Paul's leadership) pointed out that protective laws discriminated against women by keeping them out of higher paying jobs, and they objected to the dominant philosophy that women needed protection because they were "weaker." However, the proponents of the ERA did not deal with those cases in which protective legislation actually benefited women workers, nor did they offer solutions to the special oppression women suffered in the wage-work force.

Furthermore, while it might seem obvious that the solution for working women was *equality* in the workplace, and not paternalistic protection, the ERA would not necessarily provide equal rights at work. The realistic fear held by working women was that if the ERA destroyed protective legislation, it would leave women "the right" to compete with men from a position of inequality. Equal rights would touch neither women's unpaid labor in the home, nor poorer paying, less skilled jobs outside of the home. While some arguments for protective legislation relied on very conservative assumptions, the issue of women's special oppression in the work force was real.

Very few people addressed women's double oppression, which was the most important issue to come out in the protective legislation debate. Almost as important, and equally ignored, were the rights of *all* workers. However, a small minority did look at these two issues. For example, in 1923, Mary Anderson, chief of the Women's Bureau of the Department of Labor, was in favor of protective legislation because, she argued, the demand for shorter work hours, initiated by women, was in the interest of all workers. She stated:

> What the feminist objection to the labor laws for women is really based on is this: The labor laws for women put women on a different *legal* basis from men so far as their jobs are concerned, and the ultra-feminist *legal* equality means almost everything. The worker prefers *industrial* equality which is in this case actually defeated by legal equality...
>
> The whole question, it seems to me, comes down to this: Shall we let women continue working longer hours than men, for less pay than men and continue doing two jobs to their husbands' one? And is that sort of thing to continue in the name of some principle of equality? Or shall we agree that the reality of better conditions of employment is more important, both to health and to industrial equality than is a cherished theory?
>
> Women who are wage-earners with one job in the factory and another in the home have little time and energy left to carry on the fight to better their economic status. They need the help of other women, and they need labor laws. Such laws are a safeguard not only to women but also to the children. They give protection to the family and maintain more satisfactory standards of living. In short, they help to make the country a better place for its citizens.[30]

Writing in opposition to Anderson, Rheta Childe Dorr, a well known journalist and feminist, was one of the few who said that the real problem for women was not that they needed protection, a concept which was, by nature, discriminatory, but the fact that wage-working women have two jobs, wage-work and unpaid housework.

> But great numbers of poorly paid women, kept down to the lower ranks in most trades, still work long hours at home

because of poverty, seasonal trades, legal prohibitions against working overtime in seasonal trades, and always the fear of unemployment...

What I am trying to urge, in this short article, is that unequal wages and bad factory conditions, and not special laws for adult women workers, are the things in which we all should interest ourselves. Sex has nothing to do with the case...When we limit women's opportunities to work, we simply create more poverty, and we postpone the day when equal pay for equal work will be universal. Without equal work there can be no equal pay, nor anything like a fair field for men and women alike...

I don't want a single woman to relax her war against the crime of child labor, or against the exploitation of adolescent boys and girls. I want them only to turn their intelligence and their great influence in favor of better working conditions and safeguarding of hazardous trades for both men and women. For it takes healthy men as well as healthy women to rear a healthy race.[31]

Although both women were looking at the crucial issue of double oppression, they came to different conclusions. This was because the impact of protective legislation on women was and is very complex.

What did protective legislation actually do for working women? Did it protect them or hurt them? Was it a solution to the problem of double oppression? The answers to these questions are not simple because the reality is not simple. Protective legislation varied from laws and regulations about minimum wages, to limitations on hours, overtime pay, weight-lifting standards, and standards for rest and washroom facilities. Some of these laws setting minimum standards were useful to working women and should have been granted to men—as many eventually were. On the other hand, some protective laws were used to discriminate against women.

Ronnie Ratner, research director of the Center for Women in Government, State University of New York at Albany, in a paper on "The Paradox of Protection: Maximum Hours Legislation in the United States," studied the issue of protective legislation by examining maximum hour laws. She arrived at the thesis that, *"maximum hour laws were both protective and restrictive, but not simultaneously."*[32] How laws that once were protective became restrictive can be explained by the following three hypotheses:

Protective laws failed to keep pace with the profound modifications in working conditions that followed from technological change;

The content of these laws is fundamentally shaped by the constellation of interest groups supporting or opposing legislative and judicial action at critical junctures in their development; and

These sex-specific laws, themselves a reflection of conventional thinking about the sexual division of labour typical of the first half of the twentieth century, were in fact essential preconditions for later sex-neutral legislation protecting all employees.[33]

According to Ratner's study, labor laws in the early part of the twentieth century were sex-specific, in large part because by the early 1900s most trade unions had stopped campaigning for laws for men; in some cases because the unions were too weak, and in other cases because the stronger craft unions preferred collective bargaining. At the same time, women's groups—in particular the WTUL and the National Consumers' League—made protective laws for women a central political concern. Therefore, the weakness of unions in relationship to women and industrial workers, working women's vulnerability in the workplace, the influence of middle-class reform efforts, and a belief in a conservative philosophy about sex roles all led working women's groups to demand protective legislation.

The key factor in determining whether protective legislation was progressive or discriminatory seems to be who was in favor of it. In the early years of this century, most employers opposed protective legislation since it was a first step for industrial workers' rights. This trend was reversed after World War II. During World War II, most states with manufacturing firms which engaged in war production and relied heavily on female labor temporarily suspended maximum hours legislation. After the war, maximum hours and other protective laws were often used to remove women from the highly paid jobs they had during the war.[34]

Ratner makes the important point that Title VII of the 1964 Civil Rights Act, prohibiting discrimination on the basis of sex, did not automatically invalidate protective laws. In fact, the Equal Employment Opportunities Commission (EEOC) originally accepted the legitimacy of protective laws, reversing its position only as a result of pressure from women's groups, employers, and some unions. During 1967 and 1973 there were many cases in the courts challenging job restrictions and hour and weight restrictions. After a crucial case, the *Rosenfeld* case, most sex-specific federal laws were struck down and many states followed the example.[35] Organizations that had supported protective legislation for women changed their positions, reflecting the increasing number of jobs for women and the desire to open up past restrictions. Many regulations appeared outdated. As early as the 1947 WTUL convention there was a split over legislation that prevented women from working at night.[36] Elizabeth Koontz, appointed in 1969 to head the Women's Bureau of the Department of Labor, changed the agency's position to support the ERA and got the U.S. Secretary of Labor to do so as well. In the early 1970s, there was still a debate about the ERA versus protective legislation although it was quickly disappearing.

Union WAGE's
Struggle for a Labor ERA _____

From its beginnings in 1971, Union WAGE campaigned for a "Labor ERA"—an ERA qualified by the provision that it would not eliminate beneficial protective legislation for women and one which would extend these rights to working men. WAGE also supported several bills that would extend protective labor standards to all workers, arguing that the ERA was important, but not at the expense of invalidating the bulk of protective legislation. WAGE opposed what it termed the "pure ERA." WAGE did not debate the pros and cons of protective legislation itself, but stated that protective laws have been beneficial to women since the majority of women are in unorganized jobs with no other protection. For Union WAGE, equal rights had to mean "extending any beneficial law affecting one sex to the other sex: not depriving all workers of such favorable labor standards."[37] As part of its campaign, WAGE supported extending California's protective labor standards, established by the state's Industrial Welfare Commission (IWC), to all workers.

The California IWC was established in 1913 "to promote the health, safety, and welfare of women and minor workers." It has quasi-legislative power," and its orders have the effect of law.[38] As a result of IWC orders, California had the largest body of protective laws of all the states, covering 2.5 million women and minors working in fourteen industries, excluding only domestic household workers and government employees. With the exception of legislation regulating weight-lifting requirements and work hours (which had been invalidated by a federal court decision), California had more than fifty labor standards including,

> . . .such provisions as the employer providing lunch
> hours, coffee breaks, lunch rooms away from the work area
> with seating facilities, toilets, drinking water, protective
> clothing, minimum wage, premium pay which is payment at

the rate of time-and-a-half for overtime after eight hours per
day and forty hours per week, ventilation, safety standards.[39]

In the opinion of Union WAGE these laws were in the interest of all
workers. A Labor ERA and a bill extending IWC orders to all workers
was WAGE's solution to the feared consequences of an ERA passed
without a labor addition.

WAGE met with several successes in their campaign to extend
protective legislation to men. It was influential in getting the American
Federation of Teachers (AFT) and other unions to shift their support
from a "pure" ERA to the labor version. It reversed what had been a
unanimous vote of the San Francisco Board of Supervisors for an ERA,
so that Mayor Alioto then signed the San Francisco Supervisors'
Resolution for an ERA which safeguarded protective legislation:

> Whereas of the 30 million women workers in the United
> States fewer than twenty percent, roughly one out of five,
> enjoy the protection of a union contract with respect to wages,
> hours and other conditions for work, leaving over eighty
> percent dependent upon federal and state laws for such
> protection;
> Whereas, loss of such protective laws would constitute a
> heavy blow against working women, particularly in the low-
> paying industries where many minority women are employed,
> and open the door to cuts in wages and a return to sweatshop
> conditions particularly to those employed in intra-state
> occupations.[40]

WAGE's battle for a labor ERA led them into direct conflict with NOW,
which was campaigning for immediate state ratification of the federal
ERA. The WAGE women believed that an ERA without a labor proviso
would only be in the best interests of women of property, business, and
professional careers, while harming most wage-working women.[41]

NOW favored extending the IWC orders to men, but was not willing
to campaign for it at the expense of the ERA. To Union WAGE saving
and extending protective legislation to men was the priority. An article
in the May-June 1972 issue of the WAGE newspaper stated:

> . . .Now we face a new danger in the drive by some
> women's groups, spearheaded by the National Organization for
> Women, to achieve a "pure" Equal Rights Amendment
> without any safeguard to retain existing benefits for women
> workers.[42]

At a State Senate Rules Committee meeting Ann Draper asked:

> . . .[if] NOW would reiumburse farm workers if their

wages were cut back to $1 an hour. She charged that employer groups were standing in the wings, applauding while professional business and career women were doing a "hatchet" job on protective laws.[43]

Meanwhile the other side was also in action; during the week of August 21, 1972, at the California Labor Convention, women from NOW picketed convention headquarters. In their literature they attacked the California labor movement for its refusal to support a federal ERA, issues such as equal pay for work of comparable worth, and other issues directly related to male/female inequalities in the wage-work force.

Some groups supported WAGE's position and WAGE attempted to forge coalitions with the women's movement. For example, WAGE tried to get NOW chapters in San Francisco and Berkeley to join the Network for Economic Rights, a coalition of approximately twenty-five women's organizations. WAGE initiated a joint press conference of NOW and women's groups favoring extension of protective legislation. It also proposed a joint lobbying effort with NOW, as follows:

Dear Members of California N.O.W.

Greetings to you at your State Convention...Union W.A.G.E. proposes the following four points:

1. N.O.W. and Union W.A.G.E. form a California joint women's coalition to lobby for passage of both E.R.A. and A.B. 1710 [protective legislation for men] simultaneously.

2. The women's coalition would exist from its formation late October 1972 to the end of the 1972 legislative session, or until both bills were passed, whichever is earlier.

3. The women's coalition would coordinate joint actions such as press conferences, letters to legislators, personal visits to legislative offices, workshops, etc., to implement an effective lobby action.

4. The coalition would invite the support and participation of labor, women's and other organizations.

We extend to you our hope that you will welcome and adopt these proposals for joint action at your State Convention, our commitment to work together with you in good faith, and our anticipation that together we can win a major victory not only for equal rights *without* cost for all California women, but a crucial precedent for the rest of the nation.

Union W.A.G.E. October 20, 1972[44]

NOW turned these proposals down, stating that it would work on both bills, but not simultaneously.

The national ERA was ratified in California on November 13, 1972 (a state ERA was never passed), and some of WAGE's predictions about the future of protective legislation quickly became realities. For instance, immediately after ERA ratification the Bank of America announced that it would end taxi-cab service for women workers on the night shift because men complained of discrimination.[45]

WAGE's Victories Around the Extension of Protective Legislation _____

During the next few years, Union WAGE continued its persistent effort to get protective legislation extended to men. True to its previous word, NOW joined WAGE in this campaign. At Senate hearings, the state AFL-CIO, Union WAGE, and NOW all testified on behalf of a bill that would have preserved protective laws for women and minors and would have allowed the IWC to establish regulations for both men and women.

After several bills failed, including one vetoed in 1972 by then governor Ronald Reagan, the state legislature finally passed a law in 1973 requiring the IWC to extend protective laws to men. Reagan signed this bill, which gave the IWC the right to determine wages, hours, and working conditions for all Californians.[46] Union WAGE considered the bill a major victory, even though it had been watered down from earlier versions.

However, as soon as the IWC began acting on the bill, it attempted to take away from many workers important pieces of protective legislation, such as premium pay for overtime, rest periods, and others. WAGE, along with NOW and other groups, filed lawsuits against the IWC retrenchments.

For example, a state court wiped out premium overtime pay for all California workers not also covered by federal law, and a federal judge in San Francisco upheld this ruling, claiming that the California law requiring premium overtime pay for women violated the federal law concerning sex discrimination. WAGE, in cooperation with San Francisco NOW, filed a brief urging the Court of Appeals to reverse the federal district court's judgment and to accept the IWC's interpretation that time-and-a-half pay for women now means time-and-a-half for both *men and women*. In a major victory for WAGE and its allies, a lawsuit which claimed that the 1973 law gave the IWC the power to extend, not remove, protective legislation, eventually won.

Union WAGE continued to be a part of coalitions which sponsored specific legislation that would guarantee women overtime pay, rest and meal periods, etc. By the end of 1976, California was the first major industrial state to extend premium pay after eight hours, rest periods, meal periods, and other protective laws to men.

An additional important advance was that, as of 1974, household workers were included under minimum wage, and would also receive overtime pay, rest breaks, etc. Union WAGE was pivotal in getting California to be the first large industrial state to extend benefits of protective legislation to household workers and men. "The work standards adopted for household workers are really new, there is nothing comparable anywhere in the United States.[47] One WAGE statement celebrated this progress:

> While there are a great many areas in the new orders which need improvement, we think the Commission deserves credit for standing by their recommendations. While we hope to strengthen the work orders in 1978, it appears that we may find ourselves in a position where we must also defend present gains. One bright light in the picture is the establishment of the general principle that protective laws are the right of all workers, men and women alike. Equality might have meant simply dumping all the safeguards for women workers as several cases foreshadowed. In the future, men and women would find it easier to unite for their mutual interests in improving protective laws. We need this unity because we should start right now to prepare for the 1978 employer attack.[48]

After 1976, employers reacted strongly and IWC wage orders have been blocked by court injunctions on behalf of California's industries since then. WAGE organized continually for full application of wage orders. Under the attack of big business, the weaknesses of the IWC orders were apparent, leading to a debate within WAGE (and elsewhere) about the viability of the IWC.

Joyce Maupin, one of WAGE's earliest members, was active throughout the entire campaign to extend protective legislation. In the forefront of organizing household workers, she also served on the household wage board of the IWC. Maupin stated:

> I can't offer an easy solution. But I don't think the solution is to dump the Industrial Welfare Commission in favor of turning to legislation, which seems to be the alternative presented. I see the employer attack on working standards in California as part of the general right-wing drive in this country to take away many of the benefits and working conditions we have had in the past...Some people say, well,

we are not getting anywhere with the Industrial Welfare Commission and these orders are not being enforced, they are held up in courts so that half of California industries are not regulated at all. But what is going to happen when you try for legislation? You will be up against the same employer united front which obtained these injunctions. . . The basic question here is how we can find a way to assure workers in all California industries a decent minimum wage, safe working conditions and overtime provisions which give the worker something to say about how many hours he/she wants to work. You can't pull this out of a hat like a rabbit by substituting legislation for the IWC. We all have to work together to make it happen.[49]

During the last week of December 1979, employer associations went to court in four conservative California counties and got judges to sign injunctions against most of the new 1980 IWC orders.

By 1979, the WAGE strategy of fighting to extend protective legislation to men had run its course. The principle had been won; the concept of protective legislation for women no longer existed. On a state level, the IWC was clearly politically impotent; on a national level, both women's and labor groups were now supporting an ERA without a labor proviso.

This state of affairs may appear to negate WAGE's accomplishments, but in fact, WAGE had accomplished more than any other working people's group in California on the issue. Its work in this area was a splendid example of the impact that working women's organizations can have in a workers' movement.

However, one issue that was never resolved among WAGE workers was how to fight for female rights and equality, and workers' rights at the same time. While WAGE gave attention to the extension of protective legislation, the issue of equality for women in and outside of the workplace was also critical. The tension that originally existed with NOW persisted throughout other WAGE activities.

G ender Issues and Class —Could They Be Integrated?

In the early 1970s Union WAGE was the West Coast voice for women trade union activists. During the ninth constitutional convention of the California Labor Federation, AFL-CIO, held during the week of August 2, 1973, Union WAGE led and won a floor fight to establish the very first Union Women's Conference.[50] During the same period WAGE won endorsement for the Labor ERA from various national unions. WAGE participated in and often initiated coalitions of women's groups, labor unions, and social activists. A major victory, won by such a coalition, was achieved against Proposition L.

Written by the San Francisco Chamber of Commerce and spearheaded by the president of the San Francisco Board of Supervisors at the time, Dianne Feinstein, Proposition L was a charter amendment which sought to tie city clerical workers' salaries to those of underpaid clerks in private industry. "The campaign against Proposition L brought forth a new coalition...first time in the country that the defeat of union-busting legislation can be credited to the leadership and participation of feminists in coalition with organized labor."[51] Union WAGE worked with a wide spectrum of feminist and women's groups including the National Women's Political Caucus, NOW, CLUW, and others. Even Gloria Steinem worked against Proposition L, which became known as the "anti-feminist" proposition. WAGE was also very active in the Coalition for Workers' Rights, sponsored by a coalition of union locals representing clerical workers.

Another example of a cooperative activity was a conference held in November 1975 on organizing women workers, co-sponsored by WAGE, the San Francisco Women's Union, and the Berkeley Women's Union. (These were not labor unions, but women's liberation organizations.) The conference was attended by members of rank and file caucuses, independent unions, women's organizations, and individuals, and a major theme was independent organizing outside the traditional union structure. That conference was partly responsible for establishing WAGE as a resource center for working women organizers.

The Union WAGE newspaper, for example, was viewed by WAGE activists as a crucial organizing tool, and was in fact one of the outstanding working women's newspapers in the U.S. It carried internal WAGE information, analyses, and articles on working women's struggles, especially, although not exclusively, in the Bay area. In addition, WAGE put out a series of pamphlets on a variety of topics such as the life story of Jean Maddox, rank and file organizing, and Joyce Maupin's history of working women. These pamphlets, along with articles from the WAGE paper, were crucial organizing tools and form an important part of the small but growing literature on working women.

Despite its successes, WAGE ran into many problems by the mid-1970s. First, it was not able to sustain organizing projects. One inter-chapter newsletter announced the disbanding of the clerical organizing support group. Later, at a general meeting on July 16, 1978, where members of the East Bay, Mid-Peninsula, Redding, San Francisco, and

San Jose chapters reported on how the organization was doing in workplaces and unions, with experiences presented by women hospital workers, truck drivers, construction workers, and others, participants concluded that "Union WAGE had served primarily as a resource center for information, contacts, and support,"[52] rather than a center for organizing.

The second major problem was WAGE's failure to become a national organization. In 1974, a WAGE constitutional convention had voted to make Union WAGE a national organization with local chapters and a central executive board, and after 1974 (coinciding with a decision not to merge WAGE with the newly formed national CLUW—see next chapter), much energy was put into trying to build that national structure. While the bulk of the membership continued to be in the Bay Area, WAGE also developed chapters in San Jose, Redding, and the mid-peninsula area of California, as well as in the Midwest, Seattle, Oregon, and New York City. At first, local chapters were given a great deal of autonomy, but when several chapters floundered and the New York chapter was taken over by a sectarian organization, this independence was re-evaluated. During this time there were continual debates in WAGE about the relationship and activities of the chapters, and about what direction the whole organization should be taking.

By 1978, it was clear that WAGE could not sustain itself as a national organization. In the November-December 1978 issue of the WAGE newsletter an address from the Editor on "The State of Union WAGE" stated:

> During periods of reaction when working people are suffering attacks from the right and setbacks in their own struggles, it is common for organizations committed to social change to experience confusion about the direction of their work and what needs to be changed in their priorities and structure. Demoralization among members and even a splitting away of sections of the organization can occur...
>
> Union W.A.G.E. was formed to fight for the rights of working women and we have a responsibility to continue, but we are feeling the stresses and strains of this historical period; internally we are suffering from personal and organizational tensions... Seeing the nature of our organizational problems and challenges, the executive board decided to postpone our annual convention to Feb. 10-11, 1979, to leave more time for preparation.
>
> An all-day meeting will be held... to discuss chapters, their work, their tendency to form and disband, and the difficulty of establishing effective means of communication between the chapters and the executive board.[53]

According to the article, three chapters had disbanded, and other chapters were in the process of determining whether they should continue. It was becoming clear that the heart of the organization would remain in the Bay Area.

Certainly the pressures of the time could and did account for some of WAGE's difficulties. However, there was also a crisis in leadership which resulted in a lack of direction, confusion in activities, and difficulty in sustaining chapters and projects. The deaths of two of the strongest leaders, Ann Draper and Jean Maddox, contributed to a transitional period for the organization. In addition, the entrance of many younger women into the organization, accompanied by the evolution of new issues which needed new solutions, posed a challenge to the organization's early political and ideological consensus.

WAGE's initial strength came from the unity and common experience of an older generation of working women activists. As younger women came into the organization, the consensus broke down. Many women coming into WAGE carried with them different political backgrounds than the older women; many came from the feminist movement of that decade.

Many of these newer women were not in unions or even in the wage-work force and many had little or no political experience. This change was reflected in the position taken at the November 13-14, 1976 convention, which explicitly stated that "no position will be restricted only to individuals active in the organized trade union movement.[54] The effect was to lessen the leadership of union women. In her article "Keeping the Union in Union W.A.G.E.," Geraldine Daesch criticized this development.

> Although WAGE was founded by union activists and although support of rank and file organizing and striking workers remains our most important activity, our membership now includes a significant number of non-union and, in fact non wage-earning women...
>
> Ironically, I think it is the union activists whom we are in danger of losing. Although statistically we may still show a healthy percentage of union members we must face the fact that assuming responsibilities in WAGE might pose difficulties for women with responsibilities in other organizations...
>
> ...We fail to consider union work as valid WAGE work. I don't mean to imply by this that union women should assume an elite role in the organization while the envelope stuffing is left to the housewives, students, etc. who have "nothing better to do," but I think we should recognize that

stuffing envelopes at the union hall and stuffing envelopes in the WAGE office are equal contributions.[55]

Two key debates emerged as the WAGE membership changed. One surrounded the role that WAGE should play regarding issues that affect all women. The other was around the question of how best to organize unorganized wage-working women.

Pam Allen and the Struggle Over Bringing Contemporary Feminism into WAGE _____

The new feminism brought with it the challenge of organizing women *as women,* and raised a variety of issues which affected women both in and outside of the workplace, such as sexual harassment, sexual violence, and pornography. It also raised questions about WAGE's earlier consensus on women, wage-work, and unionization. Those with feminist leanings questioned the importance of unionization, and the relationship between wage-work and housework. Those feminists who wanted to address the issue of work did so from a feminist perspective, unlike the older women who tended to look at the issue of sexism from a class perspective.

Against this background a major struggle developed within WAGE between a group of women allied with Pam Allen, editor of the Union WAGE newspaper, and a second group of women who were in agreement with the older consensus. One could categorize this struggle as "women as women" versus "women as workers." For the group that supported Allen, its frame of reference, influenced by contemporary feminism, was the oppression of women as a sex, with issues of class, unionization, etc. secondary. The second group's frame of reference was the oppression of women as wage-workers. The debate sparked by Pam Allen ultimately led to a major split in the organization.

Pam Allen came out of the early radical feminist movement in New York City, where she was a prominent leader. She was author of "Free Space: A Perspective on the Small Group in Women's Liberation." Also, she had contributed to her husband Robert Allen's work, *Reluctant Reformers: The Impact of Racism on American Social Reform Movements,* and particularly to an article in that book on the suffrage movement. In 1975 Allen joined the San Francisco chapter of WAGE and soon was elected to its executive board. She worked with Jean Maddox during the last year of Maddox's life and wrote the pamphlet *Jean Maddox: The Fight for Rank and File Democracy.* During 1976, she was one of two paid staff workers at the WAGE office and in 1977, she became editor of the WAGE newspaper.

Allen's political background combined radical feminism and the ideas of the civil rights movement. She came to WAGE with a general sense of both the limitations and strengths of the feminist experience. She was deeply impressed with the leadership skills of the early WAGE leaders and contrasted what WAGE had to offer with the leaderless structure and often anti-leadership ideology of the women's movement, which she referred to as the "tyranny of structurelessness." Allen valued the action orientation of the working-class leaders, as opposed to the emphasis, in feminist consciousness-raising groups, on talking for its own sake.[56]

The older leaders, in particular Jean Maddox, provided role models that Allen never had. There were few if any teachers of the feminism of the late 1960s, since most of the women involved were approximately the same age. While Allen was one of the leaders and pioneers of radical feminism in Union WAGE, at least in the beginning of her involvement she was one of the students. Allen's work with Maddox was a turning point in her life. Through her involvement in 1975 in a WAGE-sponsored conference on working women's organizing, she learned about issues that were new to her, such as independent organizing versus working within the unions. Allen was always ready to acknowledge the influence that the older women in WAGE had on her. Unfortunately, since Jean Maddox has died, we will never know what she got from her relationship with Pam Allen. Even without talking about Allen directly, however, Maddox did attribute certain of her own personal changes to the women's liberation movement.

> Although Jean was critical of the failure of the women's liberation movement to address itself to the problems of working women, she credited the movement with raising her consciousness about herself as a woman. She also said that it was the women's movement which helped her learn how to be open and affectionate with other women.[57]

While open to what she could learn from the leaders of WAGE, Allen came into WAGE as a feminist political leader. Her political convictions, the questions she asked, and the style of her work were much closer to the recent feminist movement than to the older left, trade union, or working women's movement. Allen infused her feminist politics into WAGE's activities first through her writings for its newspaper and then in her position as its editor.

In the September/October, 1975 issue, Allen wrote "Anniversary of Women's Suffrage," the *first* article to deal with women's oppression outside the workplace. This article marked the beginning of a feminist influence in the paper.

Allen did more than simply repeat radical feminist ideas. From her work with her husband, her experiences in WAGE, and her own thinking, she explored class and race from a feminist perspective. In the article on suffrage, for example, she was extremely critical of the racism in the suffrage movement and the leadership of Susan B. Anthony, who compromised on the question of racism.

> The lessons of the suffrage movement make it clear that principles cannot be compromised, without this affecting the nature of the movement itself. Further the movement shows us the danger of exaggerating the value of a particular victory, and the weakness of making decisions on the basis of unproven assertions. In the case of Susan Anthony, her opportunism and rationalizations were not motivated by personal gain; but her failure of leadership allowed the movement to which she had dedicated her life to become narrow and concerned primarily with the rights of the most privileged women of our society, and only secondarily concerned, if at all with the needs of working women, immigrant women and non-white women.

UNITE AGAINST ALL INJUSTICE

> In the same way that the labor movement has been willing in the past to forsake working women and non-whites in order to win concessions for white male workers, so has the feminist movement been willing to compromise the needs of working women of all races. We who work in such groups as Union W.A.G.E. and in rank and file caucuses in our unions have as an imperative and commitment to stand firm on our principles, and to oppose any moves that would sacrifice the needs of any group of workers so that some individuals might win a few privileges and benefits. In the long run such betrayals hurt us all, for as women and as workers our strength lies in a united struggle against all forms of injustice and oppression.[58]

Allen's interest in the relationship between racism, class, and gender reflected the two major questions that guided her political development throughout her participation in WAGE: 1) How does one build a completely principled feminist movement that meets the needs of women of all races and classes? and 2) How does one build an all-inclusive working-class movement?

Allen's major strength was her ability to demonstrate the interconnectedness of issues and oppressions. Her overall understanding of oppression in general and the specifics of sexism in particular is rare and outstanding. For instance, under Allen's editorship, the September-October 1977 *Union WAGE* addressed "Sexism and Working Women," which brought the subject of gender and class oppression into direct focus. The issue contains articles on topics central to the women's movement.

In "Racism and Sexual Assault," Allen put forward one of the most advanced critiques on the subject. At that time she was one of the few feminists who connected the issue of sexual assault to racism and the oppression of working people. Moreover, she put the question of sexual assault into the larger context of oppression in general without sacrificing a critique of sexism. She did not fall into the usual traps of dealing with class and race to the exclusion of gender, or of concentrating on sexism while ignoring race and class. She also confronted one of feminism's key issues—its understanding of men—and directly challenged the attitude sometimes expressed in feminist thinking that "men are the enemy."

> Because men rape and assault women, there is a strong emotional reaction to see men (or at least some men) as the enemy. But if we look at the problem of sexual assault in the larger context of the historical oppression of working people, especially third world people, we can see that sexual assault is one mechanism used to keep an entire group of people demoralized and terrorized so that they will not fight against their oppression.

> Indeed, sexual assault is historically associated with the subjugation and oppression of a people. Here in the U.S. Native American women were raped as well as murdered in the genocidal war waged against their people. Black slave women were subjected to rape as well as the other forms of terrorism used to keep the slave population in fear. During Reconstruction black women were raped by groups of white men as well as beaten and sometimes killed along with their men, for the white south was determined to keep their cheap source of labor and used every conceivable means to terrorize the black population. Rape was even used as a tool against black men. During the early 1890s when black men, women and children were being lynched almost every day, the lie was put forth that all of these victims of lynch mobs were rapists of white women. Racism and sexism combined to blame black people for their own victimization.

> Poor working women of all races have found themselves

vulnerable to the attacks of their bosses and other men with power over them. Sexual assault is considered a male prerogative as long as men do not attack women with higher status. When poor men attack the women of their class, they are aping the ways of the rulers, not inventing them.

WE MUST UNITE

...We must recognize that the struggle is not against individual men per se, but against a system which perpetrates oppression, sanctions sexual abuse of women, and punishes women when they assert their human rights to self defense.[59]

Through *Union WAGE* Allen's particular form of working-class feminist politics was developed. For her, WAGE was a place to correct the limitations of contemporary feminism and develop her own unique perspective. Her greatest contribution to the cause of working-class women and people was to show the relevance of feminist issues. She refused to accept the stereotypical and classist notion that women's issues are middle-class and that feminism would never be relevant to working-class and third world women. She also believed that the women of the early consensus devalued feminist issues.

She introduced the concept of "focus" issues for the newspaper. One of the most outstanding was on reproduction, which linked many issues both in and outside of the workplace. Articles discussed daycare, abortion, reproductive rights in contracts, and workplace danger to the fetus. In line with Allen's commitment to broadening feminism and working-class women's concerns, the article on abortion dealt with many of the deeper emotional and psychological issues around abortion. It did not just reiterate the standard pro-choice argument.

Another of the focus issues Allen edited was on the family, which very explicitly introduced the issue of lifestyles and sexual preference into the organization. That issue of the newspaper was among the most explosive, judging by the reactions of key WAGE members.

In addition, Allen opened the newspaper to poetry and personal stories of women's lives and feelings, in keeping with her feminist belief that the quality of people's lives, and issues such as creativity and personal pain, are as meaningful to working-class women as to any other group. In her eyes, to limit the paper only to immediate workplace struggles was to do working-class women an injustice.

Another way in which Allen integrated the personal and political was through organizing the Women's Work Caucus, out of which came the "Word of Mouth" productions that did dramatic and personal oral histories. This way of organizing differed considerably from the style of workplace organizing used by the majority consensus. Pam said:

If we want to understand the many ways in which we have come to tolerate a society of inequality and oppression, we must look to where tolerance is first created in us. Change has to grow in our hearts and minds. We have to start investigating what for centuries has been holding us back and keeping us apart—checking out the pieces of the picture that most often don't get looked at, the ones that are private and "none of each other's business." We have to look critically at our family experience.[60]

This emphasis on the personal came very much out of Allen's early consciousness-raising experience in the women's movement. The exploration of feelings, of the personal pain involved in oppression, and of choosing new ways to live were all integral to a feminist perspective. However, this orientation was utterly foreign to most of the older women who had been part of WAGE's founding group and a group of younger women to whom personal experience did not seem politically relevant. For example, in the pamphlet that she wrote about Jean Maddox, Allen said:

Unfortunately, none of the interviews I found among Jean's possessions spoke about her personal life: the feelings and thoughts she had about herself as a woman or the price she had to pay for being politically active. She married twice and divorced twice. Once she told me it was her political work which had split up her marriages.[61]

Last and most important, Allen tried to develop her own working women's feminism into one that broadened the definition of working women to include unpaid workers, that questioned WAGE's previous focus on wage-work, and that broadened the concerns of working women beyond immediate workplace issues.

I believe that what we need in this country is a working women's organization which encompasses all the problems and needs and struggles. WAGE is not that organization but we need to be working towards that goal.

All things hang together in this society. Yes, they do and that is why we need an organization for working women which is open to all and addresses the problems of all. Yes, we need a theory which enables us to see the connections. Yes, specific problems need to be addressed in the context of understanding their causes and implications.

We are in one system and we need an organization which is able to analyze the different situations of women and their interconnectedness.

I tend to operate on the assumption that "working women" is a euphemism for working-class women which is why I see working women meaning the whole class rather than the employed sector. Who is the working class? That's one of the questions which causes great debate but an operating definition in WAGE is everyone who is not an owner of the means of production or their direct servants (whom we loosely call bosses and management).

About half of us are working in the paid labor force at the present time, but almost all of us have or will do wage labor and many of us would be working now if we could. Work place problems and struggles are clearly of importance to us all.

I have an acute sense of injustice and elitism when I hear people talk about limiting our work and newspaper to paid workers. If there are not enough jobs to go around, having a job is sort of privilege, even when it is terribly oppressive and poorly paid. Do we repeat society's valuation of those who are employed and essentially ignore or devalue those who are unemployed?

Part of the reason I worked so hard putting together the Reproduction issue was feeling that this issue crosses those categories of employed—unemployed. But not all activists in the Bay Area agree with you that "having a whole issue of *Union WAGE* focus on reproduction was an excellent idea."

Working women need an organization which unifies and broadens the perspective of its members and allies. They also need an organization which aids them in their specific struggles. How can WAGE meet that challenge? The problems of women in the paid labor force are overwhelming. How can we also address the problems and struggles of those other categories of women? And aren't there other organizations to address the issues of sexism outside the workplace?[62]

The majority of the organization responded to Allen by restating and reformulating the initial position that Union WAGE's key focus should be women as wage-workers. The issues they emphasized—such as organizing the unorganized, the unionization of women, and protective legislation—came out of that focus. During the 1970s, certain feminist issues such as abortion were added to the program, but very little was actually done about these concerns.

The most extreme statement of opposition to "middle-class feminism" had been made back in 1973 by Ann Draper, in her article "Women in Struggle: A Point of View."

By pitching its appeal in terms of "all sisters" only, the mainstream of the women's movement blurred over—when it did not consciously gloss over—the differences in economic and social alignments which did in fact exist among women.

Working women can be most solidly organized only through the work place not by consciousness-raising in abstraction of their working lives but by raising their consciousness of their condition as workers. The "hate-man" bag is the typical malady of the middle-class women whose relationship to men is concrete mainly in a home where the husband appears as the "master" or "boss." It is typically in the middle-class family—husband, or the "breadwinner," wife the "homemaker,"—that the concept of "boss" becomes necessarily sex-linked.

This is not in the least to deny or derogate the reality of the types of sexist oppression that get chronicled in the "diaries of mad housewives". . . It is only to say that however conscious the victims may become of their situations, they have only a choice of blind-alleys as their revolt remains within the same social framework.

We point in a different direction. We point away from the preoccupations and obsessions that fill the pages of *Ms.* written by career-women who identify their own minority life-situation with the "sisterhood" of the mass. We emphasize that the most important place to organize women for their liberation is at their work place. This means putting the spotlight on a goal which is unfortunately alien to the feminist "star" movement; the goal of integrating the women's trade union movement—integrating the organization of women against social exploitation (sexism) and the organization of women against economic exploitation.[63]

Not everyone was in complete agreement with Draper. However, her article did express the feeling, evident in the early WAGE consensus, that feminism was irrelevant to working women.

Allen and her caucus responded by criticizing WAGE's founding goals—the unionization of women, specifically rank and file organizing. In one issue of the newspaper, Allen stated:

The second point of purpose and goals promotes rank and file activism but privately many WAGE members talk about their confusion and demoralization with the contradictions which keep cropping up. We tend to want "success stories" but that's not what's happening right now. WAGE should be looking clearly and ruthlessly at the truth: that rank and file people get corrupted or coopted when they are elected to office...

I continue to believe that our members should try to work
to change their unions because we can learn from those
struggles, not necessarily because the unions can be changed
right now. It is in the process of analyzing our experiences that
we will develop the clarity we need.[64]

Joyce Maupin, a leader of the majority, differed sharply from Allen
on the issue of unions, reaffirming the original consensus. While
acknowledging many of the criticisms of unions, she claimed that
unions could change.

Encouraging women to join unions and participate in
internal conflict which you don't believe they can win creates
demoralization because it inhibits action. Workers don't get
into union struggles for the experience but to win something.
From the start Union WAGE has been committed to a primary
goal of organizing women into unions. Are we still committed?[65]

Newly elected WAGE president Jan Arnold was also a prominent
spokeswoman for the "woman as worker" position. She was central in
reformulating the older consensus in newer terms and she spoke out
directly against Allen's ideas.

Our present crisis in Union WAGE cannot be solved without
a look at the assumption that underlies our organization...

STRONGEST AT THE WORKPLACE

Working people have been able to build long-lasting and
comparatively powerful unions because unions are based on
the workplace, where workers' power is greatest, because
employed workers can strike. We expect our members to join
and be active in a union when that is possible, to work to form
unions in non-union workplaces, and to build rank and file
caucuses within unions when needed to promote the interests
of especially oppressed groups. Too often, unions are concerned only with the employed workers in their craft or
industry. They are seldom involved in the struggles of the
unemployed, the aged, housewives, or the disabled. We know
we need class-wide, class-conscious organizations, but we still
support unions against employers, despite their limitations.

We are not loyal to union bureaucracy but to the ideals of
unionism, and only to those leaders who advance those ideals
of struggle or solidarity. We support women union leaders
only when they advance the interests of working women and

working people as a whole. A woman bureaucrat is still a bureaucrat, just as a woman boss is still a boss.

EMPLOYED FIGHT FOR ALL

In our non-working lives, our greatest strength lies in alliances with the employed. For example, the patients at a nursing home are almost powerless to demand improved care.[66]

Debate also centered around Allen's efforts to extend the focus of the WAGE newspaper to areas broader than just workplace-related topics. In 1978 she proposed three future "focus" issues: on health, education, and the family. Sally Floyd, one of the paper's production managers, responded to Allen's proposal:

I do not support the proposal that the WAGE newspaper have three major focus areas for the next year. This opposition, for me, is based on several operating principles: first that Union WAGE should primarily be concerned with women's concerns at the workplace; second that the newspaper should print news, analysis, and information of use to working women in as diverse a manner as possible; and third, that the newspaper should be rooted in, though not restricted to, the practice and concerns of the organization...

The three new proposed focus areas—the health industry, the education industry, and the family are all significant topics for WAGE to discuss. Health and education are fields where large numbers of women work, in both unionized and non-unionized workplaces, and the services they provide directly affect our lives. A women's organization can hardly ignore the family and hopefully this topic will be integrated into all the work we do...

I am not opposed to the content of these three focus proposals—I am opposed to them as major focuses in the WAGE newspaper.

These focuses are not tied to proposed focuses of the organization. The newspaper should have a broader range than the organization as a whole, including cultural reviews, or international news, but the newspaper should be seen as one way to direct and reflect the needs of the organization.

Most important, I think that there is an important role WAGE can perform with its newspaper—to carry news of women's organizing efforts, to share stories of how other women deal with their jobs, to uncover women's history, to provide information about contract language or other women's organizations, to contribute analysis about what is to be done. The newspaper needs a diversity that can appeal to a wide range of working women. It cannot do this and be a journal at the same time.

If WAGE decided to publish, in addition to the newspaper, pamphlets on several special topics, I think that would be fine, but the newspaper's basic function should not have to be sacrificed.[67]

It was finally agreed that Allen's contribution, extending the WAGE newspaper's concerns to women's demands and interests outside the workplace, was a positive step. However, the fear remained that to continually make women's issues, especially those that were not integral to workplace organizing, the focus of some WAGE papers would significantly alter both the paper—and, by implication—WAGE itself. Representing the original consensus, Sally Floyd believed that the newspaper should be, in the strict sense of the word, an organizing tool for workplace struggles, not an "educational publication" for women's liberation *per se*.

In the January-February 1979 issue an open debate began over the politics of Union WAGE, focusing on the content and scope of the newspaper and Pam Allen's editorship.

How do we work within the trade union movement? Should the primary focus of Union WAGE be women in the paid labor force? Should we include the problems and struggles of the unemployed, retired housewives and welfare women, and if so, in what way? How should WAGE address the problems we all face as women, whether employed or not?[68]

The exchange took place between a group organized around Pam Allen, and another consisting of founding member Joyce Maupin, newly elected WAGE President Jan Arnold, and other women who supported the early consensus.

A "Women's Work Caucus" supported Allen's editorship of the paper and also what they and Pam in particular called "a broad perspective for the paper." This group wanted to broaden WAGE's focus from the wage-work force to all the places that women worked—the home, community, and workplace. It wanted WAGE to deal with women as wives, mothers, and non-paid workers, as well as paid workers, and it wanted to expand WAGE's focus to all issues that pertained to women's lives in the broadest sense and to show the interconnection between these issues.

I believe we need an organization which is able to analyze the different situations of women and their interconnections, thus unifying and broadening the understanding of its members and allies. Without developing such an overview, the organization cannot grow in a healthy manner.[69]

At the WAGE convention on February 9-11, 1979, attended by about fifty members, compromises were negotiated between the two groups, with the original consensus in the dominant position.

The Saturday session seemed to create an understanding of Union WAGE as an organization with a broad conception of our membership and our goals and concerns—and a unique emphasis on workplace and union organizing as a vital part of working women's liberation. The newspaper will reflect both our workplace emphasis and our broad concerns as women.[70]

The convention included a dramatic reading emphasizing feelings. "Whatever you do there will be pain—the pain of reality, or the pain of dreams." Nine Union WAGE members presented additional readings reflecting the wide variety of working women's concerns. These ranged from a nineteenth century woman's feelings as she begins a strike, to Pam Allen's poem, written that morning on hearing of her father's death.

Editor Pam Allen's proposal for three "focus issues" (details in January-February Union WAGE) passed after several important amendments were accepted. There will be *four* "focus issues": Health Industry, Education Industry, the Family and Third World Women. The Publications Committee will postpone these focus issues if Union WAGE activity, or other important organizing efforts, need newspaper space. Focuses will take about half the paper, leaving room in each issue of the paper for news of Union WAGE and news of organizing struggles. Focuses will be tied to organizing attempts as much as possible, and will reflect the activities of Union WAGE and its members. Focus issues will try to present our broader political vision and connections between various struggles.[71]

As in previous instances, Allen's effect was to extend the conception and range of WAGE's concerns, but not to change the group's essential focus. "We agreed to add a section to the 'Purpose and Goals,' proposed by Jan Arnold, summarizing the main activities of Union WAGE."

THE MAIN ACTIVITIES OF UNION WAGE ARE:

1) Encouraging the organization of working women into unions and caucuses. Encouraging women unionists to take greater responsibility and leadership roles, to end male domination in unions, and to promote class-conscious trade unionism. Helping working-class women build self-confidence and skills so we can organize and lead, especially in unions, organizing drives, and rank-and-file caucuses, and in other organizations of working women.

2) Joining or leading campaigns around issues which especially affect working women, such as the fight to keep protective laws, including higher minimum wages and shorter hours.

3) Using our newspaper *Union WAGE* and our office to further our goals through education, linking up people in struggle with others who can help them, and similar activities.[72]

The convention seemed to resolve the conflict, at least temporarily. However, in the July-August paper, a letter from the editor and from WAGE president Jan Arnold announced that the WAGE executive board had made the decision not to reappoint Allen as editor of the newspaper. According to Pam Allen:

[O]riginally issues such as finances, job rotation and paid versus volunteer editor were put forth as the reasons. However, the actual discussions at two consecutive Board meetings demonstrated that the Board members were in disagreement with the content and direction of the newspaper.

In our Jan.-Feb. 1979 paper we indicated the developing divisions within the organization. We formulated the major issue as whether Union WAGE should address the broad range of issues and problems affecting working-class women or limit its focus to trade union and organizing struggles. At the convention in February we believed we had worked out a compromise, reiterating that our main activities would continue to be in support of women workers' organizing activities and rank and file work. At the same time, we reconfirmed our commitment to the broad purpose and goals and that the organization was available to working women who wanted to write and organize around other issues.

Now however, the majority of the Executive Board has said no to a newspaper which represents this broader view and which embraces the struggles of working women who are not active members of the organization. These Board members want a paper which primarily centers on union and work-place issues and news about Union WAGE activities.

Concretely, the Executive Board is challenging the right of the third world, unemployed and poor women to share their concerns and their struggles because these do not fit into a trade union context nor always address issues at the workplace. The Board is saying no at the same time as we are seeing our newspaper reaching out to precisely these women.[73]

In her statement, President Jan Arnold raised several issues, such as the executive board's belief that Allen fostered "professionalism" in her relationship to the newspaper (i.e. Allen wanted to be paid for work as editor; and it was felt that she discouraged active participation from the rank-and-file); and that the manner in which she ran the paper conflicted with the way decisions should be made in the organization. However, the major reasons for Allen's dismissal still had to do with the conflicting political views.

In the process of debating Pam's editorship, a majority of the Board finds we have serious differences with Pam's concept of the newspaper and its relationship to the organization. Politically and structurally, our newspaper is part of Union WAGE. The newspaper is not a substitute for organizing, but a tool for helping women organize, and a reflection of the activities and struggles of our members and other working women.[74]

In the May-June 1979 issue, each side wrote final statements concerning this debate. The Women's Work Caucus, in support of Allen restated its commitment to changing *all* aspects of women's lives by exploring the interconnectedness of issues, and they remained skeptical that trade unions would be the place for change.

We understand that in order to rebuild society based on human values, organizing for change at the workplace is essential. But it is not enough. . . With only one-quarter of the women in the U.S. employed and only 12 percent of employed women in unions, restricting our struggles to the workplace alone and trade unions would be class suicide. Many are learning not to depend on trade unions for change, much less support.[75]

One of Allen's major criticisms regarding unionization was her belief that concentrating solely on unions would be both elitist and racist since most unions do not express the needs of the most oppressed sectors of society, particularly black and poor women. Joyce Maupin addressed that challenge in her article "Third World Women Lead in Organizing."

In her recent statement, the editor sets up a false conflict between the interests of women, at the workplace engaged in organizing and union activity, and Black, Asian and Chicana women. She claims Third World women are 'excluded' by a newspaper whose primary focus is on workplace struggle.

She implies that white women work, organize and join unions while Third World women do *not* work or organize. This is inaccurate and insulting to Black, Chicana and Asian women who have been in the front of union struggles ...These are the women who have taken the lead in workplace organizing and union struggle.

Tying our newspaper to actual struggle is the key to achieving the goals of Union WAGE. The newspaper is not a literary publication. It is a tool as they confront both employers and union bureaucrats. We are all in this together—no one is excluded from the fight to change our workplaces, our lives and our world.[76]

Pam Allen and the women who agreed with her left the organization.

Feminist Changes in WAGE

Despite the fact that feminist issues and their implications led to extreme conflict within the organization, it is nevertheless true that throughout its history WAGE was gradually being changed by the influence of the larger feminist movement. For example, a constitutional convention held November 2 and 3, 1974, made significant changes in WAGE's statement of purpose and goals. Most notably, WAGE changed its self-definition from *an organization of women trade unionists*, to an organization of *working women, including the unemployed, the retired, and those on welfare.* The following new goals were also added:

1. Added to number one [which was equal pay. . .] "with effective affirmative action programs, and jobs for all who want them."

2. Organizing working women into unions and caucuses, and encouraging women unionists to take greater responsibility and leadership roles; and to end male domination in the unions.

3. Interpretation of the ERA to guarantee the extension to men of labor standards covering women, and national protective legislation includ-

ing health and safety standards reflecting the needs of workers, not employers.

4. Fighting racism. Recognizing the need for minority women, who are double oppressed, to take leadership in unions and in Union WAGE; supporting the struggle of all minority sisters and brothers.

5. Ending sex and age discrimination in health and welfare and pension plans with pension portability for all workers.

6. Minimum wage of $4.00 per hour to be escalated in proportion to rate of inflation, guaranteed to all workers without exception. Work week of thirty hours or less at forty hours' pay with voluntary overtime at tripple pay.

7. Free national comprehensive health care.

8. Free abortion on demand. Free contraceptive of choice. No forced sterilization.

9. Social security benefits with an inflation escalator for every adult and child.

10. An end to economic and social discrimination on the basis of sexual orientation.[77]

By January-February 1982, the following had also been added under goals.

11. An end to sexual harassment in the workplace and in society.

12. An end to economic and social discrimination on the basis of age or disability.

13. Trade union wages and unemployment insurance for prisoner-workers.[78]

During the late 1970s WAGE was involved in coalitions that fought sexual and racial discrimination, and organized against attempts to restrict or end women's right to choose abortion.

In 1982, the very last issue of *Union WAGE* stated:

> The concerns of women workers reach far beyond the workplace, and are not strictly limited to wages and hours... feminist issues cannot be quickly or easily solved at a negotiating table.[79]

Unions for Women
—Establishment or Independent? _____

Another major issue that WAGE members debated throughout their history was unionization. The original consensus believed that: 1) unions were crucial for the betterment of all working people; 2) wage-working women should be organized into unions; 3) existing unions needed to be changed because of their sexism, racism, and frequent lack of democracy; 4) the way to change unions was by organizing rank and file women within existing unions.

In a 1973 statement supporting this approach, Ann Draper wrote that:

> To begin with, we union women insist that it is basic to our goal to devote our energies to unionize the over 33 million working women who work in the lowest-paid and lowest status jobs. This is a job that has to be done both against the opposition of the employers and (at least in many cases) against the apathy or resistance of trade-union leaderships....

> The dynamic thrust of women organizing on the job will shake up the corroded bureaucratic apparatuses that want to restrain the swelling rank-and-file movement: it will break through the encrusted layers of the entrenched establishments. The women's component of the trade-union movement can be the cutting edge of its struggles; if it is given its full scope, it can weld together the brotherhood and sisterhood of unionism on a new level.[80]

During the subsequent history of Union WAGE, two developments occurred which caused the organization to rethink policy on rank and file organizing. The first issue was one in which Jean Maddox had been prominent: trusteeship.

> An international union takes control of a local by placing it under trusteeship and appoints a trustee who has sole and total control of the affairs of the local union. This means that the trustee can rule illegal, null and void any and/or all decisions by the rank and file membership. The trustee can choose to hold no membership meetings, disband all elected officers, dismiss all union staffers, and spend the members' dues as the trustee sees fit. The trustee has ultimate power to make all decisions regarding a local union despite any wishes of the rank and file membership.[81]

Trusteeship was originally developed as an antidote to local union corruption. It has also been used to limit rank and file independence.

Jean Maddox's own union, Local 29 of the Office and Professional Employees International Union, AFL-CIO, was placed in trusteeship three times from 1973 to 1976 because the International disagreed with some of the Local's more radical political positions. Maddox strongly believed that trusteeship was being used nationwide to curb rank and file attempts to gain control of their unions, many of which were composed mainly of women. She wrote:

> Illegal trusteeship is a very serious problem. Union members must begin to deal with it seriously and decisively if the labor movement is to properly fulfill its role of defending the rights of all working people, thus bringing about social reform in our society.[82]

This experience made many WAGE women take another look at their support for organizing women into existing unions.

Another experience that led WAGE to re-examine independent organizing was a case in which two rank and file women leaders affiliated their local with a union that was apparently controlled by organized crime. SEIU—Service Employees Local 400, which was originally formed to represent San Francisco City and County Employees, initiated a major campaign in 1974 to organize clerks. Soon afterwards, this local, now including many clerks, became involved in a successful strike.

Maxine Jenkins, one of the organizers hired by the local, was highly effective. The SEIU's executive board included only one clerical representative, and Jenkins, with the clerks, urged more representation, as well as other programs that favored clerks and would democratize the union. However, she and another organizer, Louise Statzer, were fired shortly after advocating these reforms.[83]

The membership used their power to get Jenkins and Statzer rehired, but again they were fired. With the help of women's groups, including WAGE, the clerks were successful in ousting Jerry Hipps, the man responsible for the firings. However, after Hipps' forced resignation, the union was placed in trusteeship by the International. Jenkins, Statzer, and other activists then formed a new union, the Union of City Employees (UCE).

WAGE and segments of the women's movement were enthusiastic about the formation of a new union. In the July/August 1975 issue of *Union WAGE*, a front page article, "New Union Forms," declared:

> The new union was greeted with considerable relief and joy by women's groups concerned with organizing the great mass of unorganized women. They had been anxiously awaiting such a breakthrough to give future impetus to

> organizing women workers in private industry. About 80% of UCE potential members are female clerical workers. Maxine Jenkins, who brought to public attention the need to organize the downtown "office ghettos" will be doing what she does best in the new organization—organize![84]

However, on the third page of the same issue an opposing view was offered by a member who was extremely critical of Maxine Jenkins' new union. The writer claimed that under trusteeship, the Rank and File Caucus was growing within the existing local. She expressed a crucial need for rank and file unity, especially because they were being raided by the new union.

> It's hard to believe that Maxine Jenkins, who began the Local 400 Clerks Council to unite clerical workers, is now willing to drop the rank and file clerks and their organization.
>
> ### WHY ANOTHER UNION?
> If the leadership of the new union supports rank and file trade unionism, why did they leave the rank and file caucus behind them to begin another City Workers' Union over our protests? What happens to our hopes for an agency shop? The new Union certainly can't hope to bring in all of 400's membership. Why are they taking their case to the Press and not to the rank and file? Why can't they tell any one where they are getting their money from? Why, in all their news releases, is only one rank and file clerical worker mentioned as opposed to at least four business agents.[85]

In the very next issue of the *Union WAGE*, under the headline "Jenkins/Statzer Betray City Clerks," is a statement from the Union Wage executive board:

> On August 6, the Union of City Employees (UCE), founded only a few weeks earlier as an independent union which would fight for principles of rank and file democracy, voted to affiliate with the Laborers Union—the Laborers is a union with a grim record of violence and corruption, male chauvinism and racism, and alleged gangster associations. It was an incredible shock to learn that former feminists had decided to join such a union, a union which will prove as destructive to them as it will to the people they have led into it. It is an injury to the women's movement of San Francisco which looked to Maxine Jenkins and Louise Statzer as leaders in the fight for rank and file democracy, for women's rights and feminist demands in the labor movement.
>
> Union WAGE disassociates itself from this betrayal of

city workers, especially women in San Francisco, by the women who chose to go into the Laborers. Jenkins and Statzer sold out not only the sisters who followed and aided them but any kind of principled position in either the labor movement or movement for women's liberation. . . .

. . .Union Wage and organizations associated with us will use every means to discredit the Laborers leadership and we promise we will give no opportunity to organize downtown. . . .They will have no support from the women's movement which they have so completely alienated by their actions.

Union WAGE, too, is due for some criticism in regard to our supportive attitude towards Jenkins and Statzer. We believed that in their conflict with the Service Employees International Union Local 400 they were taking a progressive position by building a rank and file caucus and fighting for the restoration of their jobs. We sympathized and protested when Jenkins was again fired, and many of us had hoped that out of this chaos a new democratic unionism would be born, controlled by the rank and file. This was not a unanimous point of view. Those who read the last issue of WAGE knew that there were two articles published about the new union with sharply differing positions. Many issues have since been raised which cannot be answered in an editorial. . . questions of trusteeship, of dual unionism, of independent organizing. . .

. . .We feel that some of us became enthusiastic without sufficient investigation of the facts of the struggle within the Local 400 caucus, and whether the new union was set up in the democratic fashion which its founders claimed.[86]

WAGE leaders were now confronted by two new questions: 1) What safeguards protect the integrity of rank and file leaders? 2) In order to facilitate change, does one organize from within, or build new unions? These questions were prominently debated when WAGE was faced with a major new decision: what should their relationship be with the newly organized Coalition of Labor Union Women (CLUW)—a national group of union women which had come out of the existing union movement and intended to work with it (in particular within the AFL-CIO)?

Eighteen WAGE members attended the founding convention of CLUW, held in Chicago on March 23-24, 1974. Over 3,000 women in all attended this convention, at which it became clear that CLUW had the potential to become *the* working women's organization in the U.S. The question for WAGE was whether it should disband and its members join CLUW.

Ann Lipow, then the president of Union WAGE, enthusiastically supported CLUW. In "A Giant Step Forward," she wrote:

> Every so often in history, as in nature, there occur quantum leaps by which new forces and new relationships are brought into existence.
>
> The formation of CLUW represents just such an historic opportunity for the members and friends of Union WAGE. The pioneering work of which every WAGE member can rightly be proud, along with stirrings and activities in other pockets throughout the country, have now jelled into the beginnings of a genuine movement.
>
> . . . Union WAGE's program is excellent, but an excellent 10 point program and a relatively small group of union women do not constitute a movement. CLUW, too, has. . . a program but more important, it has the potential of being a broad nation-wide organization of trade union and working women.
>
> An organization which reaches deep into the rank and file of the trade unions will not be controlled by "bureaucrats" (real or imagined). Only such an organization will be able to accomplish what is probably the most important task facing working women today; the organization into the labor movement of the millions upon millions of working women who are cheated out of a decent existence because they are not organized.[87]

The majority of women of the original consensus were extremely critical of CLUW, seeing it as the "ladies' auxiliary" of the existing trade union movement, and in that same issue Joyce Maupin wrote an opposing point of view to Lipow's. She saw that:

> The significance of the CLUW Conference is that it brought together 3,300 enthusiastic working women when the planning committee estimated an attendance of 800. The high spirits and militancy of the delegates contrasted sharply with the heavy-handed control and rigid regulations of the committee in charge. . . there is no question that female bureaucrats are in every respect the equal of male bureaucrats. CLUW has been organized because of the ferment among working women in this country and the role of the present leadership will undoubtedly be to contain this movement within acceptable channels. But the rank and file women at the conference were not so easily led, and they may be able to overcome bureaucratic control. Another possibility is that

they will seek an alternative form of organization which will include the unorganized, the unemployed and women on welfare and fight for the interests of all working women.[88]

Within the larger debate about WAGE's relationship to CLUW were two very specific issues. The first was whether CLUW should support the United Farm Workers Union (UFW) in a dispute with the Teamsters. WAGE was in favor of supporting the UFW, as a union representing a highly oppressed group; the CLUW leadership did not want to intervene. According to Joyce Maupin there were many petitions and motions presented to CLUW; the Farm Workers carried by an overwhelming majority.

> The success of the rank and file rebellion testifies to the fighting temper of the women at the conference. But on Sunday morning, in spite of a standing ovation when women from the United Farmworkers addressed the conference, parliamentary maneuvers blocked a positive motion of support.[89]

The second issue was whether CLUW should be open to non-union women. CLUW's leadership voted that the organization would be for union women only. WAGE's leadership believed that since the majority of wage-working women are not yet in unions, this stand would be unwise. They not only opposed CLUW's decision, but the *way* in which the decision was made, which they saw as another example of a lack of democracy among established union leaders. Kay Eisenhower, a WAGE activist, claimed:

> The necessity for CLUW being formed comes out of this neglect of women workers by the official union structure; to mirror the failure of the union movement to organize women workers by preventing those same women from belonging to the organization that now hopes to remedy that situation seems foolish at best. CLUW holds the possibility of organizing and leading the militant activity of millions of women workers, but it cannot do that as an elitist organization closed to the women it hopes to lead; rather we should be aggressively seeking the membership of unorganized women...as full members of CLUW that can learn the skills....
> The real damage to CLUW is not from the 90 percent of those women workers, but from those female bureaucrats, who want to use CLUW to build their own careers within the official union structure.[90]

Although it was clear to WAGE members that CLUW had some problems, they remained split as to whether or not they should join

CLUW. The ensuing debate centered around whether WAGE should continue to organize independently, build its own chapters and even become a national organization, or whether to disband and join forces with CLUW. On one side of the question, Ann Lipow stated: "Astonishingly, some WAGE members have reacted to the founding of CLUW with the idea of building new WAGE chapters. Whether it is intended or not such a perspective leads to WAGE identifying its separateness and hence its rivalry to CLUW."[91] On the other side Joyce Maupin argued, "CLUW is not the only organization of working women in existence today. Further, many of us who attended the founding convention of CLUW thought it was a bureaucratic still birth [sic] which never had any promise. We did not see it as a sign of an independent movement among women workers, but as a reaction to that movement, an attempt by the labor establishment to contour and control it."[92]

This issue could have split the organization. Jean Maddox, who represented the majority that opposed joining CLUW, ran again for WAGE president in an attempt to keep the organization together. Ann Lipow, who was in favor of merging with CLUW, was not re-elected. Some WAGE members left WAGE and joined CLUW, but WAGE as an organization remained intact.

WAGE members then addressed a crucial internal debate over the question of whether they should continue to support organizing women's rank and file caucuses within existing unions, or whether they should promote women workers' independent organizing.

In November of 1975, Union WAGE, in cooperation with the San Francisco and Berkeley-Oakland Women's Unions (two feminist organizations), co-sponsored a conference on organizing women workers. According to WAGE: "The conference's main themes will deal with the question of organizing the unorganized; how to build strong membership unions; and developing a coalition for political action."[93] One of the major purposes of the conference was to discuss and consider independent organization.

The conference drew more than 500 people from all areas of California as well as from Washington and Vancouver, Canada. Participants included members of rank and file caucuses, independent unions, women's organizations, and, in particular, many unaffiliated individuals. This program dealt with specific experiences of independent unions as well as rank and file struggles against the leadership of traditional unions.[94]

In her keynote speech, Joyce Maupin laid down her indictment of the labor movement. While stressing her belief in unionization, she also clearly stated that labor had failed in many instances.

The present union leadership is not promoting class conscious trade unionism. In fact, they're more likely to be cooperating with the employers than fighting them. Independent unions are particularly irritating to union officials because they aren't getting any dues into the AFL-CIO Treasury. These unions, the independents that we'll be talking about this afternoon, are predominantly unions of women workers or minorities whom nobody wanted to organize. They were considered unorganizable.

Clerical workers have been in the "unorganizable" class from the point of view of labor leadership and yet half of the women in the Bay area work in big downtown offices—"paper."

Clerical work is the fastest growing occupation because of the spread of U.S. imperialism. The banks and insurance companies have a world empire.

Historically the record of unions on racism and sexism is dismal. By the end of the 19th century the AFL had taken over pretty much...on organizing skilled white men. Until the thirties with the rise of the CIO, minorities and women were almost completely excluded from unions. The CIO organized all workers in mass industries, skilled, unskilled, blacks and women. The trouble is that very few blacks and women were in mass industries so not very many got organized.[95]

In the eyes of WAGE activists, the challenge was: given the sexist practices of the unions, their lack of democracy, and their inability to organize unorganized workers—many of whom are blacks and women—what should be the strategy of working women? There were two answers: rank and file organizing within established unions and independent organizing.

Conference reports described "two forms of organizing taking place among women workers." The first form was evidenced in a report given by the Service, Office and Retail Workers Union of Canada (SORWUC), which represented a new model of independent feminist union organizing. SORWUC, not affiliated with any existing international, is a union organized by working women which has negotiated contracts with such unique features as: a thirty-hour work week to be worked in four days with flexible hours, double pay for overtime, and International Women's Day as a paid holiday. The other form of organizing was rank and file struggle within an existing union: the Cannery Workers Committee in Hayward and San Jose, California was praised for fighting against the "racist and sexist practices of both their employers and Teamster local bureaucrats."[96]

The afternoon of the conference was devoted completely to discussing the pros and cons of organizing outside the traditional labor movement. A panel included representatives from the National Alliance of Postal and Federal Employees (an organization of black postal workers), the California Homemakers (who organized attendant care workers), United Workers Union Independent, Seattle (organizing on campuses along with AFSCME), and the Clerical and Allied Service Employees Union, which was independent for ten years before affiliating with AFSCME.[97]

The conference was considered a great success. It established WAGE as a major—if not *the* major—resource for both rank and file and independent organizing among working women. However, the questions concerning independent organizing were not resolved. The betrayal of Jenkins and Statzer had just occurred, illustrating, among other things, the conflicts that could occur between rank and file organizing from within and independent organizing. That question would continue to be debated. At the November 1976 WAGE convention, a resolution was proposed discouraging independent organizing of women workers:

> A substantial number of women have sought a solution
> to their problems by turning to unions. But many of these
> trade unions, imbued with racist and sexist policies, have
> rejected them.

TACTICS

> One answer to this rejection has been the organization of
> independent unions of women. Independent unionism is not
> a new phenomenon. But before the CIO, for instance, an
> independent union was formed to force industrial union
> organization. In addition black workers formed their own
> unions when racism in the trade unions barred them from
> membership. And the Farm Workers were independent and
> they were accepted into the AFL-CIO. However, these were
> *temporary* formations which were discontinued when the
> *tactic* of independent unionism was instrumental in achieving
> the desired goals.
>
> Tactically, there is no question 'that women should
> initially organize themselves if no union cooperation is
> forthcoming. Once this is accomplished, however, to achieve
> strength and to protect its members, affiliation with an
> established union is necessary.
>
> Today when workers must contend with monopolies,
> conglomerates and multi-national corporations, splinter
> unions don't stand a chance. The fact is that International
> Unions are probing amalgamations to keep afloat.

RANK AND FILE

Admittedly, democratic rank and file participation in today's unions is limited, although there are major exceptions such as in the Steel Workers Unions and the United Mine Workers. Regardless of size, rank and file activity *within* the unions is the key to:

1. unite the working class by fighting against racism and for the equal rights of women;

2. organize the unorganized;

3. achieve a labor leadership responsible to the membership's needs which will confront employers rather than establish a partnership with them.[98]

The debate begun at this convention continued within WAGE chapters and was carried in the *Union WAGE*. It was primarily between those who thought that women should organize independently only if there were no existing union (as a temporary solution until they could affiliate with an existing union), and those who favored organizing completely outside of the existing union structure. For example, while the San Jose chapter espoused the former position, the Seattle chapter put forth the latter. The Seattle chapter argued that:

Independent union organizing is one of the most exciting current aspects of women's organizing. We of Seattle Union WAGE think that it is [necessary] to analyze the impact and direction of this trend.

We strongly urge that Union WAGE not pass this—or any other—resolution which ties the organizing to one or another method of union organizing. We would like to see the field open for experimentation and to see Union WAGE as a group in which experiences and experiments are shared and delegated as we grow together to find new answers to old problems.

The Seattle activists challenged what was considered the traditional labor view that "to achieve strength and protect its members, affiliation with an established union is necessary."[99] In their opinion, that strategy might be best for production workers but might not be appropriate for many areas of women's work, in particular service and clerical areas.

In the next issue of *Union WAGE*, the San Jose chapter replied that independent unions, in particular the ones that Seattle supported, were harmful because they created competition with the existing unions. (This is called "dual unionism.") They noted that during the 1930s, when AFL craft unions did not organize the vast majority of workers, the

Trade Union Educational League (TUEL), organized by the Communist Party, not only pressed for industrial unionism, but trained large
numbers of organizers who were decisive in the successful organizing of
the CIO. After organizing temporarily, TUEL members were integrated
into the CIO, and the TUEL unions, having served their purpose, were
disbanded. "These were temporary formations which were discontinued
when the tactic of independent unions was instrumental in achieving the
desired goals [of building up the established unions]."[100]

Throughout the WAGE debate over unionization and the merits
and difficulties of independent organizing, *Union WAGE* published
articles concerning the organizing strategies and experiences of women
organizers. In "Strategies for Clerical Workers," Karen Nussbaum wrote
about the office workers' organization "9 to 5," formed in September
1973. Not originally designed as a union, "9 to 5" members came to
realize the importance of unionizing through their organizing efforts.
They considered the possibility of an independent union for office
workers, but felt that the early battles of clerical unions would be tough
and they would need very powerful resources. At the same time, they
noted that in the cities where they were organizing, "it is very difficult to
find a local that has the necessary size and strength and will also represent
the interests of clerical workers."[101]

The solution they found was chartering a *new* local of an established
union. Nussbaum wrote:

> Seeking the most effective route to collective bargaining,
> office workers in Boston recently obtained a charter for a new
> local of the Service Employees International, AFL-CIO...
> Our strategic choice has been confirmed by the response
> in our organizing drives. Office workers have something of
> their own, while at the same time bringing to bear an outside
> power whose seriousness cannot be questioned. The unioniza-
> tion of clerical workers in Boston will not proceed quickly. It
> will require painstaking effort and a delicate balance of self-
> sufficiency and support from the broader national movement.
> We are confident that this combination is being developed
> here.[102]

In July-August 1977, WAGE's discussion of organizing women
continued as Joyce Maupin stated:

> The most vital and difficult question today is how to
> organize workers in spite of the union leadership.
> In the 1970s the direction of the women's movement
> changed. Working women began to build their own organiza-

tions, Union WAGE, 9 to 5, Women Employ, Women Office Workers, Women's Organization for Employment. Some limit their goals to affirmative action and the advancement of individual women while others, like WAGE, fight to improve the wages and conditions of all working women. With the exception of CLUW, none of these groups has ties with the official labor movement. The need for independence becomes very clear when you read about the Women's Trade Union League at the beginning of this century. A few years ago, an organization in San Diego similar to Union WAGE decided to affiliate with the Central Labor Council. That's the last anyone heard about them.

The sexism of the union movement encourages the growth of separate women's organizations and the bureaucrats correctly see it as a threat. Independent unions, organized by the women who met with hostility or indifference when they approached the traditional labor movement, are another development. Many of these seek affiliation but feel that by building their own organizations they make it possible to negotiate with interested unions from a position of strength. They hope to gain greater local autonomy and rank and file control.

Despite reports that the women's movement is falling apart, independent organizations of working women have been growing and gaining strength.[103]

As another example, in the November-December 1977 issue of *Union WAGE*, an article on "Feminism and Unionism: A Different Approach" described the Service Office and Retail Workers Union of Canada (SORWUC). "If a small independent union of working women can take on the Canadian banking establishment, women can obviously do anything."[104]

SORWUC, founded in the early 1970s, was an outgrowth of another women's organization. After several union organizing experiences in which they got very little help from the existing trade union movement, they decided to form their own union, one which women could control. In 1976, when SORWUC was three years old, employees at a Vancouver branch of the Canadian Imperial Bank of Commerce joined and applied to the Canadian Labor Relations Board for union certification. Hundreds of bank workers joined the union. After that SORWUC received certification for thirteen bank branches and represented workers in those branches.

The women of SORWUC organized as feminists. They saw, however, the limitations of a feminist movement which did not organize economic power bases:

How does our approach differ from other feminist
strategies?

The organization of women around social demands—
health, rape, violence in general, educational stereotyping,
child care, maternity benefits and the whole range of questioning social roles which reinforce dependency and sub-
mission—are vital to the achievement of feminist goals!
However, it is imperative to recognize the need for a power
base if we are to have success that goes beyond creating an
awareness of the problems.[105]

SORWUC's analysis was pivotal since they articulated a feminism
which understood the importance and potential power of unionism.
They recognized the limitations of present unions in relationship to
women workers around issues such as unions' promotion of wage
differences, and the lack of collective bargaining and contracts around
women's issues.

Further the structure and organization of most unions
often does not recognize our roles as workers and homemakers....

Trade unions have not shown any particular interest in
going out and approaching unorganized women from a point
of view which these women could understand.[106]

Thus, from their feminist perspective, SORWUC saw that economic
power would come from independent unions, not the established
unions. "We consider independent unions a complement to other
unions, not a competition. Many of the unions to which women
presently belong have helped those women win benefits and wages
which have improved their lives immensely."[107]

In *Union WAGE*, feminism became increasingly associated with
independent organization. Sherna Gluck, a feminist historian, contributed an article titled "We are the Majority," in which she analyzed early
twentieth century women's locals of the Amalgamated Clothing Workers
in Chicago. She drew the following conclusion:

The same questions about organizing which we raise today
were faced by them: can women be more effective in the
mainstream of their unions or should they organize on their
own? "Looking back, the women who formed the Women's
Local in Chicago in 1920 are clear." In my day, the women
lacked experience, they lacked knowledge. We first had to be
organized ourselves...we had to get our own house in order.

We may have more experience and more knowledge now,
half a century later, but is our house in order yet?[108]

While many of the advantages of independent unions were reported and discussed, articles also reported on successful rank and file activities within existing unions. Denise D'Anne, one of the founders of the Union of City Employees with Maxine Jenkins, left it when it joined the Laborers. She went back to Local 400 of SEIU, the original local that Maxine Jenkins had been part of when it went into trusteeship. In "Turning a Union Around: Autocracy to Democracy in SEIU 400," D'Anne describes how Local 400 was able to get the trusteeship lifted and become the bargaining agent for city workers. After this victory it corrected many of its past mistakes and ensured greater union democracy.

> Clerical organizing has again become the major focus of the union. Clerks are again recognizing their potential power and have taken every precaution to hold onto this power. They are a strong and viable group with a clear road ahead and may become a model for organizing clericals in other sectors of the economy.[109]

In Local 29 of the Office and Professional Employees International Union (OPEIU—which had also been put into trusteeship), the Rank and File Caucus was also able to rebuild itself after the trusteeship was lifted and rank and file candidates won almost every office.

The issue was finally fully discussed at the WAGE convention held in Oakland on November 12 and 13, 1977, when a resolution on independent unions was proposed. It stated that "women should initially organize themselves if no union cooperation is forthcoming. Once this is accomplished however, to achieve strength and protect its members, *affiliation with an established union is necessary.*"[110] This resolution was rejected by delegates on the grounds that the underlined words were restrictive and therefore not in keeping with Union WAGE's purpose and goals.

Rather than choosing one strategy over another, Union WAGE's policy then became to give individuals and groups information about *all* of the different possibilities. WAGE itself became a resource center that offered appropriate help, rather than a place where much organizing was initiated. This was true particularly in its later years.

While the conclusion to these lengthy discussions about independent organizing may have been disappointing, the fact that they happened at all was significant. These debates within WAGE were historic. How to organize unorganized women workers? How can women control their own unions? What does feminism imply about the form that unions should take? There have been very few places where these kinds of discussions have taken place so openly. While WAGE was critical of many aspects of feminism, it advocated a strong relationship between feminism and independent unions and explored women's economic power and control over their lives. These were significant steps.

Conclusion

Union WAGE deserves to be recognized as one of the pioneer women's organizations of the 1970s. It helped pave the way for the formation of CLUW and other working women's activities that came afterward. It was a major voice for working women in Northern California during the early 1970s.

One of the crucial struggles led by WAGE was the fight to extend California's protective laws to men. This was achieved in 1976, due in large part to WAGE's efforts. Other WAGE accomplishments include a highly successful conference on women held in 1975, a bi-monthly newspaper, and other literature about and for working women. The WAGE newspaper was the major forum during the 1970s where crucial issues facing working women, women's liberation, and trade unionism could be discussed.

WAGE also became a resource center for women organizing women workers into unions. During the last years of WAGE's existence, it was involved in several coalitions that fought sexual and racial discrimination, such as "anti-Bakke" and "anti-Briggs" coalitions. (The Bakke decision was a U.S. Supreme Court case aimed at striking down minority admissions quotas in medical schools; the Briggs initiative was a referendum question that attempted to ban homosexual "advocates" from teaching in California schools.) Finally, WAGE set up a Household Workers' Rights Project to do advocacy work for household workers.[111]

WAGE represented a crucial historical stage in the development of working women's organizations. It was the first major voice since the WTUL to raise questions about women and unions and also to support integrating women's liberation with trade unionism. Within the larger women's movement, WAGE continually raised working women's issues and the importance of organizing unorganized workers. Within the labor movement, WAGE supported feminist goals and rank and file activism.

Despite WAGE's significant contributions, it remained a relatively small organization, disbanding in 1982 because of lack of resources and a tiny membership. The last issue of the newspaper stated:

Union WAGE has neither lost its commitment to unionizing women workers, nor have we decided that there are
better ways for women to gain control and dignity in the
workplace. We recognize that the labor movement in this
country has a proud history and heritage of struggle for its
members; but we are impatient to see this heritage extended to
women workers. . . .

WAGE encourages its supporters to keep our vision alive:
providing a women's perspective in the labor movement, and
a labor perspective in the women's movement.[112]

Analysis

Union WAGE's Theory and
Practice Around Double Oppression

Opposing double oppression in theory

The women of the original consensus of Union WAGE developed
an explicit analysis of the double oppression of wage-working women,
but did not consider a theory of the double oppression of *all* women.
Although non-wage forms of female labor like unpaid housework were
acknowledged, WAGE's focal point was wage-working women. For
example, in the very first issue of their newspaper, January-February
1972, WAGE stated:

Over 30 million working women endure double discrimination and exploitation: as women and as workers. Most
carry the burden of two jobs: at work and then at home. Such is
the pattern for most of California's 3 million women workers.

Women workers constitute 40% of the work force but their
pay averages 59 cents to the dollar paid to men workers for full
time work. Only one woman out of five is organized into a
union; and women workers are clustered in the low-paying
jobs of society: clerical, service, and manufacturing, and the
"women's work" of nursing, teaching, housekeeping, etc.
Trade unions are dominated by male leadership and largely
ignore the needs of women workers.[113]

From the beginning, WAGE had an excellent understanding of the
dual oppression of wage-working women: they are oppressed both at

home and in the wage-work force; being female very much affects their treatment at work.

The strength of the majority consensus was this understanding of wage-workers' double oppression, their agreement about the importance wage-workers could have in implementing a women's liberation program in the workplace and women workers' potential role in changing unions.

However, WAGE was weakest in its understanding of the oppression and unity of *all* women. Women were seen as fundamentally divided between middle class and working class, rather than as oppressed primarily as a gender group. By dismissing the struggles of non-wage-working women as "middle-class," particularly in the early years, WAGE weakened its potential for alliance with other women's groups. It also diminished women wage-workers' ability to fight against sexism in the workplace by not incorporating demands that affected them as women outside the workplace. The WAGE leaders missed or underestimated the potential power of women from all classes and races to change society and to ally themselves with working people.

Pam Allen agreed with the other women in WAGE about the double oppression of wage-working women. However, as a feminist, Pam believed that *all* women are oppressed. From Allen's thinking emerged the beginnings of a *working women's feminism* that contrasted in important ways with the theories of the majority of WAGE leaders. Although Pam Allen did not fully develop a theory and a program of working women's feminism, she did lay out several component parts. First, she believed that women needed to be organized about all of the kinds of work that they perform, including housework, childrearing, and consumption, as well as their work in the wage economy. Her analysis put at least as much attention on women's unpaid labor as on their paid labor. Second, she thought that *all* issues that affect working women's lives need to be addressed, including gender issues outside of the wage-workplace, such as reproductive rights, and violence against women, and community issues such as education, housing, etc. Third, Allen asserted that the subjective quality of women's lives needed to be explored and integrated into a political program.

Allen brought fresh ideas to the issue of gender and class. She understood the role that consciousness plays in people's lives, the interlocking nature of oppressions, and the necessity for working women to fight for a better quality of life and human relationships in addition to improved material conditions. While she took the best of contemporary feminism, such as the idea that the "personal is political," and applied it to her understanding of a working women's feminism, she did not hesitate to question some feminist ideas such as the sometimes prevalent view that "men are the enemy," and she pointed out how that view has often coincided with race and class biases. (In this attitude she was in complete agreement with women of the majority group.)

She was weakest in her seeming lack of understanding of the potential power of wage-working women and the importance of unions for women and for all working people. In addition, she was not always able to maintain a balance between the work of organizing around specific issues and a concentration on consciousness, personal relationships, and feelings.

Allen's arguments could have been interpreted as coinciding with the general anti-union sentiment held by some branches of feminism and by society as a whole. She did not share Union WAGE's most important understanding that integrating women's liberation into trade unions was key to transforming both movements. While she understood the exploitation of women as houseworkers, she underestimated the growing impact that wage-work was having on women's lives, and she did not see how getting unorganized women into unions could be beneficial for women's liberation.

Each faction in WAGE—the majority consensus and the group that shared Allen's ideas—represented the best of their respective generations. It is unfortunate that their views could not be synthesized. This would have made it possible to achieve a program that focused on wage-working women, stressed organizing all other groups of women workers, and asserted the importance of all women's issues for working women.

Opposing double oppression in practice

WAGE's platform was broad, covering issues related to all workers, issues related especially to women workers, gender issues in the workplace, and (somewhat less) issues related to all women. In practice, however, WAGE only worked on a small part of this platform. Despite its increasing sympathy with feminist issues over the years, the major focus of WAGE's organizing was on *women as wage-workers*. This was clarified in the debate with Pam Allen when Jan Arnold emphasized what the major activities of WAGE included. Never explicitly stated before, WAGE's principal activities were now recorded in the Union WAGE newspaper as follows:

1. Encouraging the organizing of working women into unions and caucuses. Encouraging women unionists to take greater responsibility and leadership roles, to end male domination in unions and to promote class-conscious trade unionism. Helping working-class women build self-con-

fidence and skills so we can organize and lead, especially in unions, organizing drives, and rank and file caucuses, and in other organizations of working women.

2. Joining or leading campaigns around issues which especially affect working women, such as the fight to keep protective laws, including higher minimum wages and shorter hours.

3. Using our newspaper, Union Wage, and our office, to further our goals through education, linking up people in struggle with others who can help them, and similar activities.[114]

WAGE's most outstanding successes in these areas were their struggles for a "labor ERA" and the extension of protective legislation to men. Their goals regarding the labor ERA were to make sure both that an ERA would pass and that it did not harm either male or female workers. The labor ERA was also an attempt to end an old conflict between working-class and middle-class women by including the interests of both in the ERA. As a result, WAGE's goals around the labor ERA were a major step forward in confronting women's double oppression. In addition, by winning the support of labor, women's groups, and others (such as the San Francisco Board of Supervisors) for their labor ERA, they raised the consciousness of a range of constituencies around working women's double oppression, and they united such groups via their effort to deal with this oppression.

While the labor ERA never passed on either a national or state level, WAGE was successful in getting California's protective legislation extended to men, which was an exceptional accomplishment.

WAGE's major sortcoming was that its position in favor of a labor ERA put it in opposition to NOW and the advocates of a "pure ERA." It was incorrect to assume that a pure ERA would not benefit working women. In fact, the ERA has been crucial for working women in their fight for equality because it has laid the basis for such essential programs as pay equity. (By the mid-1970s, recognizing that the ERA is a first step in fighting for equality in the workplace, many working women's groups and unions had reversed their earlier positions from supporting protective legislation to supporting an ERA.)

WAGE's Approach to Unionizing Women

There has been no other organization in the present period that looked at questions concerning women's liberation and unionism as thoroughly and decisively as WAGE. While WAGE may have been critical of many aspects of feminism, they saw that it was crucial for feminism and trade unionism to become integrated with each other. They understood the importance of unionization for women and the necessity for women to lead the way in building grassroots, democratically run unions. WAGE leaders saw that feminism could be the major force in building a new trade union movement in the United States. Although they were not able to accomplish their goals, their discussion of the issues had great value.

Their failure to actually organize working women into the kinds of unions they envisioned can be attributed to several factors. To some extent, external factors occurring in the 1970s, such as the general attacks on labor, the weakening of labor legislation, more sophisticated union-busting methods, a defensive rather than an offensive labor movement, and the general economic conditions of the time all inhibited WAGE's ability to act successfully. However, there were a number of internal reasons why WAGE was not more successful.

Very few of WAGE's later leaders were active union organizers, or even active organizers among non-union working women. They spent much of their time involved in internal debates, and/or dealing with the mechanics of the organization and were unable to provide inspiration for women in the workplace. WAGE was severely weakened by its isolation from both the existing trade union movement and the existing feminist movement (as will be described in the next section in more detail). Also, WAGE never attempted to deal with the gender aspect of women's double oppression in practice. They cut themselves off from women outside the wage-work force. While organizing within the wage-work force, they did not include such gender-related demands as daycare, maternity benefits, reproductive freedom, and so on. Thus, they did not help women gain a firm and equal base from which to struggle in the workplace. Lastly, WAGE lacked a *clear policy* about how to organize unorganized women. After a long debate about the virtues of independent versus internal union organizing, no decision or policy was ever arrived at, except to judge each case uniquely. While there is some value in examining every situation on its own merits, not having a strategy made it almost impossible for WAGE to organize. In practice, groups that were successful in organizing working women, such as "9 to 5," followed a particular strategy and had a focus group to organize.

Union WAGE's Approach to Stimulating Change Within the Feminist and Labor Movements and Facilitating Alliances Between the Two Movements

It is difficult to estimate what kind of changes WAGE has facilitated. In its early days it was a clear champion of women within the union movement, particularly when few other such organizations existed. It was responsible for getting labor sponsorship for the first statewide conference of women trade unionists, and within the larger women's movement it was an important advocate for workers' rights. More than that, WAGE was one of the many new working women's organizations which emerged in the 1970s, and it shared with them the total effect of building an independent working women's movement.

Throughout its history WAGE worked in coalition both with individual unions and with women's organizations, yet at the same time it was largely isolated from both movements. With regard to the labor movement, WAGE's isolation was caused both by its critical attitude towards established labor, as well as the "anti-left" bias that exists in parts of the labor movement. WAGE's independence allowed it to experiment, to debate ideas, and gave it the potential to create the kind of unions it wanted. However, its criticism of organized labor's existing leadership made it almost impossible to work with many of the unions. The question that remained unanswered was how a working women's organization could remain independent and at the same time maintain ties with the existing labor movement.

WAGE's relationship to the women's movement was different, since feminists did not have the same bias against an independent working women's organization as labor did. As a result, WAGE played an important role in forging unity between the women's movement and working women by forming coalitions, by reaching out to women's groups with the issues of working-class women, by speaking up for women's concerns within the union movement, by changing some of its attitudes towards feminism, and by tying feminism to independent unionism. At the same time, WAGE had a number of serious conflicts with the dominant women's movement. There was, of course, the specific conflict with NOW over the ERA and the criticisms WAGE repeated of the "middle-class" women's movement. While WAGE became much more sympathetic to feminism during the 1970s, the decision, explicitly stated during the struggle with Pam Allen, was the WAGE's focus was not on *all* women's issues. This severely limited the group's ability to form alliances with women's organizations.

It is doubtful that WAGE by itself made profound changes within either the women's or the labor movement, despite its original goals.

Development of a Broad Political Program

WAGE moved the development of a program around work/gender issues a step forward and articulated the needs of working women. Like working women's organizations of the past, WAGE's stated program was very broad and progressive. Its demands included a guaranteed monthly income, free national comprehensive health care, an end to sexual harassment in the workplace and in society, free abortion on demand, and many other—most of which remained on paper. WAGE did not have the power to make its political program reality.

Coalition of Labor Union Women

7

Introduction

The Coalition of Labor Union Women, or CLUW, founded in 1974, is the largest national organization of trade union women in the United States, and the first inter-union organization with an agenda for women. Since its inception, CLUW has become the major voice of trade union women, bringing women's issues to unions and forming the links between women and organized labor.

CLUW was born as a result of the women's liberation movement, the increase in activities among union women and working women (such as the formation of women's committees in unions), and the increasing interaction between these two trends. This newly forming relationship between women's liberation and union women was marked most dramatically by a change in union attitudes towards the ERA.

The United Auto Workers (UAW) was the first large union to support the ERA. Speaking on behalf of the ERA (before the Senate Committee on Constitutional Amendments on May 7, 1970), UAW vice-president Olga Madar said,

> I wanted to thank you for accommodating your schedule for me to appear, because frankly about three weeks ago in Atlantic City, 3,000 delegates representing over 1,700,000 men and women of the United Auto Workers took action in adopting a very comprehensive resolution which put us four square on the record not only for opposing all discriminatory patterns as far as women are concerned and for programs which would provide additional opportunities for them to partici-

pate at an equal level with all other individuals, but *also put us squarely on record favoring the Equal Rights Amendment.*

FEW UNIONS OPPOSE THE ERA

I was very much interested in the unions which were represented here in opposition to the Equal Rights Amendment particularly those labor leaders who represent the waitresses in the Detroit area.

I do have an opportunity to eat out occasionally. I sometimes go to what is commonly referred to as the better restaurants as well as those which are not so good, and I find that many times in the restaurants where the salaries are higher and the gratuities greater, that there are very few women employed...

MEN SUPPORT WOMEN IN UAW

And I further want to say to you that the 3,000 delegates who were at the convention represent a union with predominantly a male membership. We would never have been able to improve our programs and our policies, adopt the resolution and now to go ahead and implement it if it wasn't that we also have many males who believe that something ought to be done about this.

These hearings take place on the eve of Mother's Day, a ritual observance which celebrates not so much mothers and motherhood as the American genius for wedding sentimentality and profitable commercialism... But Mother's Day, 1970 may usher in a new era, for it comes at a time when a very strong tide is running in behalf of the proposition that American women, while they may like candy and roses, really need basic rights still denied them. *Rights not roses is the watchword for an increasing number of American women,* and the UAW believes that the Equal Rights Amendment to the Constitution is essential in any serious effort to make equal rights for women a reality...

"PROTECTIVE" LAWS OUT-MODED

Now, that [hours limitations] is one that I think we really have gone at in the wrong way for a long time. I think it is because of the so-called protective legislation for women that we have been unable to move faster in terms of getting legislation for voluntary overtime provisions not only in state legislation but on a Federal level. Overtime in this country has been excessive in many cases and not necessary. It is as bad for men as it is for the women. It makes chattel of all people not just females. And what we need to have is Federal Legislation

making the right of determining the whole question of overtime hours on a voluntary basis by the employee rather than in
terms of the employer regulating that proposition.

   . . . the kind of protective legislation that we have now
that supposedly protects women has not protected them, as
you have heard many times, and discriminates against them. I
do think that we do need to have protective legislation for
people at the workplace, and this is one of the issues, for
instance, that we are dealing with right now as we are talking
about bringing the whole question of in-plant environmental
pollution to the collective bargaining table. We need to have
protective legislation in certain kinds of instances but the kind
of legislation that we have had as far as the women are concerned has not really protected them. It has worked against
them.[1]

In her statement, Madar took a strong position on behalf of women's
rights, and presented the ERA as a strategy for attaining economic
justice. Moreover, she opposed protective legislation for women only.
Like Union WAGE, Madar and the UAW favored protective legislation
for all workers.

In 1973, the AFL-CIO officially reversed its opposition to the ERA
and came out in support of it, thereby taking a major step in contribut-
ing to links between women and labor.

Events Preceding the Formation of the Coalition of Labor Union Women

In the early 1970s, activities among union women grew, and there was
every indication that a national women's trade union organization
would form. For example, in 1970 at the National Rank and File Action
Conference in Chicago, "A Declaration of Rights of Women Workers"
was drawn up calling upon the labor movement to take up the interests
of women workers.[2] The leaders of Union WAGE hoped that their
group, founded in 1971, would grow into a national organization. And
at a women's conference called by the California State Labor Federation
held in March 1973 in San Francisco (initiated by Union WAGE
members), a resolution was adopted calling for a national trade union
women's conference in 1974.

In April 1973 in Chicago, eight trade union women got together for
an historic meeting. Although all of them were trade union leaders,
many were getting to know each other for the first time. They included
Addie Wyatt of the Amalgamated Meat Cutters and Butcher Workmen,

Ola Kennedy of the United Steelworkers, Olga Madar and Edith Van Horn of the United Auto Workers, Alice Weatherwax and Jean Thurmond of the American Federation of Teachers, Joyce Miller of the Amalgamated Clothing Workers, and Helga Nesbitt of the Communication Workers of America.[3] They agreed to arrange a Midwest regional conference of women unionists.

Although ninety-nine women were invited to the subsequent regional conference held in Chicago in June 1973, 200 women attended, a strong indicator of interest in union women's organization.[4] In her opening speech, Olga Madar proposed a national conference for the following year which would have as its express purpose the formation of a national coalition of trade union women. By the end of the conference, her proposal had been unanimously endorsed.[5] Conference coordinators were elected and plans were made for further conferences.

One of the highlights of the Chicago conference was a floor discussion which allowed women to speak up about the problems they faced as working women. An observer described the floor discussion as: "The biggest consciousness raising session ever held... It helped the women come to some awareness that they shared a lot of problems as trade unionists and women and that one of the ways of solving them was to work together in a big fashion... It was a very astute way of selling the idea."[6] This conference, as well as others held around the same time, gave union women the opportunity to connect with other union women and to explore their own experiences. These conferences provided some of the same functions that early consciousness-raising groups had for "middle-class" feminists.

At a St. Louis Women's Labor Conference held on November 17, 1973, the participants voted to develop an ongoing organization, and a national conference committee met soon afterwards. March 22-24, 1974 was chosen as the date for the convention which would form the Coalition of Labor Union Women.

Independent but parallel to the planning of CLUW, was the New York Trade Union Women's Conference, held on January 19, 1974. Its more than 500 participants expressed great excitement for the organizing of an ongoing organization of trade union women. Addie Wyatt, director of the women's division of the Amalgamated Meat Cutters and Butcher Workmen of North America, and a leader in the formation of CLUW, gave the keynote address.

> For many years I have longed to see women of the trade union movement, like women of other movements, get together and begin dealing with their own problems and with their own needs. And we have been so endeavoring with some successes and yes, with some failures...today and for the last several

months, I see women all over this country excited about getting together in the labor movement. The excitement comes because we are here with great purpose. Our needs are great, and we have decided that we will no longer wait for others to focus in on our needs and decide what they are going to do about it...

Why are women so concerned across the nation? Because women work for the same reasons that men work—we have to work. We join unions for the same reasons men join unions. We need the protection. We need the security. We need the promotion and job advancement opportunities. We need the better wages and working conditions that the labor movement can help us achieve. In spite of the labor movement's commitment to all of these goals, and in spite of all the benefits that we have derived as members of organized labor, women in the trade union movement know very well that we have not achieved our maximum goals. We have not had equal opportunity for jobs. We have not had equal opportunity for leadership roles in our unions. We know that until every member can enjoy those opportunities, the trade union movement will be incomplete and never be as strong as it can be.

I am one that is in total support of the labor movement and I want the record to show it. In spite of the fact that there are those who feel threatened rather than strengthened by our coming together, let the record show that our intent and our goals are to build a labor movement stronger than we ever had before. Our objectives are to build it and not destroy it, to unify it where it has been divided and to strengthen the participation of women members at all levels of the trade union movement.

I cannot help but be a strong supporter of the labor movement... Before I knew about any other women's liberation movement, I heard the union talking about equal pay for equal work. As a worker with already one strike against me for being a worker, and with two strikes against me for being black, and with three strikes against me for being female, I needed as much union as I could get. I would be the first to say that I have not always been happy and satisfied with the things that the union did. I've never been so dissatisfied that I thought I would desert it. In spite of the weaknesses of the labor movement, its strengths are much greater. It is our strongest instrument to achieve our economic, our political and our social goals.

Sisters, there are great problems. The decisions are made in places where we are not sitting. What the union is going to

do for us is often decided behind closed doors. It isn't all the
fault of the leadership; much of it is our fault. Women must
become available, ready and capable of working in the union.

We are not concerned with taking our brother's place—
we just want to fill our own places. We are concerned about
filling a partnership role in the labor movement. Together we
can share our experiences, find ways to fulfill its commitment
to us. The union is pledged to make this a better way of life for
all workers, regardless of race, color, creed or sex. I am
inspired, and I hope you are, by what unions have already
done and by what the labor movement must and can do in the
future... I would like to call upon you to say to every sister in
this room: 'I am your sister.' 'Reach out and touch your sister's
hand. Make this world a better place for her if you can...the
union is all of us together (Wyatt then chanted "Solidarity
Forever").[7]

Addie Wyatt, along with other trade union women leaders, asserted both
the importance of unionism and the recognition of women workers'
special needs. Sisterhood, she asserted, was a strong, complementary
force to solidarity.

At the same time, Wyatt acknowledged the problems in trade unionism and in particular those related to sexism and racism. One of the
most obvious weaknesses of the labor movement was the lack of women
in leadership positions. Nevertheless, while recognizing the sexism of
the established trade union movement, Addie Wyatt's consistent policy
and the policy of the future CLUW leadership was their belief in
working within the established labor movement. Their goal was as much
to strengthen trade unionism by supporting it, as it was to gain equality
for women. They saw that women needed the trade union movement and
that the labor movement could be strengthened by giving women an
equal place. Judy Berek of Local 1199, National Union of Hospital and
Health Care Employees, and co-chair of the New York conference,
continued this theme:

Organized labor can provide leadership in the struggle
for equality. As working women who are in trade unions, we
believe we can speak best to our problems. That is why we are
holding this conference. To share our experiences as trade
union women; to encourage members to seek leadership at all
levels of trade union activity; to discuss organizing unorganized women; and to explore how union machinery can
accomplish women's goals.[8]

At the New York conference, gender issues in the workplace, such as
maternity benefits, equal pay, and better working conditions for women

workers were discussed. A central concern was organizing unorganized workers, expressed by Margie Albert of District 65 of Distributive Workers of America (who was later to become the co-chair of the "Organizing the Unorganized" Committee of CLUW). Albert said:

> We should speculate on why there are not more women in unions. How many women would be organized today if unions had worked as vigorously in female-dominated fields of work as in male-dominated fields? How many women would be organized today if on union staffs there had been as many women organizers as our ratio in the work force which is now 40 percent? How many women would be organized today if unions appeared to be organizations where men and women participated and were recognized equally? What if unions had struggled to find the answers to the special problems women have in participating?
>
> Who are these unorganized women? By and large, we are clustered in low-paid fields. Did the unions stay away from these fields because they were low paid? Or are they low paid because the unions stayed away?[9]

Albert spoke highly of the independent working women's organization. Because "unionism is still a dirty word to a lot of office women" and because of unions' lack of initiative towards women office workers, the independent working women's movement has been vital, she said. In her analysis, the combination of the women's movement and labor is what will organize the many women now unorganized.

> I believe when the fire and energy of the women's movement combine with the labor movement, we will bring hundreds of thousands and millions of women into trade union ranks and benefit all of us. We should make a commitment to each other that we're sisters. We owe it to each other to organize unorganized women.[10]

Like many women at this conference, Margie Albert believed in working within the framework of the established union structure. However, there were also those at the conference who challenged the present leadership. For example, a caucus of female cab drivers protested the scheduled appearance of Harry Van Arsdale, president of the New York Central Labor Council and of the Taxidrivers' Union, with such statements as "He runs an undemocratic union that's oppressive to both men and women." "He shouldn't be here." (It turned out that Van Arsdale was not able to come and sent a female member of the Central Labor Council in his place.)[11] Although the question of whether to be involved did not take much time at the conference, it did signify a major struggle that would absorb a great deal of energy in the early years of CLUW.

The Founding of the
Coalition of Labor Union Women _____

The call for the first national conference of CLUW, issued in January 1974, stated that its purpose was,

> to bring together women union members and retirees of bonafide collective bargaining organizations to deal with our special concerns as unionists and women, in the labor force... In an inter-union framework, the Conference will consider positive action in the areas of equal pay, equal rights and equal opportunity...education about women's legal rights, adequate maternity benefits and child care, equitable hiring and promotion practices, adequate minimum wage, upgrading and affirmative action, organizing the unorganized women workers and equitable representation of women in union structures and policy making decisions. (Adopted at the CLUW National Planning Committee meeting held January 25-26, 1974, Chicago, Illinois.)[12]

CLUW's founding conference included 3,200 trade union women, more than four times the number expected. It was considered an historic occasion. Participants were of all ages and races, and from all parts of the country. Some came as individuals; some came with their unions. There were large contingents of women from the UAW, American Federation of Teachers, AFSCME, Office and Professional Employees, members of the UFW and others.[13] From a show of hands, it was estimated that more than 50 percent of the women present were rank and file union women who had never before attended a convention. According to one of the leaders, "some women walked to get there... Some women had no money and had to sleep on the floor, but there was enthusiasm, there was excitement and there was sisterhood."[14]

The conference chair was Addie Wyatt, who told the attendees: "Union women are getting together because it is about time for us to engage in affirmative action on our own needs... That stupid commercial that says 'You've come a long way, baby' is a lie!"[15] One of her major points was that women's wages relative to men's have declined, going from 63.9 percent of men's earnings in 1960 to 59.4 percent in 1970. Wyatt continually stressed the need for union women to solve their common problems, such as dead end jobs, low wages, unemployment, and underrepresentation in unions and unions' decision-making boards. Part of the fight, Wyatt claimed, is for "equitable representation of women in union policy decisions."[16] The empowerment of women at all levels of union decision-making became a major focus of CLUW's activities.

Another major issue, particularly during the organization's formative years, was the relationship between CLUW and the union movement. Many leftists at the founding conference believed that the established union leadership structure was as much the enemy of workers and of women as were the bosses and felt that CLUW should be independent of the labor establishment. In contrast, some leading conference organizers, while critical of the sexism in the labor *establishment,* were loyal to the labor *movement* and consistently voiced the need to work *within* it. In order to keep this position, they had to balance the need to change the union movement on behalf of women with the fear of many people in labor that fighting for women's rights was divisive. During the conference, Wyatt, for example, stressed that "this is not a divisive event. This is a move to unify what has been in too many instances already divided."[17]

The conference participants were serious about women's concerns. One of the most famous quotes from the convention came from Myra Wolfgang: "When you go back to your unions you'll be able to tell Meany and Woodcock and Fitzsimmons that 3,200 women met in Chicago—and we didn't come to swap recipes."[18] Leonard Woodcock of the UAW sent the convention a good luck telegram, but nothing came from either George Meany, president of the AFL-CIO or Frank Fitzsimmons of the Teamsters. The top union leadership was less than enthusiastic and was waiting to see how CLUW would develop.

CLUW's relationship to feminism also emerged as a major and largely non-controversial theme throughout the conference. Speakers consistently acknowledged both the debt CLUW owed to feminist organizations and the general importance of the women's movement. Olga Madar expressed total unity with the women's movement. Union women, she said, "were the first 'women's libbers' but often their successful fights for equal pay, for single unified seniority lists and other forms of equality did not move out into other areas...the women's movement gave an impetus to our moving ahead."[19] She praised groups such as the National Women's Political Caucus, the Women's Equity Action League, and NOW. Although she noted that there may be disagreement over attitudes towards men, Madar asserted that the women's movement "has been helpful in making union women and blue-collar wives aware that there was blatant discrimination against women just because they were female... One of the results of this meeting is that fewer and fewer union women will be saying 'We are not women's libbers.' By coming here, they have proved that they are."[20]

Participants anticipated controversy over the decision of whether to allow men to join CLUW, but in fact, there was little debate, and it was quickly decided that men could be members. Olga Madar said that the coalition was a woman's organization but "we do not discriminate . . . any men who want to join can."[21] The leadership wanted to shape a working women's feminism that supported women's rights but that was not anti-male. Gender issues, both in and outside of the workplace, were among the least controversial issues at the conference.

Gloria Steinem attended as a representative of the American Federation of Television and Radio Artists. Although Steinem intentionally played a very low-key role, Edith Van Horn, international representative for UAW, noted, "What [Steinem] shows [is that] we are feminists. Her being here is a great bridge to the 'outside' feminist movement... The media has kept us apart. It has put down the feminist movement so that many [union] women have been reluctant to identify with it." Van Horn added, "We are here because of the Gloria Steinems."[22] Likewise, Steinem described the conference with great enthusiasm: "Union women have a lot of organizational expertise that we don't have...so it works both ways. We can make more progress if we all work together."[23] The historical tone of working women's organizations—assuming conflicts between middle-class feminists and working women—was reversed. CLUW identified with the women's movement from the very beginning.

The conference also adopted a statement of purpose as well as structural and organizational guidelines for CLUW. The statement of purpose reads as follows:

> Of the 34 million women in the work force, little more than 4 million women are members of unions. It is imperative that within the framework of the union movement, we take aggressive steps to more effectively address ourselves to the critical needs of 30 million unorganized sisters and to make our unions more responsible to the needs of all women, especially the needs of minority women who have been traditionally singled out for particularly blatant oppression.

> Women unionists work in almost every industry, in almost every part of the country. Despite their geographical, industrial and occupational separations, union women share common concerns and goals.

> Full equality of opportunity and rights in the labor force require the full attention of the labor movement...and especially, the full attention of women who are part of the labor movement.

> The primary purpose of this new national coalition is to unify union women in a viable organization to determine, first—our common problems and concerns and second—to develop action programs within the framework of our unions to deal effectively with our objectives.

We recognize that our struggle goes beyond the borders of this nation and seek to link up with our working sisters and brothers throughout the world through concrete action of international workers' solidarity.

Through unity of purpose, the Coalition of Labor Union Women will seek to accomplish these goals.

ORGANIZING UNORGANIZED WOMEN

Since less than twelve percent of the women in today's labor force are enrolled in labor unions, it is obvious that most working women are suffering economically. Statistics clearly demonstrate that the union member enjoys higher wages, better fringe benefits and working conditions and greater job security than the unorganized workers.

The Coalition of Labor Union Women seeks to promote unionism and to encourage unions to be more aggressive in their efforts to bring unorganized women under collective bargaining agreements, particularly in those areas where there are large numbers of unorganized and/or minority women.

CLUW will seek to create a greater awareness of the benefits of union membership. Within our intra-, inter- and emerging union structure, we will work to encourage non-union women to join us in the trade union movement.

AFFIRMATIVE ACTION IN THE WORK PLACE

Employers continue to profit by dividing workers on sexual, racial and age lines. This encourages the segregation of job classifications and results in wage and benefit losses to women. The power of unions must increasingly be brought to bear, through the process of collective bargaining, to correct these inequities. The Coalition will seek to encourage women, through their unions, to recognize and take positive action against job discrimination in hiring, promotion, classification and other aspects of work.

Women must learn what their rights are under law. They must become more knowledgeable of the specifics of collective bargaining, and of the contract clauses and work place practices which discriminate against them. They must be informed about what is and what can be done within the labor movement to correct these situations.

POLITICAL ACTION AND LEGISLATION

It is imperative that union women, through action programs of the Coalition, become more active participants in the political and legislative processes of our unions. Movements for

full employment and job opportunities, child care legislation, a livable minimum wage, improved health and safety
coverage, expanded educational opportunities, mass action
for final ratification of the Equal Rights Amendment (ERA),
guaranteed collective bargaining rights for all workers, the
right to strike, and an extension of truly protective legislation
for all workers are only a few of the political action programs
in which CLUW must participate. CLUW should encourage
women trade unionists to run for office on all levels of
government.

PARTICIPATION OF WOMEN WITHIN THEIR UNIONS

The Coalition seeks to inspire and educate union women to
insure and strengthen their participation, through full and
complete democratic procedures, to encourage their leadership and their movement into policy-making roles within
their own unions and within the union movement in all areas.
The Coalition will encourage democratic procedures in all
unions.[24]

There are many significant aspects to the statement of purpose. The
first sentence is crucial in terms of stating the critical purpose and
strategy of CLUW: "It is imperative that within the framework of the
union movement, we take aggressive steps to more effectively address
ourselves to the critical needs of 30 million unorganized sisters and to
make our unions more responsible to the needs of all women, especially
the needs of minority women..."[25] The combination that CLUW leaders aimed for was to *work within the framework* of the union movement
and at the same time take *aggressive steps to meet the needs of women,
and in particular minority women and unorganized women workers.*
The statement highlighted both unorganized women and minority
women, acknowledging the importance of unity for all union women.
Its largest portion, however, directly pertained to women in their role as
workers. It is only in the section on political action and legislation that
gender issues outside the workplace—particularly the ERA—are mentioned. Other vital feminist issues, such as reproductive freedom, on
which CLUW later took a position, are not mentioned at all.

There were several areas of debate within the convention. One that
did not come to the floor was whether or not CLUW would be open to
non-union women. Many women from the left campaigned for "open"
membership, while the CLUW leadership advocated limiting membership to union members. Although from the start CLUW was an
organization for union women, the issue was not completely resolved
until the Detroit constitutional convention in 1975, when open membership was finally defeated.

At the founding conference there were two floor votes on controversial questions. The first concerned a proposed amendment to the "Statement of Purpose" which called upon CLUW to fight for democracy in all unions. Many women present, especially union officials and members of the International Ladies Garment Workers specifically, believed that this amendment was anti-union because it implied criticism of the established union structure. However, leftists and progressives believed that rank and file democracy was crucial. The underlying tension was related to the question of CLUW's relationship to the established labor movement. This tension centered around how the labor movement would have to change in order for women to assume an equal role. For left-wing feminists, feminism required democracy within the unions. For the CLUW leadership, an attack on the existing leadership was counter to women's broader interests. Despite the opposition of the CLUW leadership, the pro-democracy amendment passed, and in the last section of the statement of purpose, the following sentence was added: "Additionally, the Coalition will encourage democratic procedures in all unions."[26]

The second floor vote, which proved to be even more controversial, was over support for the UFW and its boycott. Section 14 of the statement of purpose stated that "National CLUW and area CLUW chapters shall not be involved in issues or activities which a union involved identifies as related to a jurisdictional dispute." This guideline was included because women from the Teamsters threatened to walk out if explicit support was given to the UFW. UFW supporters, however, accused the Teamsters of raiding and claiming jurisdiction in areas organized by the UFW. Throughout the convention, there was a tremendous amount of support for the Farm Workers. When the name of Dolores Huerta, UFW vice-president, was read from a list of women who had helped to build the conference, "hundreds of women spontaneously rose to their feet in a standing ovation."[27]

For the CLUW leadership, the issue of the UFW and the Teamsters was complicated. To support one union over another would jeopardize the potential unity among union women and CLUW's support within the union movement. However, not to support a union that had made a major contribution to organizing unorganized workers, many of whom were women and almost all of whom were third world, would make it difficult for CLUW to gain support and be effective in achieving its goals.

Supporters of the UFW and its boycott continually tried to strike Section 14 from the statement of purpose and were finally successful. They then sought to gain explicit support for the UFW boycott. Early Sunday morning, women from the Farm Workers and the Teamsters got together with one of the conference leaders in order to work through the issue, since they did not want to divide the convention. The next day, Josephine Glores, a UFW member, addressed the delegates. "You know, sisters, we have been struggling for a long time. . .not one day, not one year or ten years. Please, sisters, the Farm Workers put everything on your table." She added, "this is not a fight with the Teamster sisters. This is a fight with the growers." Clara Day, from the Teamsters, was standing next to her and "in the most touching display of trade union unity to be seen in many decades, the two women turned suddenly toward each other and embraced. The entire audience rose and cheered, some with tears streaming down their faces. And Edith Van Horn, UAW staff representative for many years, tried to carry on. 'This is what CLUW is all about,' she said, her voice choked with emotion. And then she added, 'In 54 years, I've never been prouder to be a woman.' "[28]

Delegates, still pushing for a formal resolution, jumped up chanting, "Huelga!" (Strike!) A delegate from the floor moved that CLUW go on record in support of the farm boycott. She was ruled out of order. Olga Madar then announced that an agreement had been reached by the Teamsters, the UFW women, and the conference organizers. Consideration of the resolution would be postponed and it would instead be referred to the newly chosen CLUW National Coordinating Committee, along with other unresolved questions such as criteria for CLUW membership and action proposals for the ERA. The last action of the conference was the election of union representatives, state conveners, and national officers. The national officers chosen were Olga Madar, UAW, president; Addie Wyatt, Amalgamated Meat Cutters and Butcher Workmen of North America, vice-president; Linda Tarr Whelan, AFSCME, corresponding secretary; Joyce Miller, Amalgamated Clothing Workers, East Coast vice-president; Clara Day, Teamsters, Midwest vice-president; Dana Durham, Communication Workers of America, southern vice-president; Elinor Glenn, Service Employees International Union (SEIU), West Coast vice-president; Gloria Johnson, International Union of Electrical Workers, treasurer.

At the conference, the UFW issue had been at least temporarily resolved and a degree of unity had been achieved. However, there was uneasiness over a number of issues, in particular CLUW's relationship to the union establishment. That tension was reflected in some of Addie Wyatt's last words at the convention, when she said: "Remember we are not each other's enemies... Our unions are not the enemies because we are the unions... We are telling our unions that we are ready, available, and capable to fight the fight."[29]

In a powerful conclusion, Wyatt said, "I still believe that the union is the most viable and available channel through which we can win our goals... I am still committed to work within the framework." And then, reciting the words of "Solidarity Forever," she said, "For the union makes us strong..." With that, the delegates rose, hands clasped and bodies swaying, and sang "Solidarity Forever." The founding convention of CLUW was over and union women were on the move.[30]

Conflict Between the Left and Female Trade Union Leaders

Almost from the beginning, CLUW was the subject of a deep ideological struggle between two different groups of women: the female trade union leaders who had founded the organization, and the sizable minority of leftists who quickly became involved. This struggle over the nature and direction of CLUW went on for several years, often becoming bitter and featuring harsh personal attacks. Underlying this battle were several important questions regarding the nature of the established trade union movement and the best strategies for advancing the cause of working women.

The central question was: Was trade unionism, as it presently existed, the friend or foe of women and workers?

The Views of the Left

Leftists constituted a significant minority of the women active in the formation of CLUW. They included groups and individuals who defined themselves as socialists, communists, various kinds of Marxists, and, in some cases, socialist-feminists. Many leftists, both independent and members of organized left-wing groups, were also active in local chapters, especially in larger cities; some were on CLUW's national coordinating committee; one held national office. They were a significant presence during the formative period of CLUW.

In the eyes of their "adversaries," the leftists sometimes appeared to be a monolithic group, but there were in fact many different opinions and organizations represented among them. Some leftists were critical of CLUW for being only a "reformist" organization. Others thought that winning reforms could be very useful and a few opposed reforms altogether because they believed that reforms held back revolutionary struggle. Although most leftists were highly sympathetic to the struggle for the ERA, they did not all agree on its importance. (The Communist Party, for example, had an anti-ERA position at that time.) The leftists also differed in the conflict between affirmative action and seniority.

There were also wide differences among the leftists around strategies for operating within CLUW. Some were quite critical of what they termed the "sectarianism" of other left groups and there was often fighting over who had the "correct line" and who represented the true leadership of the working class. The Spartacist League was often the most extreme caricature of left-wing patterns. For example, they claimed that the "Spartacist League emerged not only as the sole consistent and outspoken critic of the undemocratic procedures, but as the sole pole of outspoken militancy at the conference."[31] The Spartacist League was not alone, however, in putting itself forward as the true leadership of the working class. The October League and other sectarian groups often did the same.

A few independent leftists believed that the behavior of many leftists and the tensions between them contributed to their eventual defeat within CLUW. For example, Ann Withorn, an editor of *Radical America*, member of the Boston CLUW Chapter, and a delegate to CLUW's National Coordinating Committee, later wrote in an article, "The Death of CLUW,"

> The divisions in the left were critical to its defeat. The SWP and the CP were not noticeable in their lack of opposition to the leadership and its Redbaiting. While they made "moderate" comments during debates, they always voted with the leadership. Although the October League was often forceful and skillful at opposing the bureaucrats at the national level, locally they often forced CLUW into being an OL support group rather than an independent organization with other goals than to endorse OL activities. Granted it would have been difficult no matter what, but October League members were not always able to see that demonstrating, educationals and leafletting around tangential issues were not the most effective outreach activities.
>
> The Spartacists and other splinter left groups were also instrumental in the loss. Their highly vocal and antagonistic presence at public activities must have discredited other Leftists and alienated many members of the rank and file. International Socialists who behaved more responsibly were active in local chapters, but by the time of the convention (the Detroit convention), at least, had to become somewhat shrill and excessively sectarian particularly in regard to OL. Independent leftists were often passive critics, individually opposing both excessive bureaucracy and sectarian tactics, but seldom offering organized alternatives.[32]

Despite the division within the Left, the provocative behavior of some leftist groups, and sectarian tactics, the Left nevertheless shared some overall policies and themes. A major common theme was antagonism to the trade union leadership. (There were some notable exceptions, such as the Communist Party and the Democratic Socialist Organizing Committee.) A chief criticism made by leftists was that CLUW, like the trade union movement in general, lacked democracy and used parliamentary procedures to stifle real discussion. One example of this "lack of democracy" was that an attempt from the floor to add a clause to the statement of purpose concerning the right to sexual preference was ruled out of order on the basis that amendments were not allowed from the floor.[33]

Coupled with the leftists' criticism of undemocratic procedures was a belief that trade union leaders were "bureaucrats" rather than genuine leaders. In the *Workers' Vanguard,* the paper of the Spartacist League, the major article about CLUW's founding convention was titled "Women Bureaucrats Rig CLUW Conference" (March 15, 1974).

> The main concern of CLUW's organizers in planning the Chicago conference, as evidenced by the undemocratic regional conference procedures and totally pre-determined limits on "permissible" topics of discussion, has been to limit or prevent participation by socialist trade union militants, gag any opposition, prevent floor discussion of resolutions and railroad through a "Statement of Purpose" that will confine women workers' struggles to a few token reforms.[34]

An article in another left journal commented:

> By the use of heavy-handed parliamentary maneuvers, the conference was run from the top down. In particular, the proposed structure of CLUW as an ongoing organization was approved with little or no debate. Resolutions on specific issues never made it to the floor of the plenary sessions.
>
> Leftists, particularly members of some of the sectarian groups often ended up in shouting floor debates and parliamentary procedure in order to get their proposals and politics on the floor of the convention. In fact, at one point some leftists felt that the leadership actually used discussion of parliamentary procedure which groups like the October League fell for, in order to wear the leftists down.[35]

Concerning a later Detroit convention, the Socialist Workers' *Militant* noted:

The perfunctory discussion and quick vote on the agenda stood in contrast to the handling of an earlier discussion on convention rules. During that discussion, in the name of "democracy," CLUW officials not only allowed, but encouraged a long, dragged-out discussion. This was designed to try the patience of the delegates and convince them that any attempt to change Madar's proposals would result in tedious, useless quibbling.

In their strategy of wearing down the delegates, the convention organizers made use of a small number of women who tried to challenge the undemocratic procedures in a sectarian way. These delegates, supporters of the Maoist October League and the International Socialists, fell into Madar's trap. They spent all their time haggling over secondary rules and articles in the constitution rather than presenting a clear political program for building CLUW.[36]

Some leftists believed that the CLUW leaders only wanted more status.

In 1973 a few women in the top levels of the union bureaucracy began to see the usefulness of a trade-union based, NOW-type organization for helping them to gain more recognition, and therefore, more "power" within their unions. Led by Olga Madar of the UAW and Addie Wyatt of the Amalgamated Meat Cutters, these women did not have an alternative vision of trade unionism, nor even broad "feminist" goals for changing the status of all women workers within the trade unions. They simply wanted more status for themselves and for other potential women bureaucrats. They saw a strategy of linking themselves to the increasingly accepted "women's movement" as a means to this end. . . .

The bureaucrats tried to build an organization which would honor them, which would legitimate them as spokespeople for women trade unionists and which would increase their stature in the eyes of George Meany, Frank Fitzsimmons, etc.[37]

The Left saw CLUW's leaders as part of the established labor bureaucracy, and felt that under their leadership CLUW had become part of the "ladies' auxiliary" of the AFL-CIO.

A slightly different, although equally condemnatory, analysis was made by Ann Withorn, who combined a left-wing feminist analysis with a more general leftist analysis. According to Withorn, the male union leadership and trade unions perpetuated the exploitation of women workers almost equally with male capitalists.

There are innumerable incidents in history where working women fought for higher wages for men. Where are comparable actions of the male proletariat? On the contrary, men so often struck against equal wages and equal work for women that it is historically correct to define trade unions as defense organizations against the intrusion of women and other minorities as well as against capitalists. The most outrageous and divisive lie in labor history, that at the beginning of the industrial revolution women flooded the market with cheap labor and took the jobs away from men, has been transported into a theory ironically by those who call fervently for proletarian unity. They still believe in it, not asking what those women had done before: The fate of the English weavers still haunts us, that of the spinners remains unheard of. The subsequent militant, organized, and sometimes bloody drives of the male workers to get or keep women out of industries, trades and unions through the nineteenth and beginning of the twentieth century are at best forgotten, at worst subsumed under "heroic working class struggles." The call for "unity" by white, male-dominated trade unions has as much credibility as the call for "industrial peace" by capitalists and governments. It means "Bow down and we will forge unity (peace) on your backs." History is to learn from, not to "speak bitterness." We uncover the dirty side of the glorified labor history to find out what is expected from today's labor movement.[38]

The left-wing feminist analysis, which was expressed by others as well, concluded that for women, the enemy was both the labor movement and capitalists. Anne Marie Troger wrote that: "The women's movement has reached a new level in spite of itself. A new consciousness has reappeared in the labor movement—against the labor unions. The Coalition of Labor Union Women (CLUW) symbolized both these developments."[39] In Troger's eyes, CLUW was the sign of unrest among working-class women who needed a militant movement independent of, and often times opposed to the existing trade union leaders. In this context it is easier to understand the issues that came to the floor at CLUW's first conference. Support for the Farm Workers was a way of giving support to unorganized workers and of taking a stand against the union establishment; the Teamsters were certainly the symbol of male union power. The issue of internal union democracy also came out of the analysis of corrupt trade unionism.

Another issue that did not come to the floor but was important to many leftists was for open membership. They thought that if CLUW was to be a genuine working women's organization, it had to be open to *all* women, organized and unorganized. The leftists believed that if CLUW did not become a militant working-class women's organization led by the rank and file, it would become a dead-end organization led by "trade union bureaucrats."

View of Trade Union Leaders

The CLUW leadership saw the leftists as a threat and a disruptive presence. Connie Kopelov, a former staffperson for the Amalgamated Clothing Workers of America, co-chairwoman of the first New York Trade Union Women's Conference, and active in the New York CLUW chapter since its inception, wrote her master's thesis on the beginning years of CLUW. She argued that the conference planners were deeply concerned about the issue of democracy and that the sectarian leftists were the biggest threat to democratic procedures since they were more interested in their own control than in CLUW.

> The major challenge in designing the conference format was to encourage participation but avoid chaos, to provide for democratic procedures but ensure the establishment of CLUW. Many committee discussions centered, in one way or another, on these dilemmas. For example, the registration fee had to be low enough to enable women paying their own way, especially rank and filers, to take part. It had to be high enough, however, to cover the costs of the conference which had to be self-supporting.
> Many committee members emphasized the importance of participation. Others stressed an expectation of disruptive tactics from women whose basic allegiance was not the formation of CLUW but to one form or another of Marxism. Experiences of CLUW organizing meetings as well as attacks on conference organizers in left-wing newspapers underscored this problem.
> In general, the desire for democratic procedures was stronger than the fear of disorder... The potential conflict between democracy and order was handled by designing the workshops to be open to ideas and debate but limiting argument in general sessions.[40]

In Kopelov's eyes, it was the radicals who had stopped substantive discussion from taking place.

Some radicals wanted to make changes in structure apparently in the hope that these would produce greater opportunity for them to control local CLUW groups. Others appeared intent upon destroying CLUW. All took part in blowing the Farm Workers issue out of proportion. As a result of parliamentary maneuvering and debate over fine points, only a few substantive issues were discussed. Whatever good might have been achieved by those workshops which had successful discussion was sharply diminished by the inability to get proposals to the floor for debate and vote. Haggling over the statement of purpose was so time-consuming that in the end the more important issue of structure was resolved with little debate. Weary delegates voted to suspend rules and adopt the proposed structure nearly intact. Radicals then charged that decisions had been rammed through. . . .[41]

A number of radicals made blatant attacks on women staff as "bureaucrats." The national staff women remarked, "It's startling to find out at this stage of your life that you're a bureaucrat."[42]

In *Labor Today*, Florence Criley, staff from United Electrical Workers, rebutted attacks made on CLUW leaders:

I feel compelled to write regarding your article on the first National Conference of Labor Union Women (April, 1974). It not only did not go into the CLUW program in depth, but this article could do much harm in picturing CLUW as an organization led by "staffers" and "bureaucrats" who give their allegiance to Meany, Fitzsimmons and Woodcock.

This is not only extremely unfair but also simply not true. I was a member of the National Planning Committee (NPC) and had an opportunity to meet and work with the women who were its members. It is true, many have full-time jobs with their international unions, some were elected officers.

This conference could not have gotten off the ground without their hard work, zeal and complete devotion to the cause of women's equality. The rank and file didn't have the money or time to go to many exhausting meetings held in Detroit and Chicago—much less the equipment, money and facilities needed to get out the volume of work necessary.

There were absolutely no "offensive bureaucratic maneuvers," and the meeting was conducted in a most democratic manner.

In stark contrast was the behavior of some of the delegates at the microphones; pushing and shoving to scream into the mikes, calling for endless questions, points of order, points of personal privilege, etc. as stalling tactics, well into the late hours of the evening.[43]

In plain contrast to the Left, the CLUW leaders were totally loyal to the trade union tradition and clear from the very beginning that CLUW was for union women only. Joyce Miller, one of CLUW's founders and current president, expressed the general sentiment: "We are trade unionists first. We are loyal to our unions. Within that framework, we want to advance the role of women."[44] These leaders saw organizing women workers into unions as a way of strengthening the entire trade union movement.

In the very beginning, CLUW's leaders expressed concern that there would be those in labor who would see CLUW as a threat. There were, in fact, conservative forces who believed that the separate organizing of black and female trade unionists might be divisive; the AFL-CIO held back any early support or recognition for CLUW. As a result, the CLUW leadership put even greater emphasis on union loyalty and on winning credibility within the labor movement. Connie Kopelov observed that the founding leaders "constantly stressed their intention to work within the trade union structure to improve the lives of working women. Loyalty to their unions and to unionism is strong. They demand redress of women's grievances but want to achieve this as a group within the labor movement. They don't want to attack their unions, they want to improve them."[45]

And Judy Berek of the New York Trade Union Conference asserted: "We are doing this from the inside. No male trade unionist should think this meeting or the ongoing organization that will come out of it is directed at him... All of us here are committed to the labor movement."[46]

According to Connie Kopelov, one of the pressing concerns in drafting the statement of purpose was to determine whether "a certain phrase would alienate the male union leadership. Was an alternative proposal weak and gutless? Was it clear we were not attacking our unions?"[47]

These women clearly had no intention of being either anti-male or anti-union. At the founding conference, Addie Wyatt, one of the chief articulators of a pro-union position, stated, "this is not a divisive event. This is a move to unify what has been in too many instances already divided." And as she said at the end, especially in relationship to the Farm Workers' struggle, "I say, the unions are not our enemies... "[48] As chair of the conference it was her responsibility more than anyone else's, to find a way to maintain unity and "handle" the Left. She urged over and over again that participants not squabble. "We are not here to have a rhetoric festival. Speak only when it is germane. We are not going to let anyone destroy the intent of this conference."[49]

Despite their support for the union establishment, CLUW leaders were aware of the sexism in the labor movement. To fight for women's rights in the work force and within unions was the reason for CLUW's existence. As Addie Wyatt said at the earlier New York conference:

> We women have special concerns. We need maternity benefits and child care. We need an upgrading of jobs. We need equal pay for equal work. We need to organize the unorganized among women workers. After all most women work for the same reasons men do: we need the same protections men have. But women in the labor movement know very well we have not achieved our goals. We have not had equal opportunities for jobs and leadership.[50]

CLUW leaders were keenly aware of male domination in unions. For example, at the Detroit convention, Madar spoke against what she termed the "chumism" among men in union leadership. "Until we have a participatory democracy in our unions' leadership, we won't be able to do anything about affirmative action."[51] Within the general framework of being pro-union and pro-women's rights, the female trade unionists nevertheless represented a spectrum of attitudes.

Some leaders—Marge Albert, Connie Kopelov, and others— saw themselves as "progressive" feminists committed to working within the union movement but were also much concerned with women's independence and feminism. Marge Albert stated:

> How independent should CLUW be from our unions? For progressive feminist CLUW members, the answer is not so simple. We don't agree with those who say CLUW should open its doors to *all* women, thus weakening its specific union orientation. Nor are we anxious to carry on struggles with our male union leaders in public thus giving ammunition to anti-union forces among employers and the press. On the other hand, we are certainly not content to simply be female voices mouthing what our male union leaders tell us we can say and do. Finding the path between those alternatives is not easy.[52]

Connie Kopelov was one of the few original leaders who explicitly stated that there could be some conflict between women workers and union officials as women fight for their rights.

> The danger posed in striving so hard for acceptance is that CLUW could lose sight of its raison d'etre. While it is

crucial that CLUW not be discredited in the eyes of the labor movement, it is equally important that this compromise be limited to those of tactics, not principles. CLUW must remember it exists because women suffer discrimination on the job, in their unions and elsewhere. CLUW women have to push their unions to fight against all forms of inequality. Some degree of conflict is inevitable between women seeking their rights and male union leadership, if it fails to respond adequately to those needs. Women in CLUW leadership should not do the bidding of male union leaders or male revolutionary leaders.[53]

At the other end of the spectrum were women whose union loyalty came first and foremost. They favored toning down anything that sounded like militancy related to women's issues. Clara Day of the Teamsters, who was a national leader of CLUW during its earliest period, represented this end of the spectrum. She said:

We have found that we have been really supported by our unions and that unions are not fearful of us because we are not an organization that is organizing within a union to be another union itself. We use the tools from which we already have [sic]. We [CLUW] have no by-laws, no constitution that is contrary to our unions. We will not be a part of an organization that goes against our union. We are Teamsters first, and then we will be CLUW members next.[54]

CLUW's leaders often found themselves doing a balancing act. They wanted to develop a working women's agenda without attacking the male labor establishment; they wanted to win support from and gain credibility within the official labor leadership. The early struggle over the Farm Workers was an important case in point. The majority of rank and file participants, officers, and staff at the CLUW conference supported the Farm Workers. However, to publicly condemn the actions of the Teamsters would automatically antagonize one of the most powerful unions in the U.S. They did find a solution—expressing support for the Farm Workers without a formal resolution. This allowed CLUW chapters to support the Farm Workers' boycott and strikes on their own.

After the 1974 convention, the national coordinating committee did, in fact, pass a resolution in support of the UFW (as part of a resolution on organizing the unorganized):

Whereas, the organization of millions of unorganized women is vital to the labor movement if it is to unite all working people and advance the cause of human dignity, economic security, equality and social progress.

Whereas, we desire unity with our union sisters.

Whereas, our fight is not with the Teamsters but with the growers who are trying to pit one union against another, we denounce the action of the growers and reach out to our sisters in the Teamsters Union and the United Farm Workers. We welcome the opportunity to work with them on issues of mutual concern... Further that CLUW go on record in support of the UFW strikes and support the boycott of grapes, head lettuce and Gallo wine.[55]

While CLUW endorsed the United Farm Workers, they made it clear that it was the bosses, not the Teamsters, who were the cause of the problem. By uniting with the Teamster women and not condemning the actions of the Teamsters, vis-a-vis the UFW, they avoided any open conflict. How satisfactory this compromise approach would be for other such issues was yet to be seen.

CLUW's First Year: Dealing with Several Conflicts

As CLUW got off the ground during its first year and chapters grew, the struggle that had started earlier also continued to grow.

Conflict Within the Chapters

The leadership claimed a large growth in membership during the first year. By the end of 1974, Olga Madar reported that there were 2,500 dues paying members and twenty-four local chapters.[56] However, given the large and enthusiastic founding convention, many observers and participants were disappointed, having expected much greater growth. Observers attributed the slower than anticipated growth to two factors: first, the effects of the deepening recession, which was particularly hard on women and minorities; and second, the constant fighting between the Left and the leadership, which tended to drive away many rank and file union women.

The view of the CLUW union leaders is typified by Connie Kopelov:

Each [left sectarian] group regards itself as the vanguard of social change. They don't view feminism or women's rights, per se, as being revolutionary, but a large group of organized women, especially working-class women, is regarded as potential political material.[57]

Many local CLUW groups have been bogged down in conflict with radicals over the local structure of CLUW chapters. Nothing can be more effective in driving the average, hard-working women unionists away than endless squabbling about by-laws and election procedures—unless it is endless squabbling over points of order, as seemed to be the case so often at the Chicago conference.[58]

Leftists had the reverse perceptions. For example, Ann Withorn in "The Death of CLUW" published in *Radical America*, March-April, 1976, gives an independent left perspective, accusing the leadership of suppressing the opposition, employing overtly bureaucratic techniques, and showing lack of real leadership for working women.

Many people came away from the convention with an understanding that although the Left and the bureaucrats would clearly remain in conflict, the organization was useful enough to both so that neither would precipitate suicidal struggle.

It was not to be so. Despite the logic supporting coexistence, lines quickly hardened. The leadership sluggishly initiated complicated certification procedures which forced new chapters into performing time-consuming non-outreach duties in order to obtain charters. Chapters received little communication or support from the national office except when they did not play by the rules—when they raised questions of membership requirements, when they criticized local unions, when they tried to address "loaded" issues like seniority or deportations. Then the reaction was harsh and dictatorial. Charters were denied; condemning letters were mailed to all members; overt and bitter red-baiting took place. Olga Madar, the President, was particularly vocal. She even went to Atlanta and vowed to start her own chapter because the local one was strongly influenced by the October League.

The Left and the rank and file were unprepared for such an offensive. At the local level complicated bureaucratic procedures frustrated them and led to splits among leftists over the proper way to fight. They argued over whether it was best to comply reluctantly and fight nationally or to stand on principle. In many chapters, such as Washington, D.C. or Detroit, the anti-Communist paranoia of the bureaucrats, and their efforts to pack committees, led many moderates to move further left. "I never thought I was a radical, but if they keep treating me like one I might as well be one," one woman said.

The more common response among the moderate rank and file, both in local chapters and in the NCC [National

Coordinating Committee], was to drop away from the increasingly bitter and intense fighting. Despite massive efforts by the bureaucrats, including Shanker's paying of his AFT members' dues, the membership did not grow rapidly. Local chapters remained small and NCC attendance dwindled. The October League, although most severely harassed by Madar, would not work with the International Socialists or with other Marxist-Leninist groups. The Socialist Workers Party and the Communist Party supported the leadership and did not condemn the red-baiting. Independents were unable to unite among themselves to influence other members to be less sectarian.

By the fall of 1975, CLUW was in tatters. Chapter membership was down. NCC meetings could no longer expect quorums. Nearly every chapter experienced difficulty with NCC rules and restrictions. Many independent Leftists and progressive rank and file members had pulled out. While the officers spent time meeting with the Presidents of the AFL-CIO, the Teamsters, and other major unions, those active members who remained pressed for a last-ditch campaign around a more meaningful constitutional convention and a constitution which would provide a less bureaucratic, more open structure.[59]

While each side blamed the other for chapter difficulties, the form that the conflict took varied from chapter to chapter. In the Boston chapter, for example, approximately 200 women attended the opening meetings, and eventually forty women remained in the core group. There were tensions between members of sectarian groups, independent leftists, and women who were part of, or sympathetic to, the established trade union leadership. One grouping within the Left tried to get the chapter involved in community anti-racist struggles. Others wanted the chapter to support some women who were fighting their local union over discriminatory layoffs.[60] A major struggle took place around the issue of open membership. Boston was one of the chapters that had decided to include women who were not yet union members but involved in organizing drives. The National CLUW responded by refusing to grant them a charter until it admitted only union members. The Boston chapter decided to go along with the NCC's decision in order to get its charter, and brought its fight for an open membership to the Detroit convention. The national leadership also opposed the Boston chapter's decision to fight the deportation of undocumented foreign workers.[61]

Conflict Over Affirmative Action and Seniority

In other chapters, such as Chicago, Houston, and Atlanta, there were conflicts between the national leadership and those who had taken "unacceptable" stands on the issue of affirmative action versus seniority. In CLUW's statement of purpose, affirmative action was one of four areas of concentration.

Employers continue to profit by dividing workers on sexual, racial and age lines. This encourages the segregation of job classifications and results in wages and benefit losses to women. The power of unions must increasingly be brought to bear, through the process of collective bargaining, to correct these inequities. The Coalition will seek to encourage women, through these unions, to recognize and take positive action against job discrimination in hiring, promotion, classification and other aspects of work. Women must learn what their rights are under the law. We must become more knowledgeable of the specifics of collective bargaining, and of the contract clauses and workplace practices which discriminate against us. We must be informed about what is and can be done within the labor movement to correct these situations. We seek to educate and inspire our union brothers to help achieve affirmative action in the work place.[62]

While CLUW consistently backed affirmative action hiring, the question of affirmative action in firing was more controversial. This tension was exacerbated because of the recession and the increasing number of layoffs. In his discussion of CLUW and affirmative action, Philip Foner quotes the U.S. Commission on Civil Rights in its booklet *Last Hired, First Fired: Layoffs and Civil Rights.*

The recent recession has had a critical impact on minorities and women. Many had only recently obtained their first promising jobs. Increasing numbers had begun to penetrate employment areas of great importance in our society, such as state and local government. Because they have not had time to acquire adequate seniority, however, minorities and women have been affected disproportionately by the personnel cutbacks occasioned by this recession and much of their limited progress has thereby been obliterated.[63]

While the trade union movement had fought hard to establish the right of seniority against arbitrary firing, women and blacks had fought hard for affirmative action. The question now was whether using seniority during times of massive layoffs was just another way of discriminating. Many feminist and black groups answered yes, while many trade unionists said no. The AFL-CIO supported seniority unequivocally. Many people, however, including some trade unionists, disagreed with the dominant union sentiment and believed that white, male, and skilled workers profited from seniority while women, blacks, and unskilled workers suffered.

During the 1970s, many suits were filed, supported by NOW and other civil rights organizations, challenging seniority on the grounds that it jeopardized the newly won jobs of women and blacks. For example, a CLUW chapter in California supported a group of women suing both a GM plant in Fremont and the UAW over "discriminatory" layoffs.[64] The plaintiffs recognized that seniority was a crucial gain for working people and it was not their intention that the men be fired. Instead they proposed a shared work plan. The AFL-CIO, however, opposed their plan.[65]

As the controversy over affirmative action versus seniority spread throughout CLUW, the Left was divided. The majority left sentiment was in favor of affirmative action even if it meant modifying the seniority principle, while a minority of leftists believed that using affirmative action in this way was divisive. The issue was discussed in local chapters and for many leftists their stand on affirmative action became part of their anti-trade union leadership program. In contrast, the CLUW leadership unanimously defended seniority rights when they conflicted with affirmative action. (This was the only major example of disagreement between CLUW and NOW and was somewhat reminiscent of the struggle between protective legislation and the ERA.)

At an NCC meeting held on May 31, 1975, a position on affirmative action and seniority was adopted. The NCC tried to work out a compromise similar to the UFW resolution by taking a position *in favor* of women, blacks, and unorganized workers *without* coming out against the unions.

AFFIRMATIVE ACTION AND SENIORITY

The Coalition of Labor Union Women, in its statement of purpose, adopted at its founding, agreed upon the following basic beliefs about affirmative action:

*Employers continue to profit by dividing workers on sexual, racial and age lines. This encourages the segregation of job classifications and results in wage and benefit losses to women.

*The power of unions must increasingly be brought to bear through collective bargaining to correct these inequities. The coalition will seek to encourage women, through their unions, to recognize and take positive action against job discrimination in hiring, promotion, classification and other aspects of work.

*We must become more knowledgeable about the specifics of collective bargaining and of contract clauses and workplace practices that discriminate against us. We must be more informed about what is and can be done within the labor movement to correct these situations.

In the 15 months since these principles were enunciated, the national economy has deteriorated, and women, particularly non-unionized women, have been pushed back many of the steps they won toward equality in the workplace. Accordingly, the Coalition of Labor Union Women adopts the following resolution in three parts:

1. In regard to employers, RESOLVED

That CLUW pledges itself to renewed efforts to organize unorganized women, noting that unionized women suffer proportionately less in layoffs and noting that a union contract provides almost the only safeguard against capricious or selective layoffs, which most harm women and minority group members;

That CLUW pledges itself to renewed efforts to inform women workers about their job rights under Title VII equal opportunity guidelines, the Equal Pay Act and pertinent executive orders;

That CLUW will support efforts to see that employers provide training and retraining programs to allow women to move into non-traditional jobs and to promote job posting and job bidding in ways that open new fields to women and minority members;

That CLUW will continue its exploration of ways to promote full employment and to place the cost of discrimination upon the employer rather than the worker, and will press for legislative action where appropriate, to bring governmental or tax support into areas under the threat of layoffs or closures.

2. In regard to our unions, RESOLVED

That CLUW and its members will take vigilant action in their unions to see that seniority for all purposes is measured on the widest possible base in any workplace, thereby safeguarding workers against layoffs that run counter to seniority;

That CLUW members will seek to improve the seniority system in their unions and eliminate those aspects that have not served women and minority workers fairly;

That CLUW members will monitor recall and rehiring actions in their unions closely to see that contract clauses are carried out;

That where unions have hiring halls or apprentice programs, CLUW members will insist that their union's control over hiring does not work to the detriment of those suffering the effects of long discrimination;

That CLUW and all its members will press our unions to put their own houses in order with regard to discrimination against women and minorities wherever it exists and will urge that the unions themselves:

a. Evaluate all contracts and eliminate provisions and practices that permit discrimination;

b. Bargain for affirmative action programs and then monitor the results;

c. Establish procedures under the union constitutions for redress of sex-discrimination problems within the rank and file or the union structures, and

d. Undertake affirmative action hiring and training in the union headquarters.

3. With regard to all women unionists, RESOLVED

That CLUW will assist women trade unionists to pursue through local union procedures any charges of discrimination, and if no satisfactory response is offered by the local union, it will assist such women to pursue methods outlined in the union's constitution for redress. To secure information about such procedures, the CLUW chapter will review the union's constitution and turn to the N.C.C. representative from the union concerned.[66]

As can be seen from this document, CLUW's leadership attempted to reconcile the conflict between affirmative action and seniority by supporting both, claiming that there does not have to be a conflict between the two since seniority applied fairly is in the interests of women. In several articles, Olga Madar explained CLUW's position. She argued that union women are better off than unorganized women, and that seniority protects women from indiscriminate firings rather than perpetuating discriminatory firing practices. The proof, she said, is that more women are losing jobs in unorganized workplaces than in unionized workplaces. Most important, neither unions, workers, nor seniority are the cause of discrimination; employers who intentionally divide workers are the cause, and should bear full responsibility for discrimination. The solution to employer discrimination is affirmative action in hiring, full employment, and monitoring seniority so that it meets the needs of all workers.

In the CLUW newsletter which printed the NCC decision, Olga Madar wrote,

> Women can retain the marginal gains they have made at the workplace and make greater progress in the future if they deal practically with the reality of their situation. Despite commonly-held assumptions and statements to the contrary, the last hired are not routinely the first fired. The victims are more apt to be older workers, particularly women, some with years of seniority.
>
> More women, young and old, are released from their jobs out of line with seniority than are laid off in line with seniority. In periods of economic stress, employers in both the private and the public sectors disregard seniority and lay off women first for the very reasons that they hired them last.[67]

In another article CLUW explicitly criticized the position taken by NOW.

> Madar said NOW promotes "a myth that makes women victims of short-sighted feminists" when NOW infers that seniority rights are responsible for layoffs of women.
>
> In companies without union contracts and no seniority system, Madar said, older women are "dumped in favor of younger personnel." Madar said that attacking the seniority system is "supportive of management's long opposition to seniority systems and a return to the law of the jungle at the work place."
>
> "May I humbly suggest," Madar wrote to the NOW president, "that you monitor those unorganized places and insist that they lay off in line with company-wide seniority. I promise that you will help save more women's jobs than by attacking the seniority system."[68]

Although CLUW supported the concept of seniority over affirmative action with regard to layoffs, in the case of *hiring* they came out strongly in favor of affirmative action. For example, in later years, in the famous Bakke and Weber cases, CLUW supported affirmative action. However, when there was any conflict between affirmative action and seniority they sided with the official labor movement in support of seniority. This issue was one of the sharpest conflicts between unions, women, and black groups.

Does seniority hurt or help the most oppressed workers? The

answer, it would seem, is that it can do both. Both sides were trying to say something important. The strength of Madar's argument was to put the ultimate responsibility with the employer; the weakness of her position was that she did not acknowledge that seniority has sometimes been used to protect white, male, skilled workers at the expense of women, minorities, and unorganized workers. While it is true that seniority is important to union women and long-term workers, the majority of women workers are unorganized. A long-term, non-divisive solution would be a program that supports both full employment and affirmative action.

Other Early Activities

Not all of CLUW's early programs and activities were controversial. Chapters sponsored training programs in organizing, leadership, the history of the labor movement, and union procedures, as well as the campaigns in support of organizing drives. Although a CLUW chapter could not organize (CLUW was not a union and did not want to be accused of dual unionism), it could actively support and participate in organizing campaigns. The New York chapter supported organizing campaigns at two publishing companies. Seattle CLUW had a rally in support of unorganized office workers. In Texas, there was support for hospital organizing and in New Jersey, there was support for a strike against a hotel and restaurant. Many chapters involved themselves in the UFW boycott and the J.P. Stevens strike.[69]

On a national level, the National Coordinating Committee took major steps in program development. At the January 1975 NCC meeting, held in St. Louis, the following program was passed.

DEPRESSION AND UNEMPLOYMENT

The deepening depression and continued rates of unemployment and inflation are the most pressing areas for trade union women. In order to show the plight of all workers—minority men and women, youth, the older worker and all women who fall into the category of "secondary workers," CLUW should develop a national program which will include the participation of CLUW chapters. A program is proposed against the depression, unemployment, and layoffs.

1. The National Coordinating Committee of CLUW calls for action on March 8, International Women's Day, to kick off a campaign against the depression, unemployment, and layoffs. We encourage all local chapters to hold activities on that day.

2. CLUW members should immediately seek union endorsement of our activity, March 8, as a part of a continuing

campaign against depression, unemployment, and layoffs.

3. Public forums will be sponsored by CLUW. These forums could be in the form of hearings or other appropriate action which could focus on the plight of women as it relates to the labor force. Legislators, women's groups, media, and unions will be asked to participate. Local chapters will interview women on the shop floor, in offices, and other work places to develop information on what is happening to the union women we wish to have as CLUW members. The proposed date for these forums will be the week of April 28-May 3, 1975. Target cities with high unemployment rates will be Detroit, Los Angeles, New York, Chicago, Seattle, Washington, D.C., Atlanta, and Cleveland. All other chapters will be encouraged to hold similar activities.

4. CLUW encourages local chapters to engage in mass lobbying and other demonstrative actions along with trade unions and other concerned organizations to government agencies, legislatures and private corporations who are responsible for maintaining full employment. In no case will any CLUW chapter engage in action against the employer without the consent and agreement of the union involved. CLUW will only work with organizations whose stated purposes and goals are not in opposition to the statement of purpose of CLUW adopted at the founding conference. All decisions are to be made by a democratic vote.

5. The National Coordinating Committee charges the Steering Committee and Officers to plan in consultation with national unions for mass lobbying on the economic crisis in Washington toward the Congress and administrative agencies by mid-June.

6. CLUW endorses the UAW demonstration in Washington on February 5, 1975.

7. CLUW endorses the proposals advanced by the Full Employment Action Council (FEAC) headed by Coretta King and Murray Finley, President of the ACWA. FEAC, which includes CLUW President Olga Madar on its Board of Directors, has called for: creating 1,000,000 new public service jobs for 1975; extending unemployment insurance to 52 weeks and substantial federal tax reduction for low and middle income earners and for permanent tax reforms emphasizing the closing of loopholes. CLUW endorses the proposals and actions by the National Coalition to Fight Inflation and Unemployment (NCFIY) headed by Sidney Von Luther, former N.Y.

Senator. NCFIU recently held public demonstrations in 35 cities, endorsed by 600 prominent people, including 100 local union presidents. These demonstrations called for jobs and comprehensive unemployment insurance and a roll-back in prices. Another action is called for in April, a nation-wide march on D. C.

8. The demands of the CLUW campaign will be:
   *shorter workweek at no loss of pay
   *no overtime as long as anyone is laid off
   *no wage controls
   *cost of living clause in all contracts
   *no speed-up or other form of job harassment
   *full SUB [Supplemental Unemployment Benefits] pay backed by the employer's assets for the duration of layoff for all workers
   *unemployment insurance raised to two thirds of gross pay, top limit removed, with no one to receive less than the minimum wage for the duration of unemployment for all categories of workers, including first time workers
   *more jobs at union wages and working conditions including public works jobs, support the Hawkins Bill for enforcement of the Full Employment Act of 1946, and other measures to create full employment
   *unions to place the burden of past discrimination of minorities and women on employers rather than workers
   *no runaway shops
   *legislation to roll back prices starting with the necessities—food, rent and utilities
   *oppose budget cuts in programs for people and recommend a cut in U.S. military spending to pay for these programs[70]

CLUW held "Jobs for All" demonstrations on International Women's Day 1975 throughout the country. It also participated in a trade union demonstration for jobs in Washington, D.C. on April 26, 1975. The NCC passed proposals in favor of the Kennedy-Corman National Health Bill, comprehensive childcare legislation, and against involuntary sterilization. A significant resolution was passed on Chile: "that the Coalition of Labor Union Women condemns the military take-over of the democratically elected Chilean government and the repression of trade union rights, and calls for the restoration of basic human rights."[71]

Conflict at the Constitutional Convention

CLUW held its constitutional convention on December 6-7, 1975 in Detroit, Michigan. The atmosphere was quite different from that of the founding conference. A thousand people attended, in contrast to the 3,200 who attended the founding conference, and the majority of those who came to Detroit were appointed or elected staff when more than 50 percent of the founding conference participants had been rank and file union members. According to Margie Albert's description of the Detroit convention:

> One could sense an air of apprehension as 1,000 women unionists arrived in Detroit for the Coalition of Labor Union Women (CLUW) convention December 5th. This rather gloomy uncertainty contrasted with the air of anticipation, even exhilaration, that characterized CLUW's founding convention almost two years ago. As CLUW began, the 3,500 women who argued, laughed and cried through its birth pains felt almost euphoric. We had put together the first national women's organization made up of "average working women" (both white- and blue-collar), a genuinely multi-racial, multi-ethnic group and one that saw women of all ages actively participating. We believed in ourselves as a force that would really shake things up: strengthening women's participation in our unions, organizing unorganized women, promoting affirmative action and engaging in political and legislative action to meet our needs. We left the first convention with high hopes.
>
> Now, in Detroit to adopt a Constitution, we admitted that our hopes had not yet been fulfilled. CLUW membership has climbed to just about 5,000, respectable enough as women's organizations go but far short of what we could achieve. We felt apprehensive because we knew that the same differences that had plagued us from the beginning and kept down our growth might erupt and even tear apart this convention.[72]

From the beginning of the conference, the union leadership was in control. Prior to the convention, Olga Madar had sent a letter out to all CLUW members with the proposed constitution agenda, proposed rules, and a warning against "the small minority of our members who have attempted to divert us from our goals" (amendment proposals were sent out separately by the opposition). "The invocation speech, in the form of a prayer, asked 'the Lord' to protect Olga Madar and the 'majority constitution' and save the convention from 'disrupters'."[73]

In her opening talks, Olga Madar stressed that the goal of CLUW was to work within the labor movement for equal partnership. The sole agenda items other than speeches were passage of the constitution and election of officers. The fight between the Left and the trade union leadership ended at this conference.

At the convention there were two major opposition groupings. One, the Houston Caucus, in which the Socialist Workers' Party was very active, had as its top priority affirmative action, followed by action proposals around the ERA and a "jobs for all" campaign. The other major opposition group, composed of various leftists, considered open membership their priority.

In her president's report, Olga Madar stated that the issue of affirmative action had been settled by the NCC. After Madar's agenda was proposed, a supporter of the Houston Caucus asked that three evening hours be set aside to discuss affirmative action, the ERA, and "jobs for all." This proposal lost, with only 30 percent voting for it. The Houston Caucus did, however, win an amendment calling for action on the ERA. Although the CLUW leaders felt that they had already expressed a strong commitment to the ERA, the Houston Caucus felt that not enough action had been taken, and that this amendment would move CLUW forward.[74]

The second opposition group proposed an alternative constitution which would give the local chapters a great deal of autonomy and national leaders very little power. It was rejected. Another proposal, to admit non-union women to membership in CLUW, was defeated, with only 25 percent in support of it. Even a compromise motion, allowing women to join who had signed union cards during organizing drives, was defeated, though very narrowly. The only issue that the Madar leadership lost was over chapter representation. Her proposal was that only CLUW chapters with 100 or more members could elect representatives to the national executive board (which at that time would have applied to very few chapters). An opposition proposal won which gave representation to chapters having fifty or more members.

In the election of officers the leftist opposition lost, four to one. The Madar slate, with Olga Madar, president, Addie Wyatt, vice-president, Gloria Johnson, treasurer, Joyce Miller, corresponding secretary, and Patsy Fryman, recording secretary, was victorious. The major left-wing candidate for president, Dana Duke, received only 168 votes against Madar's 538. Madar claimed that her slate's victory meant that CLUW had solidified its goals. According to the *New York Times*, "Miss Madar expressed the hope that the leftist women might leave the coalition and turn their attention to organizations in which they might have more influence."[75]

Sunday morning, at an "Honor Our Unions" breakfast, Representative Bella Abzug, surrounded by male leaders, declared "CLUW to be
the biggest shot in the arm" the women's movement has experienced.[76]
She challenged CLUW to be "the cutting edge not only of the women's
movement, but of the people's movement for full employment, for new
priorities, for democracy."[77] There was great applause when she said, "I
hope next year we'll be able to introduce a sister from the executive board
of the AFL-CIO."[78]

Since CLUW's inception, it has had a cooperative relationship with
the AFL-CIO. While CLUW was critical of the AFL-CIO's sexism, and
at least some sectors of the AFL-CIO were equally skeptical about
CLUW, that cooperation was growing. At the AFL-CIO conference in
October 1975, the delegates had voted down formal endorsement of
CLUW on the grounds that CLUW had members outside the AFL-
CIO.[79] However, an intention of cooperation was also expressed. While
AFL-CIO president George Meany did not send a message to CLUW's
founding conference, he sent a message to the Detroit convention one
year later which noted CLUW's "consistent progress" and stated that "as
the AFL-CIO made clear, we are ready to cooperate with CLUW on
programs of common interest, particularly passage of the Equal Rights
Amendment—a priority matter to the entire trade union movement."
Throughout the Detroit convention, CLUW's leaders expressed delight
at the AFL-CIO's endorsement of the ERA.

As a result of the overwhelming vote in support of the Madar slate,
CLUW's leadership and the majority who attended the convention felt
that the problem of "disruption" by "fringe groups" had now been
solved. Although they had been a sizable minority at CLUW's founding
conference, the leftists were defeated and departed from CLUW as an
organized presence after the Detroit convention.

The victory of the Madar slate, and the growing ties between CLUW
and the AFL-CIO, convinced the Left that CLUW was a bankrupt
organization. Following the Detroit convention, the *Guardian* wrote
that the "Coalition of Labor Union Women has moved closer to becoming the women's auxiliary of the labor bureaucracy."[80] In *Radical America*, Ann Withorn wrote that the

> first Constitutional Convention of CLUW (held in Detroit in
> December) has, for all practical purposes, ended the struggle.
> The bureaucrats have gained solid control over the organiza-
> tion, although in order to gain their victory, they were forced
> to destroy CLUW as a widely based mass organization within
> trade unions.
>
> They have won, but everyone—especially the male trade
> union bureaucracy they so hope to impress—knows that

CLUW is not just a paper organization dominated by union bureaucrats who cannot mobilize large numbers of trade union women for even the most narrow goals.[81]

Despite this prediction, CLUW did not die. It continued under the leadership of trade union women, as it sought to change and strengthen the union movement, organize women workers, and make a contribution to women's liberation.

Cooperation with the AFL-CIO and Increased Commitment to Feminism _____

After the Detroit convention, with the Left clearly out of the way, CLUW tackled issues that were both gender- and work-related. In March 1976, CLUW's national executive board held its first meeting and "began implementing the constitutional mandate that ratification of the Equal Rights Amendment is the top priority goal for CLUW."[82] It set up a force to mobilize support for the ERA among union women, and five other task forces were also formed, for the purpose of:

* Supporting health security legislation encompassed by the Kennedy-Corman bill;

* Achieving full employment through enactment of the Humphrey-Hawkins bill;

* Studying the health and safety problems of working women, meeting with federal and state health and safety agencies, and keeping abreast of existing "protective" laws that keep women out of certain industrial jobs;

* Gathering and distributing model contract provisions that deal with women's problems which CLUW members will eventually be able to propose to their individual unions. For example, in the area of health insurance several unions have made progress in their efforts to gain insurance benefits for pregnancy-related disabilities; (and)

* Seeking to open up nontraditional apprenticeship trades to women and finding out which trades need improvement.[83]

CLUW has always had a major commitment to childcare and in 1977, the organization participated in a study of childcare programs in Sweden, France, and Israel (with a $97,000 grant from the German Marshall Fund), in order to discover what needed to be established in the United States. Their final report, "A Commitment to Children," noted that the countries studied had a "commitment to children and family life" in the ready availability of a variety of childcare programs provided through public funding. The report stated that the programs in Israel, Sweden, and France were based on acceptance of the need for women to work. The study found that the number of daycare programs in these nations still did not meet the demand but that unions were playing a major role in the effort to expand facilities and improve the quality of care.[84] One of the major purposes of the study was to point out the sharp differences in programs and attitudes between the United States and the other countries. For example, at the time of the report, President Nixon had just voted a publicly-financed childcare program. Despite their many efforts, CLUW's goal to achieve national childcare legislation has not yet been achieved.

In November 1977, several hundred CLUW members participated in the first National Women's Conference, held in Houston. It was an historic occasion for the U.S. women's movement.

> Two thousand delegates (watched by thousands of observers) forged a strong national plan of action that will move women forward to full equality, economic and social justice. Over-whelming endorsement for swift ratification of the Equal Rights Amendment and for adoption of a full employment program were among the key issues approved by the dele-gates.[85]

The demands coming out of this conference were gender-related and work-related and included issues having to do with racial discrimination. Following the Houston women's conference, a national advisory committee for women, which included Joyce Miller, Addie Wyatt, and two other CLUW board members, released a twenty-six point "National Plan of Action" which had been adopted by the Houston delegates. It included a call for ratification of the ERA, reproductive freedom, and equal employment opportunities. The advisory committee's co-chair, Bella Abzug, claimed that President Carter supported a good part of the program, but not all. The major area of disagreement was reproductive freedom.

Reproductive rights had become the cutting edge of the feminist movement with the right to legalized abortion (won in 1973 with the Supreme Court decision *Roe vs. Wade*), an important victory. In spite of the backlash during the late-1970s, CLUW remained steadfast in its commitment to women's right to choose and was in fact the major working women's organization to take a stand on the issue. On this feminist issue in particular, CLUW has been willing to take a controversial position, even though the AFL-CIO has taken no position on women's reproductive rights, and most unions have steered away from the issue.

The CLUW leadership wanted to make sure that all CLUW members participated in the implementation of the Houston plan. CLUW leader Joyce Miller said, "We've got to make sure that [the] voices of American working women which were heard in Houston are heard in every part of this nation and particularly in Washington D.C."[86] CLUW supported, and in some cases even took the lead on, key feminist issues on the 1970s. The ERA and reproductive freedom stand out as two of the most important issues.

At its March 1979 meeting, CLUW's national executive board made a major commitment to the creation of a safe and healthy workplace. A major aspect of that right was the fight against what they called "reproductive hazards." In the spring of 1979, CLUW's newspaper launched a new column focusing on health and safety issues affecting women workers.[87] The first column was "Reproductive Freedom for Workers: A Right, Not a Benefit" by Sylvia Krekel (occupational health specialist for the Oil, Chemical, and Atomic Workers International Union). Krekel was working on a survey to find out the extent of reproductive damage at the workplace. One of the most dramatic cases concerned five women who had themselves sterilized after their employer, American Cynamid, announced that women able to have children would not be allowed to work in jobs which involved lead exposure. Thus women were forced to sacrifice either their childbearing capacities or their jobs. According to Krekel, however, numerous studies show that exposure to lead damages both male and female reproductive systems.

> Thus the American Cynamid case clearly illustrates the dual discrimination implicit in exclusionary placement policies based on reproductive capacity. Women transferred out of their jobs suffer economic loss and the men remaining on the job endure exposure to substances that may cause sterility or birth defects in their children.
>
> Since women have been put on the firing line and are the ones who are singled out by exclusionary placement policies, women must lead the fight to defeat this new attempt to force women out of industrial jobs.[88]

CLUW also joined the Coalition for Reproductive Freedom, one purpose of which was "to expose the corporate policy of eliminating workers rather than hazards."[89]

CLUW continued to take strong stands and important risks on feminist issues. When President Carter dismissed Bella Abzug as the co-chair of the National Advisory Committee for Women, many committee members resigned with her, among them CLUW's president, Joyce Miller. In her telegram to President Carter of January 15, 1979, Miller stated:

It is with deep regret that I must submit my resignation from the National Advisory Committee for Women.

After full discussion with the Officers of the Coalition of Labor Union Women, we feel that the National Advisory Committee for Women can no longer be an effective vehicle for implementing the National Plan of Action passed at the Houston Conference.

We respectfully urge that very strong positive action be taken by your administration to restore the confidence of American women.[90]

CLUW also protested when George Meany called for the 1979 AFL-CIO convention to be held in Florida, an unratified ERA state. Miller wrote to Meany:

One of the most effective developments on the political scene has been the formation of the coalition of labor and the women's movement which in turn has interpreted the goals of the women's movement to labor. This partnership has been effective as we found for a higher minimum wage, labor law reform, pregnancy disability, Humphrey-Hawkins and the extension of time for the ERA. We look to a continuing close working relationship as trade unionists with the women's movement. Holding the Convention in Florida would seriously weaken this continued working together in coalition.[91]

The AFL-CIO honored the request and moved its convention from Miami Beach to Washington, D.C.

As CLUW did more work on women's issues, it also moved into greater cooperation with the AFL-CIO. Immediately before its third national convention in September 1977, CLUW sponsored a two-day legislative conference in Washington, D.C. Speakers included Congresswoman Yvonne Braithwaite Burke from California, Congresswoman Barbara Mikulski from Maryland, and Senator Edward Kennedy from Massachusetts. Most important, however, was the address given by George Meany, president of the AFL-CIO.

If supporting a living wage for all workers makes me a feminist, move over sisters; I've been called a lot worse. ERA, full employment, minimum wage, labor law reform, pregnancy benefits, national health insurance—these are not women's issues. They are labor issues, trade union issues. They are fights all of us must win and win together...CLUW is an organization to benefit all working people. Labor history has many chapters about the role of women in the labor movement. You are writing a new chapter and I'm confident you intend to make it the greatest chapter yet. I'm proud to be here with you. . .[92]

Within the labor movement, your [CLUW's] efforts have encouraged women trade unionists to seek leadership roles. You have assisted them in developing the skills necessary for leadership—for dealing with the myriad problems ranging from government regulations to lobbying. You have provided special expertise to the labor movement, on such issues as day care, minimum wage, pregnancy benefits and national health insurance. CLUW has been the focal point for labor's support for the Equal Rights Amendment. That's a rough battle, as all of you here know—but it is not a lost battle. We still have a fighting chance—and we—and I am sure, you—intend to give it our best shot. . . Your officers and staff of AFL-CIO have worked closely in attempting to secure the greatest possible support for ratification, and we are ready, willing and able to continue the battle. Even together, we may not produce miracles but we can do our level best to produce ratification. And I still think ERA can be won. . . It's all one fight—with a lot of separate battles. ERA, full employment. . .[93]

For the president of the AFL-CIO to publicly refer to himself as a feminist marked a highly significant change. One might argue that it was a token or a public relations gesture; however, even as a gesture, it was an important new symbol of political alliance.

C LUW's Fourth National Convention and Further Links with the AFL-CIO

On September 13-16, 1979, CLUW's fourth national convention was held in New York City. Twelve hundred delegates, including CLUW observers, non-CLUW observers, and foreign guests attended. Joyce Miller reported that CLUW now had 8,000 members from sixty different unions. In her keynote speech she stressed one of CLUW's major themes. "Women will not achieve equality in the workplace without the collective strength of unions behind them."[94]

At the convention, there were educational and training workshops on topics such as winning the ERA, childcare, organizing the unorganized, fighting sexism in our unions, equal pay for work of comparable worth, reproductive rights, and other topics. At these workshops excellent information and strategies were given. Conference delegates also,

* Pledged stepped-up efforts to win ratification of the ERA in

three more states and urged continuation of the boycott of unratified states.

* Renewed CLUW's commitment to affirmative action programs and called upon the labor movement to implement and expand such programs, including representation at all levels within unions to reflect the membership of women members.

* Called for strengthening federal job safety and health protection and urged industry to fix the workplace and not the workers—a reference to exclusionary hiring and promotion practices that affect women.

* Urged passage of a national health security bill to provide for universal coverage, comprehensive services and effective cost controls and voted support for efforts to fight cutbacks in health services as well as closing of hospitals.

* Renewed CLUW's commitment to obtaining federally funded childcare programs.

* Called for changes in the Social Security system to provide equitable protection for all women.[95]

Delegates also reaffirmed CLUW's commitment to "comparable worth," eliminating wage discrimination against women who perform jobs similar to those of men. A resolution called for reevaluating women's jobs according to their "real worth" and urged unions to adopt the concept of equal pay for work of comparable worth in all contract negotiations.

On September 14th, convention participants joined a picket line in support of the organizing drive at Abraham and Straus department stores in Brooklyn. Abraham and Straus, whose employees were mostly women, was the largest, non-unionized New York department store.

The rally at Abraham and Straus was a strategy for drawing maximum attention to this fundamental aspect of CLUW's program: organizing the unorganized.[96] Miller strongly linked the issue of unionizing unorganized workers to that of equal pay for work of comparable worth.

Of the 4,000 workers in that store, more than 80 percent are women... A&S employees earn $20-$30 a week *less* than their organized counterparts at stores like Macy's, Gimbles and Bloomingdale's. They need the benefits and protection that a union card can bring.

Women today still earn only 57 percent of what men earn. Women are segregated into low-paying stereotyped jobs and cannot escape the wage ghetto imposed by both economic forces and long-standing patterns of discrimination.[97]

"We believe," said Miller, that "correcting discrimination in wage rates will have a major constructive impact on the economic well-being of *all* workers—men and women alike."[98]

For working women, equal attention was given to issues of work and gender. At the same time, the bonds between women and labor were emphasized and strengthened when Thomas Donahue, executive assistant to Meany, expressed the federation's "continuing support for CLUW's work."[99]

At the 1979 convention, new national officers were elected. Since Olga Madar did not seek re-election, she was given the position of president emerita. Joyce Miller was elected president; Addie Wyatt, executive vice-president; Georgie McGhee, first vice-president; Clara Day, second vice-president; Gloria Johnson, treasurer; Patsy L. Fryman, recording secretary; and Odessa Komer, corresponding secretary.

In August 1980 an historic event occurred. CLUW's president, Joyce Miller, was the first woman elected to the AFL-CIO Executive Council. This election was a major expression of CLUW's growing alliance with the AFL-CIO and also symbolized the credibility and recognition that CLUW had achieved as a force within the labor movement. In 1981, Barbara Hutchinson, director of the Women's Department of her union and vice-president of the American Federation of Government Employees, became the second woman, and the first black woman, elected to the AFL-CIO Executive Council.

There were those who believed that the elections of Joyce Miller and Barbara Hutchinson were tokenism, and in one sense they were correct. The AFL-CIO's Executive Council was still overwhelmingly white and male, and according to CLUW's report, *Absent from the Agenda*, there was still a very low percentage of women in union leadership. Nevertheless, Miller's election in particular was a significant breakthrough because she considered herself a feminist and was also president of *the* organization of labor union women, CLUW.

The alliance between labor and the women's movement continued, particularly in relationship to the ERA. At a pro-ERA rally at an Illinois labor conference held in April 1980, Joyce Miller stated: "Illinois is not a 'right-to-work' state—but in its failure to ratify the Equal Rights Amendment, the state joins the company of other states which have consistently denied the rights of working people as well as of women."[100]

Miller considered the ERA to be an economic issue. "The labor movement and the women's movement fight a common enemy: corporate power and right-wing forces intent on keeping wages low and increasing profits for a few. Sex discrimination and economic exploitation go hand in hand."[101]

Several national trade union leaders also spoke at the same rally for the ERA. For example, Lane Kirkland, president of the AFL-CIO, claimed that "working together—as a united labor movement and with our allies in the women's groups—we can turn the tide and win a victory for the ERA in Illinois and the nation at large."[102]

Further Growth of CLUW

Continued Support for Feminist Issues

From the late 1970s to the present, CLUW has continued to be a significant force in connecting labor and women. Ellie Smeal, national president of NOW, was a major speaker at both the 1981 AFL-CIO sponsored "Solidarity Day" in Washington, D.C. and at the AFL-CIO national convention that followed. Labor's ties with NOW are largely a result of the growing partnership between NOW and CLUW. The two organizations conduct joint projects, attend and speak of each other's functions and, in general, influence each other's growth. NOW also includes issues related to workers and working women in its program.

CLUW's relationship with NOW is part of its overall commitment to the women's movement. It has continued to work in coalitions around specific issues such as reproductive freedom. CLUW also has brought feminist issues to the workplace and shown their economic relevance by, for instance, emphasizing the economic implications of the ERA. Finally, CLUW (along with other women's groups) has developed a feminist agenda for the workplace. In addition to supporting "traditional" working women's concerns such as daycare and maternity benefits, CLUW has agitated for "new" feminist work issues, such as equal pay for work of comparable worth, reproductive freedom as a health and safety issue, and combatting sexual harassment in the workplace. This agenda has signifies an important new stage in working women's feminism.

Organizing the Unorganized

CLUW's 1979 national convention put great emphasis on organizing the unorganized, and on November 14-16, 1979, CLUW held a major follow-up conference on unionizing workers, co-chaired by Vicky Saporta of the Teamsters and Margie Albert of the UAW. Elmer Chatak, secretary-treasurer of the AFL-CIO's Industrial Union Department, praised the conference for being the first national conference on the topic. He expressed his belief that working women "are on the march, they are the new frontier of the labor movement." Again, Joyce Miller pledged CLUW's commitment to organizing the unorganized.

> We are committed to helping organize women workers in order to give them the chance to escape from the low-paid dead end jobs that perpetuate the wage gap between unionized women workers and those who are unorganized... Only through trade unions can that wage inequity be erased.[103]

In addition to guest speakers such as Crystal Lee Sutton (the real "Norma Rae"), the conference included a series of information-sharing workshops on organizing in various sectors such as health care, public, and industrial work. The national conference inspired local and state conferences on the same theme.

CLUW's program of organizing the unorganized meant close cooperation with the Industrial Union Department (IUD) of the AFL-CIO. On January 28, 1981, a one-day conference on organizing was sponsored by CLUW and IUD, and joint work with the IUD continued on specific projects to organize women workers.

Despite CLUW's progress in this area, it cannot organize directly since it is not a union, nor will it side with one union over another. CLUW will only support organizing drives and provide training in organizing to union women which means that its activities are defined by organized labor. As a result, CLUW members and others have asked whether support and training are sufficient to organize the unorganized.

Absent From the Agenda—Lack of Female Leadership in the Union Movement

Another area of concern for CLUW has been the overall lack of female union leadership. Although some progress has been made (partly as a result of CLUW's activities), there is still a long way to go.

In 1980, as part of a project on the empowerment of union women, the staff of CLUW's Center for Education and Research published a major report on women's participation in union leadership, titled "Absent from the Agenda: A Report on the Role of Women in American Unions." The project's explicit goal was to have women present at every level of union leadership.

> Today women constitute 30% of all organized workers in the United States (approximately 6.9 million women); yet leadership positions in almost every labor organization in America at national, regional, and local levels are still held almost entirely by men. In 1980, one woman leads only one of

the AFL-CIO's 104 international unions and only a handful serve on their governing boards. Efforts by the AFL-CIO to improve the representation of women in leadership positions include the creation of the post of "Co-ordinator of Women's Affairs" and the appointment of the first female department head (Education). More dramatically, the 35 member AFL-CIO Executive Council recently elected its first and only woman member. In doing so, the Council had to waive long-standing, informal rules requiring that a council member had to be chief officer of a member union. AFL-CIO President Lane Kirkland, who personally led the move to get a woman seated on the council, said he hoped that the time would soon come when women as well as minorities would gain elections to union presidencies and make special rules unnecessary.[104]

"Absent from the Agenda" included a detailed examination of women's participation *at every level of union leadership*. The report does not offer a concrete strategy but it concludes that women should continue working within the labor movement.

In the labor movement, as in the rest of society, discrimination and benign neglect have contributed to an under-representation of women's skills and talents. Yet unlike other institutions, the labor movement has the vision, the ability and the power to be different.[105]

The report emphasizes throughout the tension between unions' potential for change and the reality that in the present unions, as in other "power centers of institutions—women are absent from the agenda."[106]

Growing Progressivism Within CLUW

One of CLUW's strengths has been its ability to raise women's concerns from within the AFL-CIO. While highly successful on issues like the ERA and sexual harassment, feminist strategies have not worked as well in areas such as promoting union leadership and organizing the unorganized.

CLUW's leadership has tried to achieve a balance by challenging the predominantly male labor leadership on some issues but not on others. Some CLUW activists have tried to raise issues within CLUW that go beyond the organization's gender and work agendas. For instance, at the 1979 National CLUW Convention, there was much support from the floor for a resolution supporting undocumented workers. Despite resistance from some CLUW leadership, it passed. Regarding more controversial issues, such as disarmament and military expenditures, some CLUW chapters have clearly allied themselves with the more progressive wing of the labor movement.

At the 1982 National CLUW Convention, some members unsuccessfully fought for a resolution in favor of ending U.S. aid to El Salvador. In 1984, however, the tenth National CLUW Convention passed a series of resolutions on U.S. domestic and foreign policy which substantially moved CLUW's positions forward in comparison to those of the established labor movement. These resolutions included: opposition to U.S. military aid to the government of El Salvador; rejection of military intervention in El Salvador, Nicaragua, and all other Central American countries; opposition to the deployment of Euromissiles; and a statement which clearly linked reduction of the U.S. military budget with increased domestic spending and the implementation of CLUW's political and social goals. CLUW also reaffirmed its support of total reproductive freedom for women, even though many, if not most, AFL-CIO unions would still not take a stand on this controversial issue.[107]

CLUW's membership has continued to grow, with 18,000 members in 1986, and the addition of close to twenty new chapters. The organization has expanded many of its education and training programs. In addition, it has done new work on the legislative issue of "parental leave" and has sponsored nationwide voter registration drives. While organizing the unorganized remains a key concern, CLUW has not sponsored any new national efforts around this issue.*

Conclusion _____

The Role of Labor

CLUW stands out as the most successful organization for union women in the United States. It is the largest and the only *national* organization of union women. CLUW's major strengths include its commitment and ability to bring gender issues to working women at the workplace, to put union women at the forefront of union issues, to work for a progressive labor program, to ally working women with the existing women's liberation movement, and to forge relationships with the existing union movement.

---

* The bulk of this case study was written in 1983. Although CLUW has grown in membership and added some new projects since then, there have been no substantial changes in the organization's policies or programs.

There are, however, many areas where CLUW has not yet succeeded. Most women workers remain unorganized and are in the least skilled, lowest paid jobs. And while the number of women in union leadership has increased, the majority of labor leadership, especially in the higher echelons, is still predominantly male. What can we learn, then, from CLUW's history regarding women's role in changing unions and organizing women workers?

In order to evaluate CLUW, we need to develop an analysis of the role of organized labor. Unions have served both positive and negative functions with regard to their constituencies (working people, women, people of color, and other oppressed groups). Also historically, unions have been changed both by independent efforts and through changes from within.

On the positive side, unions have historically been and still are the *basic organization* for working people. Without them, there would be no gains in wages, working conditions, or in workers' ability to defend themselves against their employers. The facts suggest that in general any union, even a "bad" one, is better than no union at all. For example, no matter how sexist unions have been, when women have unionized, they have been better off than non-unionized women. Union women generally earn higher wages than non-unionized women, and have better working conditions. Even when unions are not democratically run or are overly bureaucratized, they promote women's self-empowerment.

Most important, on overall domestic issues, the labor movement has been one of the most progressive forces for change in the United States and CLUW, in its short history, has been at the forefront of promoting progressive legislation within labor. Andrew Levison, author of *The Working Class Majority*, states:

> There is simply no avoiding the conclusion that, considering its power as well as its views, labor has been the chief force for progressive domestic legislation in America. Without them, there would be no Voting Rights Act, and therefore no black caucus. In Congress, without a doubt, many of the most valuable social programs would have been defeated and the very composition of Congress would have been far more conservative, without many of the key Senate doves who received labor support despite the AFL-CIO's support for the [Vietnam] war . . .
>
> Also, the political viewpoint workers receive from their unions is solidly liberal and at times far more "radical" than that of the liberal critics who dismiss the labor movement as a force for change.[108]

There are negative aspects to the labor movement that CLUW leaders have difficulty acknowledging. For instance, the AFL-CIO's overall policy has included support for U.S. foreign policy in Vietnam and Central America. It has been difficult to get labor to speak out on issues such as military expenditures, nuclear arms, and foreign intervention. Even though there is growing support within labor to challenge U.S. military policies, such issues remain a source of tension within the labor movement. Perspectives on these issues differ within and between CLUW chapters, as they do within and between unions. While CLUW's national leaders have been hesitant to publicly take a position on U.S. foreign policy, they tend toward the more progressive end of the political spectrum.

Issues of union democracy and lack of corruption are important union concerns that CLUW needs to discuss. Morevoer, CLUW needs to take into full account that unions have often historically played a negative role in relation to unorganized workers who include the least skilled workers, women, and minorities. Today this phenomenon is most clearly seen in relationship to workers outside of the United States. Multinational corporations have increasingly used workers in the third world and in some parts of the western world to make up the pool of "cheap labor" that they require. Without an international perspective and connection to workers throughout the world, the U.S. labor movement will continue fighting for only narrow gains and will not grow stronger. For CLUW, "sisterhood and solidarity" also means establishing relationships with women and workers throughout the world and not allowing the labor force in the United States to be used against workers from other countries.

Because CLUW wants to remain loyal to the existing labor movement while at the same time fighting for women and minorities, and organizing the unorganized, their challenge is to resolve the conflicts that have existed between organized workers (usually white men) and both organized and unorganized women. Thus far, CLUW has not been able to resolve all these conflicts. This case study suggests that it will continue to be necessary to work both inside and outside the existing labor movement to make needed changes on behalf of women. This will be discussed further in the following section.

Analysis

CLUW's Theory and Practice Around Double Oppression

Opposing double oppression in theory

CLUW had no *explicit* theory about women's double oppression since it placed its emphasis on *program*. However, the organization was built on an implicit understanding of double oppression. This understanding can be seen in CLUW's platform, program, and statements.

For example, CLUW was built on the understanding that women are discriminated against in the wage-work force, and placed in the lowest paying, least skilled jobs. CLUW members know from first-hand experience that 80 percent of women work in non-professional jobs. Also, CLUW has taken a stand on equal pay for work of comparable worth, which means that they are aware of the existence of a sex-segregated work force.

Although CLUW understood that women are discriminated against in the larger society, it did not analyze the family as a place of female exploitation or discuss the kind of relationships women, men, and young people could have in an equal society. While CLUW's program of childcare, and maternity and pregnancy benefits, was based on the idea that women's traditional role in the home made it difficult for them to function equally in the wage-work force, their program was designed to *improve* the quality of the traditional family, not to *challenge* it. CLUW also did not address women in their roles as unpaid houseworkers, and there was no discussion of reorganizing family life and redistributing housework and childcare between both men and women. These factors have hindered CLUW from developing a full vision of a world without exploitation or inequality. Moreover, it has limited CLUW's ability to fight for women in the wage-work force since women can not gain equality in work outside the home without freedom within the home.

Opposing double oppression in practice

CLUW's strength was its program of action. More than any other working women's organization, its programs covered gender and work issues comprehensively. In its original statement of purpose, CLUW expressed four areas of concern: organizing unorganized women, affirmative action in the workplace, political action, and legislation.

It is impressive to review all the issues that CLUW has worked on and/or supported over the years (listed below):

1. General work issues that women share with men: full employment, a shorter work week, a livable minimum wage,

extension of protective legislation to men, national health insurance, job safety and health, amnesty for undocumented workers.

2. Work issues that are informed by the fact of being female: organizing unorganized women workers.

3. Gender issues in the workplace: affirmative action, child-care, pregnancy benefits, equal pay for work of comparable worth, reproductive rights at the workplace (e.g. investigation of and ending the use of harmful chemicals, prohibiting discrimination against women at work for their role as childbearers).

4. Gender issues outside the workplace: the ERA, abortion rights and other reproductive rights (including protection from forced sterilization), federal legislation for comprehensive childcare, support for programs for victims of domestic violence.

Two issues, however, were most strongly emphasized in CLUW's literature: the unionization of women, and the empowerment of women through their unions, especially through union leadership.

> In CLUW it has always been our belief. . .that the first step most working women need to take is to join a union. A union can offer them the legal and contractual framework within which other issues, progressively over time, can be negotiated and settled. . .
>
> CLUW has known that ultimately the best guarantee of decent working conditions, adequate salaries and an end to discrimination against women workers is a union contract. . .
> Thus CLUW has always been strongly dedicated to the principle of organizing the unorganized.[109]

To deal with these issues, CLUW has held a conference on organizing the unorganized, has worked with the AFL-CIO Industrial Union Department on organizing projects, and has published a major study on the lack of female union leadership ("Absent from the Agenda").

CLUW's unique strength was its ability to successfully involve wage-working women in the feminist struggle. CLUW made the ERA, abortion rights, and other feminist issues the issues of working women. In addition, CLUW was committed to supporting women's gender issues at the workplace, including opposition to sexual harassment and support for equal pay for work of comparable worth.

The above demands, particularly for comparable worth, are tremendously important. If won, they would have radical effects on women's lives. In particular, job segregation according to sex role is probably the major reason for disparity of wages between women and men and comparable worth is the first major attack on this disparity. CLUW, along with union women, has been successful in winning significant union support for this issue.

A related strength was CLUW's ability to promote a joint program that supports both gender and work issues (for example, both ERA *and* full employment) without having either appear to conflict with the other, and in fact showing the interrelationship of both types of issues. No other present-day working women's organization has successfully integrated demands that span a spectrum of both gender and work. In all the other organizations examined, there was conflict at some point between gender and work demands, particularly between gender demands outside of the workplace (such as suffrage or the ERA) and work demands for both male and female workers (such as the extension of protective legislation to men). CLUW's only significant exception was the conflict between seniority and affirmative action. However, that conflict did not cause any break in CLUW's relationship to feminist organizations or labor groups.

There were other areas in which CLUW was very successful. Of all the women's organizations with which I have had personal experiences, CLUW is the most racially integrated, at all levels of participation. Minority women are active members and leaders in CLUW. Also, CLUW has tended to be part of the more progressive wing of trade unionism in their overall program. For example, in their 1975 program on jobs, one of CLUW's specific demands was "opposition to budget cuts in programs for the people's needs and a cut in military spending in order to pay for these programs."[110]

How effective has CLUW been at actually winning any part of its program? It is important to note that CLUW does not have the power to require unions to bring any issues into collective bargaining. CLUW has educated union members on a variety of women's issues and, during the last few years, many more feminist issues have been included into collective bargaining—a phenomenon owed in part to CLUW's existence. However, much more still needs to be done before the majority of unions incorporate key feminist issues into their programs.

Unfortunately, major pieces of national legislation supported by CLUW, such as the ERA, full employment, and national daycare, have still not been passed. One could attribute these failures to the economic and social policies of the present national administration, the generally defensive position of unions, the Right's attacks on women and labor, and finally to the need to build a stronger working women's movement.

CLUW's Approach to Unionizing Women

CLUW understands both the importance of unions to women and the importance of women to trade unionism, and recognizes that organizing the unorganized is crucial to both groups. Previous attempts to organize unorganized women workers often failed because the organizers did not try to reach out to women workers as women. One of CLUW's major contributions to this area has been adding gender issues to workplace concerns.

However, most women workers remain unorganized, and most successful attempts at organizing in the present have still been by independent working women's groups. This is because CLUW is limited in its own ability to organize the unorganized. First, it will not take the side of one union over another, so it cannot get into jurisdictional disputes such as that between the Farm Workers and the Teamsters. This means that CLUW must ignore the needs of many smaller new unions. Second, CLUW has made the decision that it will not organize women directly since CLUW itself is not a union. Third, CLUW, unlike WAGE, can only promote existing unions which, it has been shown, are often inattentive to the needs of women.

It is this inability to unionize the majority of still unorganized women that has limited CLUW's power and its ability to succeed in its other goals, particularly in challenging the male domination of the trade unions. Women cannot be equals in labor, nor can they have power, influence, or major leadership until they are organized.

CLUW's Approach to Stimulating Change Within the Feminist and Labor Movements and Facilitating Alliances between the Two Movements
Building alliances

CLUW stands out as an organization that has built excellent relationships with both the existing feminist and labor movements. It has played an important role in facilitating cooperation between feminism and labor (with the exception of left-wing feminism), and in particular has facilitated contact between leaders of NOW and the AFL-CIO.

CLUW has worked in coalition with many different women's groups over many different issues. It was actively involved in the 1977 National Women's Conference. Joyce Miller supported Bella Abzug when she was fired by President Carter. The organization has stressed bringing gender issues to unions, gained support for the ERA, and provided an understanding of the link between gender and work issues. Furthermore, CLUW's focus on wage-working women has proved to be a successful strategy for gaining access to many women. Although there are still class divisions among women, those divisions are much less sharp than they have been in the past as more and more women work for wages and as more women are dependent on their own earnings. Despite strong cooperation, there have occasionally been conflicts between CLUW and feminist groups. These include CLUW's argument with NOW over seniority and affirmative action, its criticisms of the women's movement for frequently disregarding work-related issues, and its insistence that CLUW work within the trade union movement and consider it a potential ally, despite its male domination. Although the alliance between NOW and CLUW survived their disagreements, the relationship between CLUW and some left-wing feminists did not fare so well. Because they could not resolve their conflicts over how to relate to the existing trade union movement, CLUW lost many enthusiastic activists while the left-wing feminists lost the potential of working with the largest group of union women in the United States.

Meanwhile, CLUW has developed a successful alliance with the existing trade union movement. While the AFL-CIO did not formally endorse CLUW because CLUW's membership included women outside of the AFL-CIO, there has been, ever since 1975, a supportive relationship. There are many indications of the two organizations' mutual support: CLUW president Joyce Miller was the first woman member of the AFL-CIO executive board; the AFL-CIO sends speakers to CLUW functions and CLUW does likewise for the AFL-CIO; the AFL-CIO supported the ERA; and George Meany has gone so far as to declare himself a feminist.

While many individual unions may have little relationship to CLUW (particularly if its members do not belong—and many union women still do not belong), CLUW has legitimacy and recognition within the existing union movement in a way that no other women's group has ever had. The credibility that CLUW has gotten through its loyalty to trade unionism, and because its leaders and members are active unionists, is one of the major reasons for CLUW's success.

There are, however, problems in the alliance between CLUW and organized labor. Many women within CLUW's pro-union leadership have pointed out the dilemmas that CLUW faces working with the male-dominated unions. As Margie Albert asks,

> How independent should CLUW be from our unions? For progressive feminist CLUW members, the answer is not so simple. We don't agree with those who say CLUW should open its doors to *all* women. . . Nor are we anxious to carry on struggles with our male union leaders in public, thus giving ammunition to anti-union forces among employers and the

press. On the other hand, we are certainly not content to simply be female voices mouthing what our male union leaders tell us we can say and do.[111]

And Connie Kopelov continues in a similar vein,

> While it is crucial that CLUW not be discredited in the eyes of the labor movement. . . it is equally important that its compromises be limited to those of tactics, not principles. CLUW must remember it exists because women suffer discrimination. . . Some degree of conflict is inevitable between women seeking their rights and male union leadership.[112]

To some extent CLUW is hampered by their need to maintain credibility with the male labor leadership. The resulting limitations on CLUW's involvement in organizing the unorganized have already been noted. This need to maintain credibility also makes it difficult for CLUW to question or break with existing AFL-CIO policy on issues such as U.S. foreign policy and military policy or the conflict over seniority and affirmative action.

Finally, full equality for women within unions remains an unrealized goal. While CLUW has made some gains in all these areas, in its own eyes there is much yet to be done.

Stiumulating change

CLUW has had an important effect on both organized labor and feminism. For example, it has been vital in pushing feminists to acknowledge the importance of working women. Evidence of CLUW's influence can be seen in the package of goals for women workers that was adopted by the delegates at the April 1975 NOW convention. It pledged full support by NOW for union organizing, for full employment legislation, a comprehensive childcare act, and a guaranteed minimum income. Sara Nelson, coordinator of NOW's Labor Task Force, said: "What's emerging now is work to stimulate organizing into unions, so women workers can get some power into their own hands. We can't sit back and wait for the union movement to find us—that won't happen."[113]

Despite all of the changes in NOW, the greater openness of feminists towards unions, and the growth of several overlapping demands between feminists and working women's organizations, some important challenges still need to be met. First, most feminists do not yet see unionization for women as a central feminist issue. While unions for women are now supported, they are not yet widely understood as a crucial basis of women's strength. Second, most feminists still do not perceive themselves as able to have an impact on the existing union movement. More needs to be done in order to help feminists become aware of their potential influence on labor.

In addition to its strong impact on the women's movement, CLUW has been an important advocate for women within unions. Some of these successes have already been noted. For example there has been an increase in female union leadership and male trade union leaders often show a greater openness to feminist issues. Also, CLUW has been a force for a more progressive trade union agenda. However, this is only a beginning. According to CLUW's own analysis in *Absent from the Agenda,* women are still largely invisible in the eyes of the trade union movement. They are grossly underrepresented in union leadership positions, still concentrated in low-paid, low-skilled jobs, make fifty-nine cents for every dollar that men make, and the majority are not unionized, even though the percentage of union membership of women has increased and is at a higher rate than that of men.

The AFL-CIO itself ackholwedges many of these weaknesses; but significantly, the AFL-CIO report, "The Changing Situation of Workers and Their Unions," barely mentions women, and ignores the important role that women could play in the overall growth and development of unionism.[114]

CLUW is a striking example of the success that can be achieved by a working women's group that has a solid union base and a good working relationship with the existing male leadership. However, it is important to note that despite its positive results, forming an alliance with the labor establishment and working from within do not seem to be *sufficient* as ways of achieving full gains for women.

My analysis suggests that the existence of an active *independent* movement promoting the interests of working women is *equally* necessary. The independents are often the first ones to raise issues important to women and the existence of an independent women's movement seems to keep these issues alive. Almost all the major efforts to organize the unorganized were started independently, particularly the efforts of the CIO in the 1930s and the independent movement of working women in the 1970s, or else, as in the case of the Garment Workers at the beginning of the twentieth century, arose from the rank and file. Many of the gains for women as a gender and as workers have usually been a result of an independent women's movement and/or from an alliance between working women and independent feminists.

While in almost all cases independent or independently initiated unions sooner or later end up affiliating with the existing labor movement, they often have a better chance of organizing a union that is responsive to their members' needs, by finding some way to simultaneously maintain their independence. For instance, 9 to 5, the National Association of Working Women, an organization for office workers, which has organized at least 10,000 office worker in the U.S., has created SEIU District 925, a national local with divisions throughout the country affiliated with the Service Employees International Union. Working Women will remain an independent organization, while encouraging union projects such as District 925. Also, SEIU was chosen for this affiliation for several reasons; under its current president John Sweeney it has emphasized flexibility in negotiating affiliation agreements with independent unions, has initiated new organizing campaigns, and has a much more decentralized structure than most other unions. As a result, women office workers can have a greater degree of control in District 925 than they would have in many other unions.[115] Examples such as this suggest important implications for CLUW's potential to change the existing union movement towards its goal of equality for women.

My analysis suggests that there need to be independent groups for CLUW to work with. What these groups might be is an open question. One possibility is organizing centers for women workers. The present feminist movement could be a place to initiate organizing women workers in a similar fashion to the independent working women's organizations. The future holds important possibilities, and while CLUW has taken important steps, there is still much to be done.

Development of a Broad Political Program

CLUW has been the most successful of the three working women's organizations under consideration. It has the largest membership, the highest degree of cooperation between feminists and unions, and the highest degree of integration between work and gender issues. CLUW's greatest achievement has been bringing feminist issues to the labor movement.

During the 1970s, CLUW's major political work was formulating and organizing around a broad, inclusive program of domestic and social issues such as national childcare legislation, full employment, a shorter work week, comparable worth, the ERA, reproductive rights, etc. In contrast to WWA and WAGE, CLUW has also had the resources and numbers which enabled them to continue active lobbying for this broad spectrum of issues over many years, and to work with other groups in support of this program. In the 1980s, CLUW focused more strongly on anti-Reagan activities. Although as an organization they did not support electoral candidates, they made voter registration a priority in 1984.

While one of CLUW's most important contributions was the development of a broad political and social program, they still have not yet been able to mobilize the power to have that program successfully instituted. Women's groups and working women need to take the next steps in building that power base.

Conclusion

8

In order to create a world which reflects their vision, women need political power. Being a majority of the world's population and members of almost every oppressed group, women have the potential to exert a significant influence on world events. There is great consciousness and momentum among women that is international in scale. However, what is most critical about the current period is the growing economic power that women possess as a result of the dramatic changes in the wage-work force. The case studies in this book provide a forum for examining that economic power: how have women attempted to organize around it; what happens when women organize in their interests as women *and* as workers; and what happens when attempts are made to forge greater alliances between the feminist and labor movements?

We can summarize the findings of this book as follows:

1. There has been growing cooperation between the feminist and labor movements over the past 100 years due, in large part, to the recent dramatic increase in the number of women in the wage-work force.

Although there is a prevailing impression among much of the feminist community that there are inherent conflicts between the women's and labor movements, we have seen that this assumption is not necessarily true. The three case studies just completed in this book make it apparent that cooperation between feminism and the labor movement has not only occurred in the past, but is increasing with each year. Their alliance has brought greater, yet relatively unrecognized, growth for both movements. Despite the overall decline in trade unionism, women have been the base for what growth has occurred in trade unionism. Moreover women, because of their numbers and developing consciousness, represent the potential for new strength and resurgence for unions.

At the same time trade unionism has been, especially in recent years, the best ally of women on several significant women's issues. Most of the victories around pay equity have been the result of union initiative. ERA, reproductive health at the workplace, and childcare have all had union support. Though many of these struggles did not end in victory, they still represent the development of a solid, working alliance between the two movements.

2. There has been the growth of a working women's feminism which is a unifying agenda for all women and deeply connects women to working people. This agenda could serve as the basis for new progressive change.

In order to organize women successfully, both feminists and the labor movement have had to organize consciously around issues that speak to women as women *and* as workers. Several indices in this book have been used to show the evolution of the integration of gender and work issues. Today, there is a full program on a series of issues which includes pay equity, affirmative action, reproductive health, childcare, full employment, parental leave, and others. This program is the broadest program that has ever existed for women and points to the fact that women as workers are pivotal for major social change. The kind of progressive legislation and change that came about as a result of trade unionism in the 1930s could be paralleled today with such a political agenda.

Pay equity, or equal pay for work of comparable worth, is also an excellent example of a gender/work issue which, if instituted, could bring fundamental changes. Often, when there have been pay equity gains, there have been pay raises and upgrading of the traditional female occupations like nursing and clerical work. However, this is only the beginning. Think of the effect of applying the concept of comparable worth to all forms of labor. What if daycare workers were paid as much as truck drivers? Or mothers were treated with the same respect as doctors? Devaluing and paying less to one segment of the work force than another has been used to keep overall wages down and workers divided. Under mining the ideology of inequality would eliminate the basis of unequal compensation. There would no longer be a "need" for a sex-segregated and sex-defined work force. In other words, to apply the concept of equity in the work force would demand the complete restructuring of the work force.

3. We need to build new working women's organizations which will be broader and more inclusive than others preceeding them.

CLUW is the largest organization of union women, but the majority of women are not in unions and therefore cannot belong to CLUW. Although NOW is the largest women's rights organization in the United States, its membership represents only a very small percentage of the entire female population. Building working women's organizations that focus on organizing the majority of women and that are able to deal specifically with the other oppressions women experience (such as racism, ageism, etc.) should be prioritized as the strategy most likely to reach most women.

In addition to developing a broad and unifying working women's agenda, these organizations need to organize women around their specific occupations such as secretaries, industrial workers, nurses, teachers, domestics, and others. It is critical, however, that these organizations remember that most women have at least two jobs—unpaid homemaker and wage-worker. Many women have three jobs—unpaid mother, homemaker, and wage-worker. Today the pressures for women to work at home and in the wage-work force are great and this makes their situation particularly exploitive: they are compensated poorly for their work outside the home and not compensated at all for their work within the home. Unfortunately, there is no program which sufficiently deals with women's unpaid labor and its relationship to wage-work.

In order to change their relationship to labor in general, women need to develop programs that address their unpaid labor. Short-term programs would include paid parenting leave (the right of both male and female parents to take time off after the birth of a child and return to the same job), quality childcare, and quality maternity care. Long-term programs include the redistribution of housework and childcare.

There are indications that such programs are not far off. The major issue of the Congressional Caucus on Women's Issues is a parental leave bill (unpaid). Also, a wages-for-housework clause was included in the United Nations document that came out of the International Conference in July, 1985 in Nairobi, Kenya which ended the United Nations Decade for Women.

4. The unionization of women is key to women's political and economic power. Feminism and working women's organizations need to choose this goal as a major objective.

There have been some feminists who have glimpsed the power of unions for women, but most feminist organizations have at best developed only supportive relationships to labor women. Feminists need to see the building of unions as being in the interests of all women and as central to their organizations' efforts. We need to work with existing unions and to create unions which are led by women, are democratically run, and stress a variety of issues in women's lives. Such an effort is key to the empowerment of women.

5. *Feminists and working women's organizations need to work with the established labor movement for the unionization of women at the same time that they need to maintain a parallel, independent women's base that will keep the feminist vision clear and will provide the external pressure necessary to motivate labor's organizing of unorganized women.*

Despite the growing cooperation between feminism and labor and the emergence of a working women's feminism, there is much that needs to be done to improve unions. The majority of workers remain unorganized; most unions are now on the defensive; the top trade union leadership remains male-dominated; and neither feminism nor unionism has been able to unite with other forces to defeat the right-wing. An autonomous women's movement with its own organizations and organizing techniques has a unique contribution to make. The innovative strategies used by feminism in the last decade should be employed in the organizing of women workers. One of the strengths of the women's movement has been its ability to organize women around their personal experiences and issues which affect the quality of their lives as well as around the material conditions of their lives. This work was done in the early consciousness-raising groups and happens today in support groups. A personalized forum where women can share their feelings and attitudes about their work and their relationships allows them a chance to value their work, share difficulties, and envision change. Support groups create a greater and qualitatively different solidarity among workers and should be very useful in the building of a new unionism.

It is interesting to note that among the present union leadership, there is some recognition that unions need a resurgence and new organizational forms. This should make it easier for feminists and unionists to experiment together. Using our own history, feminists can contribute our vision and skill to help bring about necessary change.

6. *Women need to lead the union movement.*

Within the union movement, the biggest obstacle for women has been the lack of female leadership. The women's movement, working women's organizations, and trade unions all need to tackle this problem. (CLUW has identified it as *the* key concern.) While there are more women leaders today than ever before, unions' top leadership remains male-dominated, in spite of the fact that growing unions are female unions. Women have the vision and skills to provide the kind of leadership needed. And women leaders are needed if the union movement is to grow, and if women are to take charge of their economic lives.

7. *The combination of feminism and organized labor have led to broad and highly progressive political agendas serving the needs of many oppressed groups in society. Today, there is a great need for women, labor, and other oppressed groups, especially people of color, to create a working peoples' agenda that will be a clear alternative to present political priorities.*

In each of the case studies, it was shown that when feminism and labor were able to unite and when women were able to organize into working women's organizations, the political programs they developed were broader and more comprehensive than either was able to develop separately.

In the 1984 presidential election, there was a greater possibility than ever before for women, labor, and organizations of racial minorities to unite. Labor had begun early to develop a strong anti-Reagan program and to work with other groups to defeat Reagan. Women, because of the surfacing of the Gender Gap, became the hope of many in the Democratic Party. For blacks and some progressives, Jesse Jackson became the articulate spokesperson for oppressed groups.

The failure to defeat Reagan in 1984 had to do in large part with the lack of a sufficient programmatic alternative and a lack of cooperation between groups. The unity that was possible was not achieved. Each group went into the Democratic Convention and into the election fighting for its own issues and allowing itself to be vulnerable to the charge of "special interests." Labor put all its influence behind Walter Mondale without organizing around a labor platform or the needs of working people. Women put all their energy into supporting a female vice-presidential candidate and ended up confined to two issues— the ERA and the right to choose. While the Rainbow Coalition tried to develop that sufficient alternative, it was not yet able to win over allies in the majority population, or able to build the broad-based coalition of women, labor, and farmers that was needed.

However, there are lessons to be learned. There is a greater need now than ever before to provide a new and broader political program for change in the United States. Seeds of that program have been expressed in the Coalition of Labor Union Women, the Rainbow Coalition, segments of the labor movement, and parts of the women's movement. As indicated before, the emerging working women's feminism certainly contains the basis of a program that could make sweeping and qualitative changes.

Issues concerning welfare, jobs, and defense spending are going to be at the forefront of the presidential campaign of 1988. Ideas including a living wage for all people and priorities geared towards human needs and not military destruction should be strongly put forward. These are issues in which women could play a leading role. While developing a program on women's issues, we are certainly in the position to assert that all issues pertain to us as women and as working people. We have the power to initiate with other groups—blacks and labor, in particular—an alternative program that would bring greater equality and fulfillment to daily life, both at work and at home.

It is time that we take that kind of leadership.

Notes

Introduction

1. Joan Walsh, "Feminism's New Frontiers," *In These Times,* December 11-17, 1985, p. 12.

Chapter 1

1. Judith Hole and Ellen Levine, *Rebirth of Feminism,* New York, Quadrangle/New York Times Book Co., 1971, p. 117.

2. Betty Friedan, *The Feminine Mystique,* New York, Dell, 1974 (1963), p. 5.

3. Barbara J. Berg, *The Remembered Gate: Origins of American Feminism, The Woman and the City, 1800-1860,* New York, Oxford University Press, 1978, p. 5.

4. Martha Atkins, *The Hidden History of the Female: The Early Feminist Movement in the United States,* Somerville, Mass., New England Free Press, n.d., p. 6.

5. Zillah R. Eisenstein, *The Radical Future of Liberal Feminism,* New York, Longman Series in Feminist Theory, 1980, p. 155.

6. Ellen Carol DuBois, *Feminism and Suffrage: The Emergence of an Independent Women's Movement in America, 1848-1869,* Ithaca, Cornell University Press, 1978, p. 46.

7. Eleanor Smeal, *Why and How Women Will Elect the Next President,* New York, Harper & Row, 1984, p. 7.

8. *Ibid.,* p. 3.

9. Bella Abzug with Mim Kelber, *Gender Gap,* Boston, Houghton Mifflin, 1984, p. 11.

10. Smeal, *op. cit.*, p. 22.

11. Abzug and Kelber, *op. cit.*, p. 242.

12. Smeal, *op. cit.*, p. 5.

13. *Ibid.*, p. 1.

Chapter 2

1. Joan Walsh, "Feminism's New Frontiers," *In These Times*, December 11-17, 1985, p. 12.

2. *Ibid.*, p. 12.

3. Ellen DuBois, "The Radicalism of the Woman Suffrage Movement: Notes Toward the Reconstruction of Nineteenth Century Feminism," *Feminist Studies*, III, no. 1/2, 1975, p. 62.

4. Ann Oakley, *Woman's Work: The Housewife, Past and Present*, New York, Vintage, 1976, p. ix.

5. Meredith Tax, *The Rising of the Women: Feminist Solidarity and Class Conflict, 1880-1917*, New York, Monthly Review Press, 1980, p. 7.

6. Philip S. Foner, *Women and the American Labor Movement: From Colonial Times to the Eve of World War I*, New York, Free Press, 1979, p. ix.

7. Pamela Roby, *Women in the Workplace*, Cambridge, Mass., Schenkman, 1981, p. 1.

8. Foner, *op. cit.*, p. 537.

9. Margaret A. Simeral, "Women and the Reserve Army of Labor," *Insurgent Sociologist*, VIII, Fall 1978, p. 164. Quoted in Foner, *Women and the American Labor Movement: From World War I to the Present*, New York, Free Press, 1980, p. 537.

10. Heidi Hartmann, "Capitalism, Patriarchy and Job Segregation by Sex," in *Capitalist Patriarchy and the Case for Socialist Feminism*, Zillah R. Eisenstein (ed.), New York, Monthly Review Press, 1979, p. 206.

11. *Ibid.*, p. 208.

12. Barbara Wertheimer, *We Were There: The Story of Working Women in America*, New York, Pantheon, 1977, p. 195.

13. Margery Davies, "Woman's Place is at the Typewriter: The Feminization of the Clerical Force," in Eisenstein (ed.), *op. cit.*, p. 249.

14. *Ibid.*, p. 262.

15. *Daily World*, June 23, 1978. Quoted in Foner, *Women and the American Labor Movement: From World War I to the Present, op. cit.*, p. 551.

16. David M. Gordon, "Economic Dimensions of Occupational Segregation," in *Women and the Workplace: The Implications of Occupational Segregation*, Blaxall and Reagan (eds.), (Chicago: University of Chicago Press, 1976), p. 243.

17. Ruth Milkman, "Women Workers, Feminism and the Labor Movement Since the 1960s," in Ruth Milkman (ed.) *Women, Work and Protest*, Boston and London, Routledge & Kegan Paul, 1985, p. 301.

Chapter 3

1. Andrew Levison, *The Working-Class Majority*, New York, Coward, McCann & Geoghegan, 1974, pp. 209-212.

2. Ruth Milkman, *Women, Work and Protest*, Boston and London, Routledge & Kegan Paul, 1985, p. 304.

3. Rosalyn Baxandall, Linda Gordon, and Susan Reverby, (eds.), *America's Working Women: A Documentary History, 1600 to the Present*, New York, Vintage, 1976, p. 167.

4. Joyce Maupin, *Working Women and their Organizations*, Berkeley, Union WAGE Educational Committee, 1974, p. 6.

5. Alice Kessler-Harris, "Where Are the Organized Women Workers?", *Feminist Studies*, III, no. 1/2, 1975, p. 93.

6. Editorial, *The Pioneer*, May 31, 1834. Quoted in Barbara Taylor, "'The Men Are As Bad As Their Masters]]]' Socialism, Feminism and Sexual Antagonism in the London Tailoring Trade in the Early 1830's," *Feminist Studies*, V, no. 1, 1979, p. 7.

7. Heidi Hartmann, "Capitalism, Patriarchy and Job Segregation by Sex," in *Capitalist Patriarchy and the Case for Socialist Feminism*, Zillah R. Eisenstein (ed.), New York, Monthly Review Press, 1979, p. 206.

8. Kessler-Harris, *op. cit.*, p. 97.

9. Robin Miller Jacoby, "The Women's Trade Union League and American Feminism," in *Class, Sex, and the Woman Worker*, Milton Cantor and Bruce Laurie (eds.), Westport, Conn., Greenwood Press, 1977, p. 128.

10. Philip S. Foner, *Women and the American Labor Movement: From Colonial Times to the Eve of World War I*, New York, Free Press, 1979, p. 34.

11. Meredith Tax, *The Rising of the Women: Feminist Solidarity and Class Conflict, 1880-1917*, New York, Monthly Review Press, 1980, p. 283.

12. Maupin, *op. cit.*, p. 2.

13. Eleanor Flexner, *Century of Struggle: The Woman's Rights Movement in the United States*, New York, Atheneum, 1973, p. 242.

14. Maupin, *op. cit.*, p. 1.

15. Thomas Dublin, "Women, Work, and Protest in the Early Lowell Mill: 'The Oppressing Hand of Avarice Would Enslave Us,'" in Cantor and Laurie (eds.), *op. cit.*, p. 52.

16. Barbara Mayer Wertheimer, *We Were There: The Story of Working Women in America*, New York, Pantheon, 1977, p. 71.

17. *Ibid.*, p. 71.

18. *Ibid.*, p. 68.

19. Lise Vogel, "Hearts to Feel and Tongues to Speak: New England Mill Women in the Early Nineteenth Century," in Cantor and Laurie (eds.), *op. cit.*, pp. 70-71.

20. Wertheimer, *op. cit.*, p. 104.

21. Flexner, *op. cit.*, pp. 258-259.

22. James J. Kenneally, *Women and American Trade Unions*, St. Albans, Vt., Eden Press Women's Publications, 1978, p. 231.

23. *Ibid.*, p. 130.

24. Jacoby, *op. cit.*, p. 217.

25. Tax, *op. cit.*, pp. 156-163.

26. *Ibid.*, pp. 283-284.

27. Milkman, *op. cit.*, p. 304.

28. *Ibid.*, p. 304.

29. *Ibid.*, pp. 304-305.

30. "The Changing Situation of Workers and Their Unions," in *Report by the AFL-CIO Committee on the Evolution of Work*, Thomas R. Donahue, chair, Washington, D.C., AFL-CIO, 1985, p. 5.

31. *Ibid.*, p. 8.

32. *Ibid.*, pp. 30-32.

Chapter 4

1. Meredith Tax, *The Rising of the Women: Feminist Solidarity and Class Conflict, 1880-1917*, New York, Atheneum, 1973, pp. 11-12.

2. Joyce Maupin, *Working Women and their Organizations*, Berkeley, Union WAGE Educational Committee, 1974, p. 8.

3. Nancy Schrom Dye, "Feminism or Unionism? The New York Women's Trade Union League and the Labor Movement," *Feminist Studies*, III, no. 1/2, 1975, p. 111.

4. *Ibid.*, p. 114.

5. *Ibid.*, p. 122.

6. Nancy Schrom Dye, "Creating a Feminist Alliance: Sisterhood and Class Conflict in the New York Women's Trade Union League, 1903-1914," in *Class, Sex, and the Woman Worker*, Milton Cantor and Bruce Laurie (eds.), Westport, Conn., Greenwood Press, 1977, p. 22.

Chapter 5

1. Martha Atkins, *The Hidden History of the Female: The Early Feminist Movement in the United States*, Somerville, Mass., New Eng-

land Free Press, n.d., p. 6.

2. Ellen DuBois, *Feminism and Suffrage: The Emergence of an Independent Women's Movement in America, 1848-1869*, Ithaca, Cornell University Press, 1978, p. 46.

3. Atkins, *op. cit.*, pp. 6-7.

4. Judith Papachristou, *Women Together: A History in Documents of the Women's Movement in the United States*, New York, Alfred A. Knopf, 1976, pp. 57-60.

5. Atkins, *op. cit.*, p. 7.

6. *Revolution*, New York, January 1868.

7. DuBois, *op. cit.*, p. 104.

8. Israel Kugler, "The Women's Rights Movement and the National Labor Union (1866-1872)," New York University, unpublished Ph.D. dissertation, 1954, pp. 41-42.

9. DuBois, *op. cit.*, p. 120, citing Pillsbury, "Woman's Work," *Revolution*, August 27, 1868, pp. 120-121.

10. The three secondary case studies used about the National Labor Union and the Working Women's Association are the following: DuBois, *Feminism and Suffrage, op. cit.*, pp. 104-161; Philip S. Foner, *Women and the American Labor Movement: From Colonial Times to the Eve of World War I*, New York, Free Press, 1979, pp. 122-162; and Kugler, "The Women's Rights Movement," *op. cit.*

11. Foner, *op. cit.*, p. 128.

12. *Ibid.*, p. 129.

13. DuBois, *op. cit.*, p. 110, citing "The National Labor Union and U.S. Bonds," *Revolution*, April 9, 1868, p. 213.

14. *Revolution*, July 2, 1868, p. 405.

15. Foner, *op. cit.*, p. 130.

16. Ellen DuBois, "Nineteenth-Century Woman Suffrage Movement," in *Capitalist Patriarchy and the Case for Socialist Feminism*, Zillah R. Eisenstein (ed.), New York, Monthly Review Press, 1979, p. 140, citing Ellen DuBois (ed.), "On Labor and Free Love: Two Unpublished Speeches by Elizabeth Cady Stanton," *Signs: Journal of Women in Culture and Society*, I, 1975, pp. 257-268.

17. *Ibid.*, p. 141.

18. "Capital and Labor," *Revolution*, April 30, 1868, p. 264.

19. "The Degradation of Women," *Revolution*, January 15, 1868, p. 25.

20. "The Workingmen's Convention," *Revolution*, July 9, 1868, p. 9.

21. "Second Annual Session of the Labor Union," *Revolution*, September 3, 1868, p. 141.

22. Foner, *op. cit.*, p. 133.

23. *Ibid.*, p. 133.

24. DuBois, *Feminism and Suffrage, op. cit.*, p. 122.

25. Foner, *op. cit.*, p. 133, citing *Proceedings of the Second Session of the National Labor Congress in Convention Assembled at New York City, September 21, 1868*, Philadelphia, 1868, p. 4.

26. Foner, *op. cit.*, p. 133.

27. "National Labor Congress," *Revolution*, October 1, 1868, p. 200.

28. *Ibid.*

29. Foner, *op. cit.*, p. 143.

30. "Working Women's Association, Meeting at the 'Revolution' Office," *Revolution*, October 1, 1868, p. 197.

31. Kugler, *op. cit.*, p. 97, quoting *Revolution*, February 19, 1868.

32. *Revolution*, April 16, 1868, p. 227.

33. "Working Women's Association," *Revolution*, September 24, 1868, pp. 181-182.

34. "Working Women's Association, Meeting at the 'Revolution' Office," *Revolution*, October 1, 1868, p. 197.

35. DuBois, *Feminism and Suffrage, op. cit.*, pp. 132-133.

36. "Working Women's Association," *op. cit.*, p. 197.

37. Foner, *op. cit.*, p. 148.

38. *Revolution*, October 1, 1868, p. 197.

39. "Working Women's Association," *op. cit.*, pp. 196-197.

40. "Women's Typographical Union," *Revolution*, October 8, 1868, p. 231.

41. *Ibid.*

42. "Working Women's Association, No. 2 Meeting at the Working Women's Home," *Revolution*, October 1, 1868, p. 198.

43. *Ibid.*

44. DuBois, *Feminism and Suffrage, op. cit.*, pp. 145-146.

45. *Ibid.*, pp. 146-147.

46. Foner, *op. cit.*, p. 154.

47. DuBois, *Feminism and Suffrage, op. cit.*, p. 156.

48. Foner, *op. cit.*, p. 135.

49. Kugler, *op. cit.*, pp. 446-447, quoting *New York World*, August 17, 1869.

50. *Ibid.*, pp. 448-449, quoting *New York World*, August 18, 1869.

51. *Ibid.*, pp. 452-453, quoting *New York World*, August 18, 1869.

52. Foner, *op. cit.*, p. 154.

53. Kugler, *op. cit.*, pp. 456-457, quoting *New York World*, August 18, 1869.

54. DuBois, *Feminism and Suffrage, op. cit.*, pp. 157-158.

55. *Ibid.*, p. 158.

56. Kugler, *op. cit.*, p. 451, quoting *New York World*, August 18, 1869.

57. James J. Kenneally, *Women and American Trade Unions*, St. Albans, Vt., Eden Press Women's Publications, 1978, p. 6.

58. Foner, *op. cit.*, pp. 160-161, quoting *Report of Proceedings of the Nineteenth Annual Session of the International Typographical Union Held in Baltimore, Md., June 5, 6, 7 and 8, 1871*, Philadelphia, 1871, p. 68.

59. DuBois, *Feminism and Suffrage, op. cit.*, p. 161.

60. Aileen S. Kraditor, *The Ideas of the Woman Suffrage Movement, 1890-1920*, New York, Anchor Books, 1971, pp. 38-39.

61. DuBois, *Feminism and Suffrage, op. cit.*, p. 121.

62. "Working Women's Association," *op. cit.*, p. 197.

Chapter 6

1. Ann Draper, "History of Union W.A.G.E.," *Union WAGE*, San Francisco, Jan.-Feb. 1972, p. 2.

2. Pamela Allen, "Jean Maddox: Labor Heroine," in *Jean Maddox: The Fight for Rank and File Democracy*, Pamela Allen (ed.), Berkeley, Union WAGE Educational Committee, 1976, p. 18.

3. Draper, *op. cit.*, p. 2.

4. Pamela Allen of Union WAGE, private interview, San Francisco, Calif., May 1979.

5. Edith Withington and Gretchen Mackler, "State Fed. Convention: Women Win Floor Fight," *Union WAGE*, Sept.-Oct. 1972, p. 1.

6. Hal Draper, "Modern Labor Heroine Dies," *Union WAGE*, May-June 1973, p. 5.

7. Union WAGE Executive Board, "Ann Draper, 1917-1973," *Union WAGE*, May-June 1973, p. 5.

8. Manja Argue of Union WAGE, private interview, Oakland, Calif., May 1979.

9. Allen, interview, May 1979.

10. Allen, "Jean Maddox," *op. cit.*, p. 20.

11. *Ibid.*, pp. 1-20.

12. *Ibid.*, pp. 7-8.

13. *Ibid.*, p. 8.

14. *Ibid.*, p. 9.

15. *Ibid.*, pp. 10-11.

16. *Ibid.*, p. 11.

17. *Ibid.*, p. 12.

18. *Ibid.*, pp. 14-15.

19. *Ibid.*, p. 21.

20. *Ibid.*, p. 16.

21. *Ibid.*, p. 41.

22. "We Move Forward," *Union WAGE*, Jan.-Feb. 1972, p. 1.

23. Allen, "Jean Maddox," *op. cit.*, p. 17.

24. Ann Draper, "Women in Struggle: A Point of View," *Union WAGE*, March-April 1973, p. 6.

25. "Germaine Greer—," *Union WAGE*, Nov.-Dec. 1972, p. 5.

26. Lois Weiner, "The Invisible Woman: Union WAGE Looks at Ms. Magazine," *Union WAGE*, Nov.-Dec. 1972, p. 4.

27. James J. Kenneally, *Women and American Trade Unions*, St. Albans, Vt., Eden Press Women's Publications, 1978, pp. 52-53, citing Muller vs. Oregon, 208 U.S. 412 (1908).

28. Ronnie Steinberg Ratner, "The Paradox of Protection: Maximum Hours Legislation in the United States," *International Labour Review*, CXIX, no. 2, 1980, p. 190.

29. *Ibid.*, p. 196.

30. Mary Anderson, "Should There Be Labor Laws for Women? Yes," *Equal Rights*, Aug. 25, 1923. Quoted in Judith Papachristou, *Women Together: A History in Documents of the Women's Movement in the United States*, New York, Alfred A. Knopf, 1976, p. 209.

31. Rheta Childe Dorr, "Should There Be Labor Laws for Women? No," *Equal Rights*, Aug. 25, 1923. Quoted in Papachristou, *op. cit.*, pp. 205-207.

32. Ratner, *op. cit.*, p. 186.

33. *Ibid.*, pp. 186-187.

34. *Ibid.*, p. 193.

35. *Ibid.*, p. 194.

36. Keneally, *op. cit.*, p. 197.

37. "EEOC Attacks Protective Laws," *Union WAGE*, Sept.-Oct. 1972, p. 4.

38. Ann Draper, "What is the Industrial Welfare Commission?", *Union WAGE*, May-June 1972, p. 3.

39. "EEOC Attacks Protective Laws," *op. cit.*, p. 4.

40. "San Francisco Supervisors' Resolution," *Union WAGE*, Jan.-Feb. 1972, p. 3.

41. "For a Labor E.R.A.," *Union WAGE*, Jan.-Feb. 1972, p. 3.

42. Ann Draper and Luella Hansberry, "Fight Goes on For Protective Legislation," *Union WAGE*, May-June 1972, p. 1.

43. *Ibid.*

44. "W.A.G.E. Proposal to N.O.W.," *Union WAGE*, Nov.-Dec. 1972, p. 2.

45. "Clerks and Cabbies Take on Bank," *Union WAGE*, Jan.-Feb. 1973, p. 1.

46. Ann Fagan Ginger, "Struggle for Protective Laws Continues," *Union WAGE*, July-Aug. 1972, pp. 4-5.

47. "Employers Line Up for Attack," *Union WAGE*, Sept.-Oct. 1976, p. 3.

48. *Ibid.*, p. 11.

49. Joyce Maupin, "Employers Attack Labor Standards," *Union WAGE*, March-April 1980, p. 13.

50. "State Wide Union Women's Conference," *Union WAGE*, July-Aug. 1973, pp. 1, 8.

51. "Labor-Feminists Win Victory at the Polls," *Union WAGE*, Nov.-Dec. 1974, p. 1.

52. Clerical Organizing Support Committee, "History of the San Francisco Chapter's Clerical Organizing Support Committee," *Union WAGE Interchapter Newsletter* (Berkeley-San Francisco), March 1978.

53. "The State of Union W.A.G.E.," *Union WAGE*, Nov.-Dec. 1978, p. 14.

54. "WAGE Moves Forward, Convention Report," *Union WAGE*, Nov.-Dec. 1976, p. 1.

55. Geraldine Daesch, "Keeping the 'Union' in Union WAGE," *Union WAGE*, Jan.-Feb. 1979, p. 4.

56. Allen, interview, May 1979.

57. Allen, "Jean Maddox," *op. cit.*, p. 22.

58. Pamela Allen, "Anniversary of Woman Suffrage," *Union WAGE*, Sept.-Oct. 1975, pp. 7-8.

59. Pamela Allen, "Sexual Assault: To Keep Us Down," *Union WAGE*, Sept.-Oct. 1977, pp. 9-10.

60. Pamela Allen *et al.*, "WAGE Members Speak Out: Women's Work Caucus," *Union WAGE*, Sept.-Oct. 1979, p. 14.

61. Allen, "Jean Maddox," *op. cit.*, p. 22.

62. Pamela Allen, "Excerpt From An Answer," *Union WAGE Interchapter Newsletter*, March 1978, p. 2.

63. Ann Draper, "Women in Struggle: A Point of View," *Union WAGE*, March-April 1973, p. 6.

64. Pamela Allen, "Working in Unions: For a Broader Vision," *Union WAGE*, Jan.-Feb. 1979, p. 1.

65. Joyce Maupin, "Everything Can Change," *Union WAGE*, Jan.-Feb. 1979, p. 2.

66. Jan Arnold, "Why a *Union* Women's Alliance to Gain Equality?", *Union WAGE*, Jan.-Feb. 1979, p. 3.

67. Sally Floyd, "News for Working Women," *Union WAGE*, Jan.-Feb. 1979, p. 14.

68. "Wage Debates," *Union WAGE*, Jan.-Feb. 1979, p. 1.

69. Allen, "Working in Unions: For a Broader Vision," *op. cit.*, p. 1.

70. Jan Arnold, "Wage Convention: Putting Humpty Dumpty Back Together Again," *Union WAGE*, March-April 1979, p. 12.

71. *Ibid.*

72. *Ibid.*

73. Pam Allen, "From The Editor," *Union WAGE*, July-Aug. 1979, p. 14.

74. Jan Arnold, "From The President," *Union WAGE*, July-Aug. 1979, p. 14.

75. Pamela Allen *et al.*, "WAGE Members Speak Out: Women's Work Caucus," *Union WAGE*, Sept.-Oct. 1979, p. 14.

76. Joyce Maupin, "WAGE Members Speak Out: Third World Women Lead in Organizing," *Union WAGE*, Sept.-Oct. 1979, p. 14.

77. "Purpose and Goals," *Union WAGE*, Nov.-Dec. 1974, p. 2.

78. "Purpose and Goals," *Union WAGE*, Jan.-Feb. 1982, p. 15.

79. "Don't Mourn, Organize," *Union WAGE*, n.d. [final issue, 1982], p. 3.

80. Draper, "Women in Struggle," *op. cit.*, pp. 7-8.

81. Jean Maddox, "Trusteeship: Roadblock to Union Democracy," in *Jean Maddox*, Allen (ed.), *op. cit.*, p. 35.

82. *Ibid.*, p. 36.

83. Denise d'Anne, "Autocracy to Democracy in SEIU 400: Turning a Union Around," *Union WAGE*, Nov.-Dec. 1977, p. 7.

84. "Local 400 Shake-Up: New Union Forms!", *Union WAGE*, July-Aug. 1975, p. 1.

85. Joan Goldman, "Report from Rank and File for a Democratic 400," *Union WAGE*, July-Aug. 1975, p. 3.

86. "Statement of Union WAGE Executive Board," *Union WAGE*, Sept.-Oct. 1975, p. 1.

87. Ann Lipow *et al.*, "A Giant Step Forward," *Union WAGE*, May-June 1974, p. 4.

88. Joyce Maupin, "Founding Conference, Chicago, March 23-24, '74: Rank and File Victory," *Union WAGE*, May-June 1974, p. 5.

89. *Ibid.*

90. Kay Eisenhower, "Founding Conference, Chicago, March 23-24, '74: Open Membership," *Union WAGE*, May-June 1974, p. 5.

91. Lipow *et al.*, "A Giant Step Forward," *op. cit.*, p. 4.

92. Joyce Maupin, "Working Women's History—Where Do We Go From Here?", *Union WAGE*, July-Aug. 1977, p. 10.

93. "Organize! Conference for Working Women," *Union WAGE*, Nov.-Dec. 1975, p. 3.

94. "West Coast Conference Builds Unity," *Union WAGE*, Nov.-Dec. 1975, p. 3.

95. Joyce Maupin, "Working Women on the Move: Keynote Speech," *Union WAGE*, Jan.-Feb. 1976, p. 7.

96. "Organize! Conference for Working Women," *op. cit.*, p. 3.

97. *Ibid.*

98. "Rank and File Activity—The Key," *Union WAGE*, Nov.-Dec. 1976, p. 3.

99. Seattle, Union WAGE, "Opinion—Independent Organizing," *Union WAGE*, March-April 1977, p. 11.

100. *Ibid.*

101. Karen Nussbaum, "Strategies for Clerical Workers," *Union WAGE*, Jan.-Feb. 1976, p. 3.

102. *Ibid.*

103. Maupin, "Working Women's History—Where Do We Go From Here?", *op. cit.*, p. 10.

104. "Feminism and Unionism: A Different Approach," *Union WAGE*, Nov.-Dec. 1977, p. 1.

105. *Ibid.*, p. 2.

106. *Ibid.*, p. 3.

107. *Ibid.*, p. 3.

108. Sherna Gluck, "Women's Locals in the Early Twentieth Century: We Are The Majority," *Union WAGE*, Nov.-Dec. 1977, p. 10.

109. D'Anne, "Autocracy to Democracy in SEIU 400," *op. cit.*, p. 7.

110. Anita Reinthaler, "WAGE Convention," *Union WAGE*, Jan.-Feb. 1978, p. 14.

111. "Eleven Years of a Persistent Vision," *Union WAGE*, n.d. [final issue, 1982], p. 2.

112. "Don't Mourn, Organize," *op. cit.*, p. 3.

113. "Our Purpose and Goals," *Union WAGE*, Jan.-Feb. 1972, p. 1.

114. *Ibid.*

Chapter 7

1. "Statement of the UAW in support of the Equal Rights Amendment as presented by Olga Madar, UAW Vice President, before Senate Committee on Constitutional Amendments, Washington, D.C., May 7, 1970," n.p., n.d.

2. Philip S. Foner, *Women and the American Labor Movement: From World War I to the Present*, New York, Free Press, 1980, p. 498.

3. *Ibid.*, p. 506.

4. Connie Kopelov, "Trade Union Women and Women's Rights," Goddard College, unpublished M.A. thesis, August 1974, p. 91.

5. Foner, *op. cit.*, p. 507.

6. Kopelov, *op. cit.*, p. 92.

7. Connie Kopelov (ed.), *Proceedings of the First New York Trade Union Women's Conference*, New York, Trade Union Women's Studies of Cornell University's New York State School of Industrial and Labor Relations, 1974, pp. 14-17.

8. *Ibid.*, p. 12.

9. *Ibid.*, p. 18.

10. *Ibid.*, p. 18.

11. Claudia Dreifus, "Trade Union Women's Conference," *Nation*, March 30, 1974, quoted in Coalition of Labor Union Women, *Founding Conference, March 22-24, 1974, Press Clippings*, n.p., n.d. (hereinafter *CLUW Founding Conference Press Clippings*), p. 18.

12. Kopelov, "Trade Union Women," *op. cit.*, p. 92.

13. Donna E. Ledgerwood, "An Analysis of the Satisfaction/Dissatisfaction of the United States Female Unionists with their Local Trade Union Organizations: A View of the Coalition of Labor Union Women," University of Oklahoma Graduate College, unpublished Ph.D. dissertation, 1980, p. 57.

14. Cindy Jaquith, untitled article, *Militant*, April 5, 1974, quoted in *CLUW Founding Conference Press Clippings*, p. 48.

15. "Trade Union Women Meet in Chicago," *Spokeswoman*, April 15, 1974, quoted in *CLUW Founding Conference Press Clippings*, p. 35.

16. Jaquith, *op. cit.*, p. 48.

17. *Ibid.*

18. "Trade Union Women Meet," *CLUW Founding Conference Press Clippings*, p. 35.

19. Eileen Shanahan, "Three Thousand Delegates at Chicago Meeting Organize a National Coalition of Labor Union Women," *New York Times*, March 25, 1974, quoted in *CLUW Founding Conference Press Clippings*, p. 1.

20. *Ibid.*

21. Patsy Sims, "Labor Union Women Form First Coalition," *Detroit Free Press*, March 25, 1974, quoted in *CLUW Founding Conference Press Clippings*, p. 4.

22. *Ibid.*

23. *Ibid.*

24. "CLUW Statement of Purpose," *CLUW Founding Conference Press Clippings*, p. 50.

25. *Ibid.*

26. Annemarie Troger, "Coalition of Labor Union Women: Strategic Hope, Tactical Despair," *Radical America*, IX, Nov.-Dec. 1975, p. 104.

27. Jaquith, *op. cit.*, p. 49.

28. Ruth Jordan, "Women from 58 Unions Give a CLUW to Future," *Los Angeles Citizen*, official publication of L.A. County Federation of Labor, April 5, 1974, quoted in *CLUW Founding Conference Press Clippings*, p. 40.

29. *Ibid.*

30. *Ibid.*

31. "CLUW: Dead End for Working Women," *Women and Revolution*, Summer 1974, p. 20.

32. Ann Withorn, "The Death of CLUW," *Radical America*, X, March-April 1976, pp. 50-51.

33. "Women Are Ready and They Have a Message for Labor," *Philadelphia Inquirer*, March 25, 1974, quoted in *CLUW Founding Conference Press Clippings*, p. 9.

34. "Women Bureaucrats Rig CLUW Conference," *Workers Vanguard*, March 15, 1974, quoted in *CLUW Founding Conference Press Clippings*, p. 54.

35. Pat Fry, "Women Form Labor Coalition," *Fifth Estate*, April 13-26, 1974, quoted in *CLUW Founding Conference Press Clippings*, p. 54.

36. Cindy Jaquith and Ginny Hildebrand, "Women Debate Future of CLUW," *Militant*, December 19, 1975, quoted in Coalition of Labor Union Women, *Constitutional Convention, December 6-7, 1975, Detroit, Michigan, Press Clippings*, n.p., n.d. (hereinafter *CLUW Constitutional Convention Press Clippings*), p. 18.

37. Withorn, *op. cit.*, pp. 47-48.

38. *Ibid.*

39. Troger, *op. cit.*, pp. 47-48.

40. Kopelov, "Trade Union Women," *op. cit.*, pp. 102-103.

41. *Ibid.*, p. 110.

42. *Ibid.*, p. 116.

43. *Ibid.*, p. 197.

44. Ledgerwood, *op. cit.*, p. 63.

45. Kopelov, "Trade Union Women," *op. cit.*, p. 90.

46. Dreifus, *op. cit.*, p. 100.

47. Kopelov, "Trade Union Women," *op. cit.*, p. 100.

48. Jaquith, *op. cit.*, p. 48.

49. "Women Are Ready and They Have a Message," *op. cit.*, p. 9.

50. Dreifus, *op. cit.*, p. 18.

51. "Union Women Want Leadership Roles; Avoid Activist Push," *Industry Week*, Dec. 15, 1975, quoted in *CLUW Constitutional Convention Press Clippings*, p. 21.

52. Margie Albert, "Union Women Gather," *Activist*, Jan. 1976,

quoted in *CLUW Constitutional Convention Press Clippings*, p. 1.

53. Kopelov, "Trade Union Women" *op. cit.*, pp. 124-125.

54. Ledgerwood, *op. cit.*, p. 79.

55. Coalition of Labor Union Women, "Resolution on Organizing the Unorganized," Sept. 22, 1974.

56. Foner, *op. cit.*, p. 521.

57. Kopelov, "Trade Union Women," *op. cit.*, p. 115.

58. *Ibid.*, p. 119.

59. Withorn, *op. cit.*, pp. 48-49.

60. *Ibid.*, p. 49.

61. Troger, *op. cit.*, p. 112.

62. "CLUW Statement of Purpose," *CLUW Founding Conference Press Clippings*, p. 50.

63. Foner, *op. cit.*, p. 522.

64. Susan Reverby, "An Epilogue]]]Or Prologue to CLUW?", *Radical America*, IX, Nov.-Dec. 1975, p. 525.

65. Foner, *op. cit.*, p. 525.

66. Coalition of Labor Union Women, "Resolution on Affirmative Action and Seniority," adopted by National Coordinating Committee on May 31, 1975, in Houston, Texas.

67. Olga Madar, "Safeguarding What We Have," *CLUW News*, New York, Summer 1975, p. 2.

68. "CLUW Hits NOW Seniority Stand," *CLUW News*, Summer 1975, p. 3.

69. "Current Developments," The Bureau of National Affairs, Inc., quoted in *CLUW Constitutional Convention Press Clippings*, pp. 5-6.

70. Coalition of Labor Union Women, "Depression and Unemployment," Resolution adopted by National Coordinating Committee on January 19, 1975, in St. Louis, Missouri.

71. Foner, *op. cit.*, p. 524.

72. Albert, *op. cit.*, p. 1.

73. Ben Bedell, "CLUW: More of the Same," *CLUW Constitutional Convention Press Clippings*, p. 11.

74. Jaquith and Hildebrand, *op. cit.*, pp. 18-19.

75. Eileen Shanahan, "Coalition of Union Women Holds to Course in Labor Mainstream," *New York Times*, Dec. 8, 1975, quoted in *CLUW Constitutional Convention Press Clippings*, p. 6.

76. "Current Developments," *op. cit.*, p. 6.

77. Albert, *op. cit.*, p. 1.

78. Helen Fogel, "Union Women Back Moderate Position," *Detroit Free Press*, Dec. 8, 1975, quoted in *CLUW Constitutional Convention Press Clippings*, p. 9.

79. Foner, *op. cit.*, p. 527.

80. Bedell, *op. cit.*, p. 10.

81. Withorn, *op. cit.*, p. 47.

82. "CLUW Sets Goals: ERA Priority," *CLUW News*, Spring 1976, p. 1.

83. *Ibid.*

84. Ruth Jordan, *A Commitment to Children*, The Report of the Coalition of Labor Union Women Child Care Seminar, sponsored by the German Marshall Fund of the United States, 1977, pp. 1-30.

85. Diane S. Curry, "Strong Action Plan Adopted: 'Forward to Full Equality,'" *CLUW News*, Winter 1977, p. 1.

86. *Ibid.*

87. Sylvia Krekel, "Reproductive Freedom for Workers: A Right Not a Benefit," *CLUW News*, Spring 1979, p. 4.

88. *Ibid.*

89. *Ibid.*

90. Joyce D. Miller, telegram to President Jimmy Carter, Jan. 15, 1979.

91. Joyce D. Miller, letter to George Meany, President of the AFL-CIO, Dec. 27, 1978.

92. "Legislative Conference, Third Convention Held," *CLUW News*, Fall 1977, p. 2.

93. Ledgerwood, *op. cit.*, p. 66.

94. Diane S. Curry, "Union Card Key to Job Equality," *CLUW News*, Fall 1979, p. 1.

95. *Ibid.*, p. 1.

96. *Ibid.*

97. *Ibid.*, p. 1.

98. *Ibid.*

99. *Ibid.*

100. "Push on for ERA in Illinois," *CLUW News*, May-June 1980, p. 1.

101. *Ibid.*

102. *Ibid.*, p. 2.

103. Diane S. Curry, "'On the March' To Organize Unorganized," *CLUW News*, Nov.-Dec. 1980, p. 1.

104. Naomi Baden, Karin Gerstel, and Elyse Glassberg, *Absent from the Agenda: A Report on the Role of Women in American Unions*, [New York], Coalition of Labor Union Women Center for Education and Research, 1980, p. 4.

105. *Ibid.*, p. 5.

106. *Ibid.*

107. "Resolutions Adopted at the 10th Annual CLUW Convention," March 22-25, 1984.

108. Andrew Levison, *The Working-Class Majority*, New York, Coward, McCann & Geoghegan, 1974, pp. 209-212.

109. Joyce Miller, Introduction to Patricia Cayo Sexton, *The New Nightingales: Hospital Workers, Unions' New Women's Issues*, New York, Enquiry Press, 1982, p. ii.

110. Foner, *op. cit.*, p. 523.

111. Albert, *op. cit.*, p. 1.

112. Kopelov, "Trade Union Women," *op. cit.*, pp. 124-125.

113. Foner, *op. cit.*, p. 489.

114. "The Changing Situation of Workers and their Unions, A Report by the AFL-CIO Committee on the Evolution of Work," February 1985.

115. "A New Page in Labor History," *Moving On: Magazine of the New American Movement*, V, May-June 1981, pp. 9-10.

Bibliography

Books

Baxandall, Rosalyn, Gordon, Linda, and Reverby, Susan, eds. *America's Working Women: A Documentary History, 1600 to the Present.* New York: Vintage Books, 1976.

Berg, Barbara J. *The Remembered Gate: Origins of American Feminism, The Woman and the City, 1800-1860.* Oxford: Oxford University Press, 1978.

Blaxall, Martha, and Reagan, Barbara, eds. *Class, Sex, and the Woman Worker.* Westport, Connecticut: Greenwood Press, 1977.

Dubois, Ellen. *Feminism and Suffrage: The Emergence of an Independent Women's Movement in America, 1848-1869.* Ithaca: Cornell University Press, 1978.

Eisenstein, Zillah R., ed. *Capitalist Patriarchy and the Case for Socialist Feminism.* New York: Monthly Review Press, 1979.

Farley, Lin. *Sexual Shakedown: The Sexual Harassment of Women on the Job.* New York: McGraw-Hill Book Company, 1978.

Flexner, Eleanor. *Century of Struggle: The Woman's Rights Movement in the United States.* New York: Atheneum, 1973.

Foner, Philip S. *Women and the American Labor Movement: From Colonial Times to the Eve of World War I.* New York: Free Press of Macmillan Publishing Co., Inc., 1979.

Foner, Philip S. *Women and the American Labor Movement: From World War I to the Present.* New York: Free Press of Macmillan Publishing Co., Inc., 1980.

Friedan, Betty. *The Feminine Mystique.* New York: Dell Publishing Co., 1974, 1963.

Hole, Judith and Levine, Ellen. *Rebirth of Feminism*. New York: Quadrangle/The New York Times Book Co., 1971.

Kenneally, James J. *Women and American Trade Union*. St. Alban's, Vermont: Eden Press Women's Publications, Inc., 1978.

Kessler-Harris, Alice. *Women Have Always Worked: A Historical Overview*. Old Westbury, New York: Feminist Press and New York: McGraw Hill Book Company, 1981.

Kraditor, Aileen S. *The Ideas of the Woman Suffrage Movement, 1890-1920*. Garden City, Anchor Books of Doubleday and Company, Inc., 1971.

Levison, Andrew. *The Working-Class Majority*. New York: Coward, McCann & Geoghegan, Inc., 1974.

Oakley, Ann. *Woman's Work: The Housewife, Past and Present*. New York: Vintage Books, 1976.

Papachristou, Judith. *Women Together: A History in Documents of the Women's Movement in the United States*. New York: Alfred A. Knopf, Inc., 1976.

Roby, Pamela. *Women in the Workplace: Proposals for Research and Policy Concerning the Conditions in Industrial and Service Jobs*. Cambridge, Massachusetts: Schenkman Publishing Company, Inc., 1981.

Rowbotham, Sheila. *Hidden From History: Rediscovering Women in History from the 17th Century to the Present*. New York: Vintage Books, 1976.

Rowbotham, Sheila. *Women, Resistance and Revolution: A History of Women and Revolution in the Modern World*. New York: Vintage Books, 1974.

Sexton, Patricia Cayo. *The New Nightingales: Hospital Workers, Unions, New Women's Issues*. New York: Enquiry Press, 1982.

Smeal, Eleanor. *Why and How Women Will Elect the Next President*. New York: Harper & Row, Publishers, Inc., 1984.

Tax, Meredith. *The Rising of the Women: Feminist Solidarity and Class Conflict, 1880-1917*. New York: Monthly Review Press, 1980.

Wertheimer, Barbara Mayer. *We Were There: The Story of Working Women in America*. New York: Pantheon Books, 1977.

Articles

Baxandall, Rosalyn, Ewen, Elizabeth, and Gordon, Linda. "The Working Class Has Two Sexes." *Monthly Review*, XXVII, No. 3 (1974), pp. 1-134.

Buhle, Mari Jo. "Feminists Help Working Women Bridge Class Lines." *In These Times*, (September 10-16, 1980), pp. 17, 22.

"CLUW: Dead End for Working Women." *Women and Revolution* (Summer, 1974), pp. 20-22.

"CLUW Conference: Trade Union Bureaucrats Run Show." *Revolution* (May, 1974), pp. 12-14.

Davies, Margery. "Woman's Place is at the Typewriter." *Capitalist Patriarchy and the Case for Socialist Feminism.* Edited by Zillah R. Eisenstein. New York: Monthly Review Press, 1979.

Dublin, Thomas. "Women, Work, and Protest in the Early Lowell Mills: 'The Oppressing Hand of Avarice Would Enslave Us.'" *Class, Sex, and the Woman Worker.* Edited by Milton Cantor and Bruce Laurie. Westport, Connecticut: Greenwood Press, 1977.

Dubois, Ellen, "Nineteenth-Century Woman Suffrage Movement." *Capitalist Patriarchy and the Case for Socialist Feminism.* Edited by Zillah R. Eisenstein. New York: Monthly Review Press, 1979.

Dubois, Ellen, ed. "On Labor and Free Love: Two Unpublished Speeches by Elizabeth Cady Stanton." *Signs: Journal of Women in Culture and Society,* I (1975), pp. 257-68.

Dubois, Ellen, "The Radicalism of the Woman Suffrage Movement: Notes Toward the Reconstruction of Nineteenth-Century Feminism." *Feminist Studies,* III, No. 1/2 (1975), pp. 54-62.

Dye, Nancy Schrom. "Creating a Feminist Alliance:Sisterhood and Class Conflict in the New York Women's Trade Union League, 1903-1914." *Class, Sex and the Woman Worker.* Edited by Milton Cantor and Bruce Laurie. Westport, Connecticut: Greenwood Press, 1977.

Eisenstein, Zillah R. "Developing a Theory of Capitalist Patriarchy and Socialist Feminism." *Capitalist Patriarchy and the Case for Socialist Feminism.* Edited by Zillah R. Eisenstein. New York: Monthly Review Press, 1979.

Eisenstein, Zillah R. "The Sexual Politics of the New Right: Understanding the Crisis of Liberalism." *Signs: Journal of Women in Culture and Society,* VII (Spring 1982), pp. 567-588.

Gordon, David M. "Economic Dimensions of Occupational Segregation." *Women and the Workplace.* Edited by Martha Blaxall and Barbara Reagan. Chicago: University of Chicago Press, 1976.

Hartmann, Heidi. "Capitalist, Patriarchy and Job Segregation by Sex." *Capitalist Patriarchy and the Case for Socialist Feminism.* Edited by Zillah R. Eisenstein, New York: Monthly Review Press, 1979.

Jacoby, Robin Miller. "Feminism and Class Consciousness in the British and American Trade Union Leagues, 1890-1925." Edited by Bernice A. Carroll. *Liberating Women's History: Theoretical and Critical Essays.* Urbana: University of Illinois Press, 1976.

Jacoby, Robin Miller. "The Women's Trade Union League and American Feminism." *Class, Sex, and the Woman Worker.* Edited by

Milton Cantor and Bruce Laurie. Westport, Connecticut: Greenwood Press, 1977.

Kessler-Harris, Alice. "Organizing the Unorganizable: Three Jewish Women and their Union." *Class, Sex, and the Woman Worker.* Edited by Milton Cantor and Bruce Laurie. Wesport, Connecticut: Greenwood Press, 1977.

Kessler-Harris, Alice. "Where are the Organized Women Workers?" *Feminist Studies,* III, No. 1/2 (1975), pp. 92-110.

Lutz, Alma. "Susan B. Anthony for the Working Woman." *Boston Public Library Quarterly,* XI (1959), pp. 33-43.

MacKinnon, Catherine A. "Feminism, Marxism, Method, and the State: An Agenda for Theory." *Signs: Journal of Women in Culture and Society,* VII, No. 3 (1982), pp. 515-44.

"A New Page in Labor History." *Moving On: Magazine of the New American Movement,* V (May-June 1981), pp. 9-10.

Ratner, Ronnie Steinberg. "The Paradox of Protection: Maximum Hours Legislation in the United States." *International Labour Review,* CXIX, No. 2 (1980), pp. 185-98.

Reverby, Susan. "An Epilogue...Or Prologue to CLUW?" *Radical America,* III (Fall 1975), pp. 111-15.

Reverby, Susan. "The Labor and Suffrage Movements: A View of Working-class Women in the 20th Century." *Liberation NOW! Writings from the Women's Liberation Movement.* New York: Dell Publishing Co., Inc., (1971), pp. 94-101.

Taylor, Barbara. "'The Men Are as Bad as Their Masters...': Socialism, Feminism, and Sexual Antagonism in the London Tailoring Trade in the Early 1830s." *Feminist Studies,* V, No. 1 (1979), pp. 7-40.

Troger, Annemarie. "Coalition of Labor Union Women: Strategic Hope, Tactical Despair." *Radical America,* IX (November-December, 1975), pp. 85-110.

Vogel, Lise. "Hearts to Feel and Tongues to Speak: New England Mill Women in the Early Nineteenth Century." *Class, Sex, and the Woman Worker.* Edited by Milton Cantor and Bruce Laurie. Westport, Connecticut: Greenwood Press, (1977), pp. 64-82.

Walsh, Joan. "Feminism's New Frontiers." *In These Times,* (December 11-17, 1985), pp. 12-13.

Withorn, Ann. "The Death of CLUW." *Radical America* X (March-April, 1976), pp. 47-52.

Pamphlets

Allen, Pamela, ed. *Jean Maddox: The Fight for Rank and File Democracy.* Berkeley: Union WAGE Educational Committee, 1976.

Atkins, Martha. *The Hidden History of the Female: The Early Feminist Movement in the United States.* Somerville, Massachusetts: New England Free Press, n.d.

Baden, Naomi, Gerstel, Karin, and Glassberg, Elyse. *Absent from the Agenda: A Report on the Role of Women in American Unions.* New York: Coalition of Labor Union Women Center for Education and Research, 1980.

"The Changing Situation of Workers and Their Unions." *Report by The AFL-CIO Committee on the Evolution of Work.* Thomas R. Donahue, chairman. Washington, D.C.: AFL-CIO, 1985.

Jordan, Ruth. "A Commitment to Children." N.p. The report of the Coalition of Labor Union Women Child Care Seminar, sponsored by the German Marshall Fund of the United States, 1977.

Maupin, Joyce. *Working Women and Their Organizations.* Berkeley: Union WAGE Educational Committee, 1974.

Seifer, Nancy. *Absent from the Majority: Working Class Women in America.* New York: National Project on Ethnic America of the American Jewish Committee, 1973.

Interviews

Pam Allen of Union WAGE, private interview, San Francisco, California, May, 1979.

Manja Argue of Union WAGE, private interview, Oakland, California, May, 1979.

Ellen Gurzinsky of the Coalition of Labor Union Women, private interview, New York, July, 1981.

Barbara Haley of Union WAGE, private interview, San Francisco, May, 1978.

Gloria Johnson of the Coalition of Labor Union Women, private interview via telephone from Washington, D.C. to Boston, November, 1981.

Connie Kopelov of the Coalition of Labor Union Women, private interview, New York, July, 1981.

Joyce Maupin of Union WAGE, private interviews, San Francisco, California, May, 1978 and May, 1979.

Susan Reverby, private interview about the Coalition of Labor Union Women, Boston, July, 1980.

Newspapers, Newsletters

CLUW News (New York), 1975-1983.

Coalition of Labor Union Women: Founding Conference, March 22-24, 1974. (Chicago, Illinois), *Press Clippings,* n.p., n.d.

Coalition of Labor Union Women: Constitutional Convention, December 6-7, 1975, (Detroit, Michigan), *Press Clippings,* n.p., n.d.
Revolution (New York) 1868-1871.
Union WAGE (San Francisco), 1972-1982.
Union WAGE Interchapter Newsletter, (Berkeley—San Francisco), 1978-1979.

Organizational Records

Coalition of Labor Union Women Resolutions, approved by the National Coordinating Committee from September, 1974 to May, 1975.
Coalition of Labor Union Women Resolutions Passed, 1974-1979.

Proceedings, Reports, and Public Documents

Kopelov, Connie, ed. *Proceedings of the First New York Trade Union Women's Conference.* New York: Trade Union Women's Studies of Cornell University's New York State School of Industrial and Labor Relations, 1974.
　　Statement of the UAW in Support of the Equal Rights Amendment as Presented by Olga Madar, UAW Vice President before *Senate Committee on Constitutional Amendments,* Washington, D.C., May 7, 1970. n.p., n.d.
　　U.S. Department of Labor. Employment Standards Administration. Women's Bureau. *State Labor Laws in Transition: From Protection to Equal Status for Women.* Washington, D.C.: U.S. Government Printing Office, 1976.

Unpublished Correspondence

Coalition of Labor Union Women. Telegram and news article (January 15, 1979) regarding President Miller's resignation from the National Advisory Committee for Women brought about by President Carter's dismissal of Bella Abzug as co-chair. January 15, 1979.
　　Letters from Joyce Miller to George Meany, President of the AFL-CIO convention.

Unpublished Theses, Dissertations

Kopelov, Connie. "Trade Union Women and Women's Rights." Unpublished M.A. thesis, Goddard College, August, 1974.
　　Kugler, Israel. "The Women's Rights Movement and the National Labor Union (1866-1872)." Unpublished Ph.D. dissertation, New York University, 1954.

Ledgerwood, Donna E. "An Analysis of the Satisfaction/Dissatisfaction of the United States Female Unionists with their Local Trade Union Organizations: A View of the Coalition of Labor Union Women." Unpublished Ph.D. dissertation, University of Oklahoma Graduate College, 1980.

Index

List of Abbreviations

AFL—American Federation of Labor
AFSCME—American Federation of State, County, and Municipal Employees
AFT—American Federation of Teachers
CLUW—Coaltion of Labor Union Women
CIO—Congress of Industrial Organizations
ERA—Equal Rights Amendment
FEAC—Full Employment Action Council
IWC—Industrial Welfare Commission
IWW—Industrial Workers of the World
NCC—National Coordinating Committee (of CLUW)
NLU—National Labor Union
NOW—National Organization for Women
NTU—National Typographical Union
OPEIU—Office and Professional Employees International Union
SORWUC—Service, Office and Retail Workers Union of Canada
TUEL—Trade Union Educational League
UCE—Union of City Employees
WAGE—Women's Alliance to Gain Equality
UAW—United Auto Workers
UFW—United Farm Workers
WTUL—Women's Trade Union League
WTU—Women's Typographical Union
WWA—Working Women's Association

About the Author

Diane Balser has been an activist in the women's movement for the last two decades. She was one of the founders of Bread and Roses, a women's organization based in Cambridge, Massachusetts. She has a Ph.D. in Sociology from Brandeis University. Currently, Ms. Balser is the Executive Director of the Women's State-Wide Legislative Network of Massachusetts. The Network is composed of over ninety organizations committed to women's issues.

Diane Balser is the International Reference Person for women of the Re-Evaluation Counseling Communities. She leads workshops for women throughout the world on issues such as leadership, the empowerment of women, international solidarity, and others. She is author of *Women: Their Present Situation in the World.*